PRAISE FOR *THE RA* *PRODUCER'S HANDBOOK*

"A must-have for anyone in the business or considering the business!"—Kathy Hart, Co-host, *The Eric and Kathy Show*, 101.9 FM The Mix, Chicago

"Rick Kaempfer and John Swanson are at the top of a very short list of 'difference-making' radio producers. In this book they give us the secrets to their success, and it's my hope that it helps a whole new generation of radio producers create the kind of quality radio that Rick and John have been producing for the past twenty years."—Greg Solk, Vice President of Programming and Operations, WLUP-FM and WDRV-FM, Chicago

"Read, learn, and do what's in this book and you will be prepared to do a great show everyday. You also will be able to take care of any lazy, no-good talent in the biz—not that I know anyone like that."—Steve Cochran, WGN Radio, Chicago

THE RADIO

PRODUCER'S

HANDBOOK

Rick Kaempfer and John Swanson

ALLWORTH PRESS
NEW YORK

08 07 06 05 04   5 4 3 2 1

Published by Allworth Press
An imprint of Allworth Communications, Inc.
10 East 23rd Street, New York, NY 10010

Cover design by Derek Bacchus
Cover photography by Joel Puliatti
Interior design by SR Desktop Services. Ridge, NY
Page composition/typography by Integra Software Services, Pvt., Ltd., Pondicherry, India

ISBN: 1-58115-388-0

Library of Congress Cataloging-in-Publication Data

Kaempfer, Rick.
    The radio producer's handbook/Rick Kaempfer
    and John Swanson.
       p. cm.
    Includes bibliographical references and index.
    ISBN 1-58115-388-0 (pkb.)
    1. Radio—Production and direction—Handbooks, manuals etc.
    I. Swanson, John, 1963– II. Title.

PN1991.75.K34 2004
791.4402'32—dc22

                                                    2004017716

Printed in Canada

TABLE OF CONTENTS

Foreword by John Landecker   vii

Acknowledgments   ix

Introduction   xi

PART ONE   **PRODUCER EVOLUTION**

Chapter 1   The Wonderful World of Radio   3

PART TWO   **WHAT, MY BOY, DO YOU PRODUCE?**

Chapter 2   Booking Celebrity Guests   11

Chapter 3   Crafting a Great Interview   26

Chapter 4   Coming Up with Ideas   36

Chapter 5   Creating a Great Phone Segment   46

Chapter 6   Writing for Radio   61

Chapter 7   Pitching Material and Planning a Show   72

Chapter 8   Maximizing Your Time   82

PART THREE   **IN THE HEAT OF THE BATTLE**

Chapter 9   Pre-Game Show   95

Chapter 10   Showtime: A Day in a Life   105

Chapter 11   Remote Broadcasts   117

PART FOUR   **GETTING YOUR FIRST JOB**

Chapter 12   Laying Down an Educational Base   129

Chapter 13   Getting Your Foot in the Door   138

Chapter 14   Taking Advantage of Your Opportunity   149

Chapter 15   Final Preparations   156

PART FIVE   **TECHNICAL WORKSHOP**

Chapter 16   Becoming Chairman of the Board   165
Chapter 17   Digital Editing   176
Chapter 18   Creating an Audio Library   181

PART SIX   **CLIMBING THE LADDER**

Chapter 19   The Producer Ladder   193
Chapter 20   Future Careers for Ex-Producers   200

Appendix A   Glossary of Radio Terms   207
Appendix B   Schools with Student-Run
                Radio Stations (By Region)   212
Appendix C   Sample Celebrity Interview Prep Sheet   222
Appendix D   Sample Prep Sheet—*The Larry &*
                Mary Show   225
Appendix E   Useful Web Sites   230

Bibliography   231
About the Authors   232
Index   233

FOREWORD

WHEN I BEGAN MY CAREER IN RADIO OVER THIRTY YEARS AGO (DON'T TRY TO pin me down on the exact year), the position of producer was an afterthought, at best. Virtually no personality shows even had producers. We might have had a secretary to help with our personal appearances and fan mail, or an intern to get us sandwiches, but the thought of having someone who could produce the show for us wasn't even considered.

The authors of this book are among the handful of producers in America who helped redefine the position. Producers aren't just helping us get sandwiches anymore. They are essential partners. They book our guests, help us plan our shows, and help us come up with material. They also keep us on top of things, and help us direct the show while it's in progress. Any major personality would be completely lost without his producer.

Rick Kaempfer was my executive producer for ten years. I've had marriages that didn't last that long. By the end of our long run together, if Rick wasn't with me in the studio, the show didn't feel right to me. His co-author John Swanson is another producer I've gotten to know over the years. I've worked with him on select occasions and I greatly respect his abilities.

Just look at their collective resumes. In addition to working with me, the two of them have produced for the biggest radio stars in Chicago over the past twenty years, including Jonathon Brandmeier, Steve Dahl and Garry Meier, Kevin Matthews, Steve Cochran, and Eric and Kathy (John's current job). If these guys tell you this is how to produce a radio show, this is how to produce a radio show.

It's as simple as that.   —John Records Landecker

JOHN RECORDS LANDECKER has been honored for his accomplishments in radio with a display in the radio wing of the Rock and Roll Hall of Fame. During his distinguished radio career he has worked at legendary rockers like WIBG-Philadelphia, WLS-Chicago, and CFTR-Toronto. He most recently finished a ten-year run as the morning man at WJMK-Chicago. Landecker has been named the *Billboard Magazine* Radio Personality of the Year, the *Radio & Records* Oldies Morning Personality of the year (twice), and received countless other awards. He is currently the movie critic for *Chicago Tonight* on WTTW-TV in Chicago.

ACKNOWLEDGMENTS

As NOVICES IN THE PUBLISHING BUSINESS, WE WOULD HAVE BEEN LOST without the guidance and help of the professionals at Allworth Press. The senior editor Nicole Potter, the assistant editor Jessica Rozler, and the publisher Tad Crawford helped mold this book into much more than we ever thought it could be. Michael Madole of the Allworth publicity team was also encouraging and helpful. Thank you to all of you, plus our agent Lissy Peace, without whom we might never have found the perfect publisher.

When we called up our old friends and colleagues to help with this book, some people really answered the call. We'd like to thank John Landecker, Fred Winston, Bob Dearborn, Jim Wiser, Vince Argento, Tom Sochowski, Dr. Ed Dunkelblau, Dan McNeil, Brendan Sullivan, Jim McInerney, Cindy Gatziolis, Nick Harkin, Janet Treuhaft, George Economos, and Lissy Peace for going the extra mile and contributing their stories and/or help to us. Michelle Gabris from WPGU radio was also very helpful in getting us information about college radio.

Of course we also need to thank the people who gave us the radio knowledge necessary to write this book. Both of us got our producing start at WLUP-Chicago in the eighties. Those years were among the most treasured of our lives. Without the help of the great men and women who worked there, we never would have become accomplished producers. We learned just by watching and listening to people like Greg Solk, Matt Bisbee, Sandy Stahl, Larry Wert, Jimmy deCastro, Jonathon Brandmeier, Buzz Kilman, Steve Dahl, Garry Meier, Kevin Matthews, Bobby Skafish, Bob Stroud, Patty Haze, John Fisher, Scott Dirks, Wendy Snyder, Jim Wiser, John Bell, Gerri Wells, Fina Rodriguez, Kent Lewin, Mike Rugen, and Tom Knauss. Without their kindness and tutelage, we simply wouldn't be where we are today. Also, without the Loop (WLUP) we never would have met each other—brothers in the radio producing wars. Because of our common Loop heritage, we've helped each other through the highs and lows of producing over the years, and formed a bond that made this book possible.

Since we left WLUP, we've also worked with tremendous people who have taught us and guided us. We would especially like to thank John Records Landecker. Both of us have worked with and learned from the master. You richly deserve your place in the Rock and Roll

Hall of Fame. Thanks for being kind enough to write the foreword to this book.

To Eric Ferguson and Kathy Hart, we extend a humble thank you. Your success story provides the backdrop for much of what we have learned over the past decade. John Swanson is honored to produce your show.

Our colleagues on our various radio shows over the past twenty years have also taught us things that we continue to use every day. We absorbed knowledge by working alongside the likes of Vince Argento, Stan Lawrence, Richard Cantu, Leslie Keiling, David Stern, Mike Medina, Kim Strickland-Sargent, Dane Placko, Bobby Bitterman, Mike Bramel, Scott Redman, Lynee Alves, the SCS Trio (Michelle, Jeff, and Carolyn), Carrie Cochran, Maggie Brock, Laura Witek, Bruce Wolf, Bill Holub, Bonnie Greene, Tom Sochowski, Gene Beil, Mike Davis, Jim Defillippi, Randy Dry, Gehrig Peterson, Catherine Johns, Andi Kuhn, Vicki Truax, Tim Weigel, Bob Sirott, Fred Winston, Greg Brown, Bob Dearborn, Spike Manton, Dobie Maxwell, Max Bumgardner, Jim Foster, Bill Klaproth, Brendan Sullivan, Artie Kennedy, Carol Harmon, Dan Walker, Phil Duncan, Melissa McGurren, Barry Keefe, Cynthia Skolak, Dave Karwowski, Jude Corbett, Ron Carter, John Bermudez, Bob Dunsworth, Todd Manley, Todd Clark, Chris Lufitz, Steve McKenzie, Steve Cochran, and Doc Simpson.

As you can see by the long list of names, it takes a radio village to bring up a radio producer. We haven't even mentioned the scores of people in programming, management, sales, marketing, and promotions who helped us along the way. Those are some of the most talented people we know.

A special thank you is due to WTMX bosses Barry James, Drew Horowitz, and Mary Ellen Kachinske. Your support of this project has given us the courage to go for it. Kevin Robinson, one of our former bosses, also contributed information that we found helpful.

But most importantly, we need to thank our wives Bridget and Cheryl. You have sacrificed greatly over the years. For the countless hours of watching television you never wanted to watch, we thank you. For the countless times you came along to "just one more promotion," we thank you. For the times you calmly welcomed us home and didn't mention the huge bags forming under our aging eyes, we thank you.

Show biz is glamorous. Isn't it gals?

INTRODUCTION

WE REALIZE THAT NO ONE GROWS UP WITH THE DREAM OF BECOMING A radio producer. Children don't trade collectable producer cards or pretend to screen calls. We certainly didn't.

In fact, most kids have no idea what a radio producer does. They probably don't even know that a producer exists. They only hear the disc jockey or the host—the direct link to the radio audience. That job sounds so fun and glamorous; it's only natural a youngster would want to become one. It's not until he tries to break into the business that he discovers how difficult a task that really is. One of the authors of this book could have wallpapered his room with rejection letters when he tried to break into that end of the business. That's when he discovered a secret.

He became a producer. Becoming a producer is one of the best ways to open the radio door. Go ahead. Open the door. You just may find a rewarding and challenging career. It can be every bit as exciting as hosting a show. One of the reasons we wrote this book was to let you know there are other radio doors besides the one slamming shut in your face.

The main reason we wrote this book, however, is because we felt it was needed. Even people in radio don't totally understand everything a producer does, and that can cause problems. When we began in this business twenty years ago, the producer was expected to learn everything by trial and error. Very little guidance was given. It was sink or swim, survival of the fittest. The business has changed dramatically since then, and the position of producer has gained importance and prestige, but one thing has remained the same. Producer training is still not given enough attention.

This is the book we wish was handed to us on our first day as producers. We don't want another generation of producers tossed into the deep end of the radio pool without being taught how to swim. We somehow managed to swim over to the side without drowning. And while it's true we met some very interesting people, learned some valuable lessons, and developed our own producing strategies, we recognize that there has to be a better way. Hopefully by sharing the lessons we learned, you won't have to learn the way we did.

WHAT IS A RADIO PRODUCER?

Looking it up in the dictionary won't help. The Webster's definition of produce is "to make, to present, or to bring into view." That doesn't even scratch the surface. It's going to take us the whole book to fully explain the job to you, but we offer the following explanation as a jumping off point. We like to think of the word "producer" as an acronym. Each letter in the word will give a glimpse into some of the producer's daily duties.

- P is for Psychologist
- R is for Researcher
- O is for Organizer
- D is for Director
- U is for Understudy
- C is for Creative Writer
- E is for Engineer
- R is for Right-Hand Man

Of course that doesn't begin to cover all of the duties a producer is expected to master, but it's a good start. Let's take a closer look at each of those duties.

P is for Psychologist

There are very few jobs in the world where your number one duty is to figure out what someone else is thinking. One job is psychologist. Another is radio producer.

To explain why a radio producer is like a psychologist, we went to a professional. Our good friend Dr. Ed Dunkelblau is the director of the Institute for Emotionally Intelligent Learning, and has been a guest on many radio shows in his career. He has witnessed the producer-host relationship up close and personal, and describes it much more eloquently than we ever could. The following paragraph was his response.

"From what I have seen the producer needs to be a therapist, child psychologist, marital counselor, and specialist in treating post traumatic stress and addictive disorders. He needs to know the function of the Ego, the reinforcement value of praise, and the whereabouts of the liquor cabinet. All this while maintaining confidentiality, the utmost ethical behavior, and understanding that recognition of how helpful he is will be in short supply. The biggest difference between producers and psychologists is that a psychologist's effectiveness is hard to measure and at times hard to even see. The producer's effectiveness is revealed immediately, every day. The other difference is that we get paid better."

He's right. And though it sounds impossible, you need only be armed with empathy, common sense, and a passion to do your job well. We'll show you how to apply those skills in real life situations.

R is for Researcher

Ever wonder how a radio host seems to be so well versed on a subject? Perhaps you've been impressed by an interview a radio host conducted in which he wowed a guest with his knowledge of her career.

It's easy to sound authoritative about a subject or guest when a producer has spent hours researching and has given you the most interesting tidbits. It's a coup to find a person in the center of a news story and have her on your show, but without the producer doing the legwork it wouldn't have happened.

Research can seem like a daunting task. Believe it or not, it's easier today than it ever has been. Research that would have taken hours just a few years ago can now be done in minutes. We'll show you how.

O is for Organizer

Organization is the single most important skill for a producer. Why? Creative personalities are not organized. Ever. Luckily for the host, he doesn't have to be organized. He has a producer instead.

If you are a creative person considering a career as a producer, don't fret. Even a creative person can become organized if he really works at it. One of the authors of this book was one of those organizationally challenged "creative guys" when he began working as a producer. When he learned how to organize, he didn't lose his creative abilities. In fact, he found that he could apply his new organizational skills to his creative endeavors, greatly improving his output.

Don't think you need to be organized? A producer knows what is coming up on any given show. He knows what is coming up next week, next month, and next season. He knows who is coming to town, and when they are coming. He knows what is happening in town, and what is happening on television. He knows what is happening at the radio station and when it is happening. He knows popular culture, and politics, and music, and sports, and weather, and any other subject matter the listeners might enjoy. He has to know all of these things for his own sake and that of the host.

Organization can be taught, even to the most hopeless of our creative friends. You'll find some very helpful hints within the pages of this book.

D is for Director

During the show, someone needs to be running things. The optimum person for this task is the producer. The host has to concentrate on entertaining, performing, or informing. If he has someone he can trust to take him by the hand from one segment to the next, he'll perform his duties much more effectively.

Getting to this level of producing doesn't happen overnight. A host develops trust in his producer over time. If you are dependable and you defend him, you will eventually become his director. Even the prickliest of personalities is looking for someone he can trust to direct him. And you can direct even the prickliest of personalities.

This book not only tells you how to earn the trust of your host, it offers tips on how to direct a show once you've acquired that trust. These are two separate skills, and they are both covered rather thoroughly in the chapters ahead.

U is for Understudy

The producer has his own job to do, but he also must understand everyone else's job. For instance, he has to know what it takes to become a host. Often a station will have a producer host the show when the personality is ill or on vacation. There are scores of producers who became full-time hosts after getting their big break as an understudy. We'll mention several examples throughout the book.

While being the understudy for the host can be exciting, a producer must be understudy to everyone else on the show as well. Who is going to help the newsperson fix her news wire or computer when it breaks down during the show? The producer. Believe us, it happens nearly every day. If you don't learn the problems the newsperson faces, you won't be able to help. What about the traffic person? The producer has to know the numbers to call when the traffic information isn't coming in. The same is true of sports and weather.

The producer doesn't only need to know the jobs of everyone else on the show. He must keep in mind the priorities of the program director and help her implement those plans. The producer must also know what is happening in the sales department so that the clients are schmoozed properly. The other people doing the show are too busy with their own assignments to keep up with these things.

By the time you finish reading this book you'll have a better understanding of what every department in a radio station does. We'll speed up the learning curve so that you can serve as understudy if needed.

But don't worry. Becoming proficient enough at any of these jobs will only come with experience. No one expects you to be able to do it all on your first day.

C is for Creative Writer

The host is paid big bucks to write material for the show, right? Wrong. The host is paid big bucks to perform it. This is a very specialized skill in itself.

Often the producer comes up with material for the host or, at the very least, helps the host come up with additional material. There are some incredible hosts who handle all of the creative material. We've worked with some of them. On the other hand, it's a never-ending job to fill a four-hour radio show with quality material. If you are doing a comedy show, the producer will probably come up with the topics, the angles, and often even the punch line.

One host we worked for used to say, "I need you to be the frosting and the cake."

Another host often said, "Get me the meat."

Where do you find the meat, the frosting, and the cake? It's really not that complicated when you know where to look. We're not sure which is the meat, the frosting, or the cake, but we'll serve all three.

E is for Engineer

The fact is, the chief engineer of a radio station is not always on duty or available. This is particularly true during a morning show. In the age of radio consolidation, there are some big companies that don't even designate an engineer for every radio station. They have group engineers. This leads to some crisis moments.

When a component or piece of equipment breaks down during the show, who has to fix it or find a contingency plan? The producer. When a computer goes down, who has to get it working again? The producer.

The more you know about equipment, the better off the show will be. That's just the way it is in the modern-day radio station. A producer is like an additional member of the engineering staff. You may not know how to fix everything on your first day of the job, but through trial and error you'll definitely know how to fix it by your last day. Hopefully, we'll speed up that process significantly with the advice we give you in this book.

R is for Right-Hand Man

The producer is the host's Man Friday—and also his Man Monday, Man Tuesday, Man Wednesday, and Man Thursday. With what we've already told you, it's pretty easy to see why the host would count on his producer. A host may feel lost or naked when his producer isn't there. The producer is a security blanket.

The host knows the producer's ego will never get out of hand. He knows that the producer has seen the best and worst of the host's behavior, so he doesn't have to mince words or pretend to be nice when he doesn't feel like it. He knows the producer is there for him. The producer is on his side, and that means everything.

To illustrate this point, we have to tell you a story about one of our previous hosts. He was doing a live broadcast in Hawaii and found a toenail in his hotel room. He was horrified and couldn't get out of that room fast enough. Instead of picking up his phone and dialing nine to ask the front desk if he could change rooms, or walking three doors down the hall and asking the promotion director to change his room for him, he called his producer in Chicago. The producer was the only person he trusted to understand how disgusted he was to be sleeping in a room with a discarded toenail. After three long distance phone calls, the situation was handled. He got a better room.

BEYOND THE ACRONYM

We've been doing this job a long time now, so this is as good a time as any to apologize in advance for using terminology you've never heard. If you are a technical novice, some of the things we write about in the first three parts of the book may go completely over your head. Don't worry, because part 5 of this book will take you by the hand and walk you through a technical workshop. Before you reach part 5, however, and you run across a technical term that you don't understand, check appendix A. Your answer will probably be in our glossary. We've compiled a pretty comprehensive list of radio jargon.

The rest of your answers begin with the acronym p.r.o.d.u.c.e.r. Over the next twenty chapters, we will help you become the *p*, the *r*, the *o*, the *d*, the *u*, the *c*, the *e*, and the other *r*. If we've done our job correctly we'll have explained the rest of the alphabet to you as well. Except for the *x* and the *q*. Those are top secret. You'll have to buy our next book for those.

PART ONE

PRODUCER EVOLUTION

In the nine decades that radio has been a staple of American life, it has undergone some dramatic changes. From an exciting new medium found in only a few lucky homes, to a network-dominated medium that was the centerpiece of every home, to a format-driven medium that tried to serve everyone, to a niche-market medium serving a narrowly defined audience, radio has changed with the times. The producer position has also undergone striking changes.

In part 1 we'll explain the evolution of the position, and the hierarchy of the modern-day radio station. This will lay the foundation for the nuts and bolts discussion of a producer's duties found in parts 2 and 3.

1

THE WONDERFUL WORLD OF RADIO

IN THE DAYS BEFORE TELEVISION, A RADIO WAS THE CENTERPIECE OF everyone's home. Families gathered around the radio and listened to the same types of programs that dominate the television landscape today: dramas, comedies, variety shows, and news programs run by the big national radio networks. Like television today, radio prime time before 1955 was the evening hours when the whole family was home.

When shows like *I Love Lucy* (known on the radio as *My Favorite Husband*) were converted into television shows, and people were able to see the faces that went along with their favorite radio stars, television quickly replaced the radio as the centerpiece of the American home. Radio was forced to change, and it had to change dramatically. It could no longer offer the type of entertainment it had provided for nearly thirty years.

In the early fifties, two radio programmers came up with the innovation that rescued radio from oblivion: the format. Todd Storz (from KOWH in Omaha) and Gordon McLendon (from KILF-AM in Dallas) were at a bar having a few cocktails when they noticed that the waitress kept playing the same record on the jukebox over and over again. When they asked her why she did that, she simply replied that she liked the song. Over drinks that day, those two executives came up with the concept of Top 40 radio; playing the top hits of the day over and over again. In so doing, they also created something else—the radio format.

Over the next few years, radio gave America something television could never give them; a steady diet of their favorite records. Radio prime time was no longer in the evening; that was written off and ceded to television. The home was no longer the primary place people listened to the radio; the captive audience in the car on the way to and from work became the target audience. Prime time was now morning drive and afternoon drive; and radio was a local phenomenon.

RADIO SINCE 1955

From the early sixties through the mid- to late seventies, AM radio was still dominant. Powerful AM signals belting out the hits of the day from coast to coast and all-talk stations like KMOX-St. Louis, KABC-Los Angeles, and KVOR-Denver shared the lion's share of the radio audience. These were mass audience radio stations, trying to reach the maximum number of people of all ages. The biggest radio stars were the hosts on these AM radio powerhouses. Legendary DJs like Wolfman Jack, Casey Kasem, Dick Biondi, Murray the K, Cousin Brucie, John Records Landecker, and Larry Lujack shared the air with hosts like Don McNeil (host of the Breakfast Club) and Wally Phillips (who at one time had a Chicago audience of more than 1 million). Some of them had astounding audience shares hovering around 40 percent of the market. But they also had precious little competition.

In the late seventies, the emergence of FM radio began to change the radio landscape once again. Radio stations began to target more specific audiences, and FM radio with its virtually static-free signal became the major player in music radio. Top-40 radio died a slow death over the next ten years as FM radio divided the market more and more. Classical (created by Gordon McLendon, the first real FM format), AOR (album-oriented rock), MOR (middle-of-the-road), country, jazz, oldies, and many other formats were created and began to flourish. By the late eighties, AM music stations were nearly obsolete, and AM primarily became a venue for talk radio.

Because each market now had so many different radio stations with so many different formats to choose from, the biggest radio stars were now only attracting a fraction of the audience they once attracted. To become a radio star, the host had to be more outrageous simply to attract attention. In every major market in America, a new breed of morning radio star emerged on FM radio. Howard Stern and Scott Shannon in New York; Rick Dees, and Mark and Brian in Los Angeles; Jonathon Brandmeier, and Steve Dahl and Garry Meier in Chicago; Kidd Kraddick in Dallas; The Greaseman in Washington D.C.; Bob and Tom in Indianapolis; Jeff and Jer in San Diego; and Matt Siegel in Boston were on the vanguard of this new FM radio wave.

While the media deregulation frenzy of the mid-nineties has altered the radio landscape into an arguably less creatively competitive environment, it has also raised the stakes financially. A few major corporations like Viacom and Clear Channel now own the vast majority of the radio stations in America. Radio stars are syndicated on stations all over the country. There are fewer radio stars today than there were twenty years ago, but now each of those radio stars presides over a multi-million dollar enterprise. And the need for having a quality radio producer has never been greater.

THE EVOLUTION OF THE RADIO PRODUCER

Radio producers have been around in some form since the beginning of radio formats in the 1960s, but they were merely an afterthought at the time. The radio host was often a disc jockey who played the biggest records and tried to interject personality in short bursts between records. Major market stars did have producers, but their roles were nothing comparable to what they do today. In addition to a producer, many daytime major-market radio shows also had an engineer and a turntable operator (TTO).

Bob Dearborn was a personality on WIND radio in Chicago in 1970. He still remembers the cumbersome way the show was executed in those days:

"The engineer, in his own separate room with a glass window looking into the studio, had most of the controls. He started the commercials, jingles, and every recorded program element except the music. He also turned on the host's microphone. The TTO played all the music—on vinyl from two turntables located in the studio. The producer was positioned in the studio, physically between the host and the TTO along a long counter, and it was his job to suggest and coordinate the various program elements, keeping everything on time and according to the program log. I remember it well. After discussing the next moves in the program with three other players during a song, even something as simple as talking over a music intro would be a highly orchestrated event, and always with arms flailing."

When radio stations began to play taped cartridges, the TTO went the way of the dinosaur. The definition of the engineer changed dramatically too. The engineer of the seventies has slowly become what is now considered a board operator. (For more information on board operators, read chapter 16.) The engineer of today is the person that maintains and fixes all of the equipment in a radio station. The producer position, on the other hand, eventually evolved into a much more important position.

Radio legend Fred Winston was a morning radio star in Chicago for a decade before he encountered this new kind of producer. He remembers it distinctly:

"My first encounter with a real producer was when I switched over to mornings at WCFL in 1980. My program director Dave Martin hired a young fellow named Steve Dale. Steve greeted me by informing me that he doesn't make coffee. We would brainstorm before and after the show, he would contact guests, work press contacts, strip the papers, and contribute to the show on a new level; a higher level."

Today the radio producer does all of that and more. Over the next two parts of this book we'll go into those duties in great detail.

THE HIERARCHY OF A RADIO STATION

In order to understand the producer's place in the bigger world of radio, it's necessary to understand the hierarchy of the radio station. This has changed over the years, but today there are essentially only two different sides to a radio station; the programming side and the sales side. These two sides of a radio station are often literally physically separated from one another and they often operate autonomously.

To understand where everybody stands in the station hierarchy we have constructed Diagram 1A. Some stations will have extra layers of management and some will have fewer, but you get the general idea.

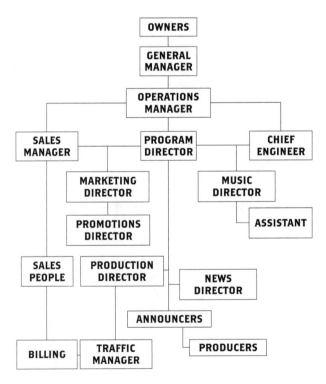

Diagram 1A

The Sales Side of Radio

As you can see by Diagram 1A, the owner is the ultimate boss of the radio station. However, in today's media landscape, the owner is nearly always a corporation. Therefore, the real power within the radio station is the general manager. He usually comes up from the sales side of the radio station and works closely with the titular head of sales, the general sales manager. Because most general managers come up through sales, and because modern day corporate reality means each station has nearly unattainable sales goals, the sales department has more power today than ever before.

The Programming Side

While the producer does deal extensively with the sales side of the business, the vast majority of his dealings come with the programming side. The producer is considered part of programming, and he must understand his place in the programming hierarchy.

His immediate boss is the host. While the producer will be dealing with the host most of the time, he must remember that the host is not the boss of the program. The host's immediate superior is the program director, and the program director's immediate superior is the general manager. Because the general manager most often deals with the sales side of the equation, the program director is essentially the king of programming. Throughout the book we will explain situations where the program director will deal directly with the producer. It's essential that the producer treat the program director with the respect he deserves.

THE PRODUCING CHALLENGE

Producing a radio show in the modern media landscape can be one of the most exciting jobs you will ever encounter. More so than producers of the past, today's radio producers are an essential part of the radio station. In our three decades of producing radio programs, we've been witnesses to the evolution of the position. In the next two parts of the book we will methodically examine each and every producer duty, and then we'll show you how it all comes together during a typical radio show. By the time you finish those parts of the book, we hope to have whetted your appetite for producing.

PART TWO

WHAT, MY BOY, DO YOU PRODUCE?

This simple question was asked to one of the authors of
this book by famous illustrator and director Chuck Jones
many years ago. It's a good question, too. Unfortunately, it's
not something we could answer in a sentence or two.
We don't think Chuck would have stuck around
to hear our complete answer anyway.

That's going to take us seven chapters. But you'll never find
a more comprehensive answer anywhere. Too
bad Chuck Jones isn't around anymore to read it.

2

BOOKING CELEBRITY GUESTS

A CELEBRITY GUEST IS THE ONLY TANGIBLE EVIDENCE THAT A SHOW EVEN has a producer. It's the only part of your job that people understand. In fact, your abilities as a producer will probably be judged based on the number and quality of celebrity guests you can book. In this chapter we're not going to debate whether or not that is fair or right. We're just going to accept that it's true and give you all the information you'll need to pass this test.

Why celebrity guests? Do people really care what celebrities have to say? The polls tell us that they don't care at all. The ratings tell us otherwise. People aren't telling the truth when they say they don't care what celebrities have to say. The proof is in the sales figures. Celebrities sell movies, they sell magazines, they sell television shows, they sell tabloids, and they sell radio shows. They know it, the producers know it, and the audience knows it.

What if your show is a hard-hitting news program? Surely the presence of celebrity guests won't be necessary on a show like that, right? Wrong. Politicians may not be Hollywood celebrities, but they are celebrities in their field. Do you think *Meet the Press* would be so respected if that show's producers didn't line up the biggest celebrity politicians? What about a sports show? It's the same concept, except you're booking celebrity athletes. A financial program will be booking Wall Street celebrities. There is no getting around this. And, of course, a music show will have famous musicians, singers, and performers.

In this chapter we'll tell you how to get all of these celebrities to appear on your show. We'll give you real-life examples from our producing careers, and we'll explain the different ways your show can accommodate a celebrity guest. If you expand the way you think, there's no telling whom you can convince to come on your program.

THE MERGING OF INTERESTS

Now that you understand the importance of getting a celebrity on your show, the next question is obvious. What's in it for the celebrity? This is where the merging of interests comes in to play. A celebrity will inevitably have something to promote, and you will offer her the opportunity to promote it for free. Whether it's her latest film, show, book, album, business venture, charity, issue, or cause, a celebrity recognizes that her celebrity status will ensure she can promote something on your show without paying for advertising. It's the classic case of "you wash my back, and I'll wash yours."

If you don't have a merging of interests like this, it becomes very difficult to book a celebrity. Even Leno and Letterman rarely have guests with nothing to promote. Once you understand the way the system works, it's just a matter of keeping an eye on who has something to promote and figuring out whom to contact. It certainly won't be the celebrity herself. It will be a public relations person representing the celebrity.

Does this book have an appendix with all of the phone numbers you'll need? No. We're not going to hand over the fish. We'll teach you to fish instead. It's not difficult if you think logically. Remember that you need to find someone whose interests merge with yours.

Let's say you know that a celebrity has something to promote. Try to figure out who else will benefit from the celebrity promoting it. Is it a local venue, a publisher, a movie company, a record company, or somebody else? Depending on the situation, you can find someone else who will have interests that merge with yours. Working with that public relations person will give you the best chance of booking the celebrity on the show. Why? Because both of you will benefit.

The key is to remember that you have something to offer as well. You have the free airtime. Don't be intimidated by celebrity status. That's how this business works. Celebrities don't pay for advertising. Radio stations don't pay for interviews. Everyone benefits.

But how do you find out who these public relations people are? We'll go over the process step-by-step, type-by-type. Most of your celebrity guests will come through local venues, book tours, movie publicity tours, and television publicity tours. Let's take a look at all of those possibilities.

LOCAL VENUES

If you discover that a celebrity is coming to town for a performance of some kind, call the local venue. Ask for the name and phone number of the person handling publicity for the venue. This person's name isn't a secret. The venue will gladly give it to you. Once you talk to the publicist directly, you can take the next step. She may be handling the booking of the celebrity herself, or she may not be, but one thing is certain. She will know who is. And you will have begun to establish a relationship with the publicist from the local venue.

It's very much like making a sales call. If you call these publicists enough, they will get to know you. You have to make them like you. Be nice. Be friendly. Don't try to intimidate or use bullying tactics. Try to make a new friend. It may take some time, but eventually you will make the sale. Before you know it, she will begin calling you.

If you are working on a show with no ratings and no presence in the market, establishing a relationship with the local PR person is essential. At first you may have to get creative to convince her that you have something to offer. Maybe the demographics of your listeners are perfect for a certain celebrity's performance. Maybe your show is not controversial, and the celebrity won't have to worry about being ambushed. There must be something. Be prepared to use that information in your pitch.

You should be doing the same thing with the PR person from every venue in town. Make a list. Make contact. Make friends. That's the best advice we can offer. A PR person from a local venue may help get you the inside track to basically three types of celebrity guests: musicians, comedians, and actors. Let's take a closer look at all three.

Musicians

The local venue probably won't be able to secure the musical guest for you, but they will be able to give you a heads up on who is coming to town. Remember that concerts are booked months in advance. Any advance knowledge you have may make the difference, because when it comes right down to it, the key to landing a musician is still the format of your radio station. If your station plays the musician's music, you step to the front of the line. If your station doesn't, you are going to have a very tough sell.

If you see right away that your format is incompatible with the guest, but you still think she would make a good guest for your show, there are a few ways around the format issue. For instance, in the era of large radio conglomerates, it may be good enough if your sister station plays the music of the musician.

Sometimes your sister station has the musician in for an interview, and your station is right down the hallway. If you are the musician, wouldn't you rather just pop in the studio down the hall for another interview than drive all the way across town to another station?

You're just making the musician's life easier. You have to use whatever weapon you have in your arsenal and you'd be shocked how many times "we're right down the hall" is good enough to get someone booked.

There are other ways to book musical guests outside of your format, but you have to get creative. If you find out the musician's pet cause or passion, you may bypass what seems to be a dead end. Paul McCartney loves to talk about animal rights. Ted Nugent loves hunting. Kid Rock is a die-hard sports fan. You get the picture. Don't give up just because your first try hits a dead end.

WORKING YOUR FORMAT

If your station does have a format match, you'll still need a little help. Musicians are usually booked through record companies or independent promoters. While you may not have a relationship with an independent promoter or someone at a record company, you can bet that your music director or program director does. They talk to those guys every single day. It's all about relationships. Use this relationship to help you book the musician for your show. All you have to do is ask your colleague. She'll be more than happy to help you out.

Some formats do this particularly well. The country music industry, for instance, is like a well-oiled machine. Country music artists will nearly always appear on country music stations. The artists don't question it. The record companies, the radio stations, and the country music artists are all part of one team. They even give out awards to radio personalities at the Country Music Awards. If you are producing a country music radio show and you can't get country music guests, something is very wrong.

The other music formats are not like that. Their formats have been sliced and diced into so many tiny little pieces that particular artists overlap onto many different stations. This is especially true of rock, pop, and rap. You may be competing against five other music stations with similar formats. Because the competition is so fierce, the industries haven't been able to mobilize the marketplace like the country music stations have.

Ironically, some formats that have a monopoly are also particularly bad at promoting their own product. The oldies market is one of the worst. There are several reasons for this. For one thing, many of the artists are dead; two of the Beatles, four of the Temptations, Elvis Presley, etc. For another thing, the surviving groups don't consider themselves oldies artists, even groups like the Beach Boys and the Rolling Stones, and individuals like Chubby Checker and Little Richard. Lastly, many of the record companies that signed these artists originally signed them to contracts that are considered unfair by today's standards. The artists aren't motivated to help the record companies, and the record companies may not even have contact with the artists anymore.

John Swanson is the producer of *The Eric and Kathy Show* on WTMX in Chicago. Their format is called "Today's New Music." Acts like Matchbox Twenty, Train, the Goo Goo Dolls, David Bowie, and Sting, were booked on *The Eric and Kathy Show* mainly because WTMX played the music from each of these artists. While other radio stations also played music from every one of these artists, none of them had a powerhouse morning show. The combination of format and ratings scored some of the biggest names in the music business.

▶ ▶ ▶

Rick Kaempfer was the producer of *The Steve Dahl and Garry Meier Show* on WLUP-AM, a comedy-talk show. Music was rarely if ever played on his station. However, WLUP-FM was their sister station, and it was a rock and roll–radio powerhouse. Because of the close proximity to the rock station (right down the hall), artists at the height of their popularity (like Aerosmith) made appearances on the talk show Rick produced.

▶ ▶ ▶

Sometimes getting a big name musician is as easy as asking the musician you already have in your studio to call up his friends. Eagles guitarist Joe Walsh was a guest on a show produced by Rick Kaempfer. At the time, Joe was touring as part of Ringo Starr's All-Star Band. The host asked Joe if he wouldn't mind calling Ringo. Joe agreed and suddenly one of the Beatles was a guest on the show.

Comedians

To find a merging of interests in the comedy world, you probably have to look beyond the sold-out arena shows by a comedy giant. If he doesn't need to sell tickets, he won't want to come on a radio show and do his act. (The exception to this rule is if the host and the comedian have a relationship that goes way back.)

To find the pearls in the comedy oyster, look no further than the comedy club. Nearly every town in America has a comedy club, and from time to time they also bring in big-name acts. Comedians may be playing the smaller venues to work out new material, or they may be doing it as a favor to the club owner who booked them when they were still unknown. Nearly every comedian working in show business today has worked the comedy club circuit. Some very well-known names may be willing to come on your show just to help out the club. (Some of the comedians booked by the authors of this book include Tim Allen, Wayne Brady, David Brenner, George Carlin, Jay Leno, Richard Lewis, Bill Maher, Steve Martin, Dennis Miller, Bob Newhart, Joan Rivers, Adam Sandler, Harry Shearer, Martin Short, Jerry Seinfeld, and Tommy Smothers.)

Booking these comedians can be as easy as calling the comedy club. The club will either have a local publicity person who handles this, or the owner does it himself. Call the club and introduce yourself. Ask to be put on the club's mailing list. Comedy clubs are very cooperative. They understand the power of free publicity.

Sometimes it pays to take a chance on an up-and-coming comedian, as well. The club will know who is really funny and may strongly recommend a comedian to you. Ask if the publicist can send you a CD or a tape of a cable television appearance. It's worth your while to listen to them. The unknown comedian of today is the David Letterman or Jay Leno of tomorrow.

> It pays to treat the up-and-coming comedian with respect. In the comedy club boom of the eighties, two comedians who are now very well known appeared on a popular Chicago radio show a few months apart. One of these comedians didn't want to do his act on the air. The host threatened to throw him off the show. He started doing his act, but he never forgot the treatment he received. The other comedian was tossed off the show because the host didn't think he was funny enough. We won't embarrass the host by divulging his name, but we will mention the names of the comedians. They both got a television show a few years later: Jerry Seinfeld and Tim Allen.

Actors

Many actors who achieved a certain level of fame in the past make a living in the present by doing theater. These actors may be coming to your town. Again, a call to your local venue public relations person will be your first move. Are you beginning to see why it's important to cultivate these relationships? There are only a handful of venues in each town and you should have established a relationship with the publicist for each one. If you haven't added a few of the bigger theaters in town to your list of venues, do so at once.

Famous and semi-famous actors or actresses may be doing a touring version of *Love Letters* or *The Vagina Monologues* or may be appearing in a musical. The process involved in getting these people on your show is the same as it is with the other venues. Call the PR person. These actors usually have to sign some sort of agreement in which they agree to do publicity for the show. That means you can get them to appear on your show.

The list of celebrities who have done local theater in the past few years includes names you'll recognize from the last four decades, including stars from the sixties like Barbara Eden, Marlo Thomas, and Dick Van Dyke, stars from the seventies like Bea Arthur, Maureen McCormick, Mary Tyler Moore, and Marion Ross, and stars from the eighties like Marilu Henner, Shelley Long, Bronson Pinchot, and George Wendt.

BOOK TOURS

There are only a few bookstores where celebrities appear for book signings. These are usually the big guns like Borders and Barnes & Noble. Once again, there is usually a local (or regional) person that handles the local publicity for these book tours. A simple call to the bookstore will let you know who handles publicity for the store. If she can't personally book the celebrity for you, she will do whatever she can to hook you up with the person who does. It is advantageous to cultivate a relationship with the bookstore PR person for this reason alone.

However, the publisher books most book tours. These are almost always in New York. It's a little more difficult to cultivate a relationship with someone like this, but it pays off big-time if you can do it. The most frustrating thing that a producer encounters is when he calls a publicist the day he finds out about a book tour and the celebrity is already booked solid. How does this happen? The publicist in New York calls producers before the information becomes known. That's how. If you cultivate a relationship with the New York publicists, you will be the one taking that call.

We always recommend sending out a mass letter to the publicity director of every publisher in New York to alert her that you have taken the producer job. (The big publishing houses are major conglomerates now too. There aren't that many. Check online for names and addresses.) In your letter introducing yourself, you should also be selling the show you produce. Follow up that letter with a phone call introducing yourself, and explain to the publisher's publicist the types of guests that you might be interested in booking.

You'd be amazed how much of an impact this can have. At the very least you'll get on everyone's mailing list and start receiving the books and press releases before that information becomes public. You may not be getting a call offering the author as a guest, but you'll be getting a heads up to call and ask.

One of the reasons celebrities get signed to book deals is that they will be sought-after guests. One of the most expensive parts of selling a book is the marketing and promotion. With a celebrity author the publisher gets tons of free publicity. What celebrities have done book tours in recent years? Tom Brokaw, Mel Brooks, Kim Cattrall, Cindy Crawford, Walter Cronkite, Jamie Lee Curtis, Tony Curtis, Bo Derek, Roger Ebert, Patricia Heaton, Hugh Heffner, Charlton Heston, Eric Idle, Larry King, Karl Malden, Dan Rather, Paul Reiser, Ray Romano, Carl Reiner, Cybil Sheppard, Richard Simmons, and Martha Stewart. That's where you come in. Your interests merge with their interests. That's the way this business works.

Sometimes being aced out of the book tour isn't the end of the line. Martha Stewart was appearing in Chicago but only agreed to do television interviews to publicize her book. When *The John Landecker Show* discovered this, they contacted the television show and asked if John could come in and serenade Martha on camera with a song he wrote for her. The TV producer loved the idea and let the radio host into the television interview with a boom box. Landecker proceeded to sing his parody song for her. She loved it, the host loved it, the TV show loved it, the audience loved it, and the entire thing was taped and played back on the radio the next day.

MOVIE PUBLICITY

Of course, the biggest stars are the most difficult to get. Movie stars often only do publicity in the biggest markets, and often don't do radio at all. There will generally be one or two PR firms in every town that deal with the movie companies. You need to find out who these firms are. These are the people that put together movie screenings for critics and sneak preview audiences. If you are having a hard time finding this information, call the local movie critic's office and ask him. His people will be able to tell you right away.

Once you find out whom to contact, you have the key to getting the biggest names in the business. Again, you have to establish a relationship. This time it's going to be a little harder because the merging of interests isn't as equal. Tom Cruise doesn't need your show to sell tickets as much you need him to boost your ratings. However, you can help the movie companies by sponsoring movie screenings or sneak peaks. You can help them by doing giveaways when movies come out on DVD. Do what you can to cultivate this relationship.

We suggest you try to find a way to get the host or yourself on the "critic list" to see the movies. The PR firm may not tell you this, but movie stars will not come on your show if you haven't seen their films. And the catch-22 is that they promote the movie before it comes out in the theaters. If you aren't on the critic list, or you haven't been part of a sponsored "sneak peak" you have no chance at booking the movie star. It's a little trick they use to make sure that if you do get an interview with the star, you'll only ask him about that movie.

There are times when lightning strikes and you actually do get an interview. Don't get too excited. It won't be an in-studio visit to your show unless your show is huge like Howard Stern's. And it won't be live. And it probably won't be one-on-one.

However, the movie companies will accommodate you if you can go to the star's hotel and tape an interview. If you've ever seen the film *Notting Hill* with Julia Roberts and Hugh Grant, there's a great scene in that movie that shows you how this process works. The star is in her suite, and the interviewers are brought in one after the other. They are usually given five or ten minutes, and they're cut off if the topic strays too far from the subject of the movie.

It's more likely that they do a mini press conference (also known as a "roundtable"). They'll have five or six press people in the room at once, and you have to fight for the star's attention. Or, they'll have a full-fledged press conference for all the members of the press. Luckily, you are considered part of the press. However, in this kind of scenario, you're lucky if you get to ask more than one or two questions.

So why go? Because with creative editing, it will sound like you had a one-on-one interview with one of the biggest stars in the world. Some of the movie stars booked by the authors of this book include Ben Affleck, Julie Andrews, Sandra Bullock, James Cromwell, Tom Cruise, Penelope Cruz, John Cusack, Joan Cusack, Matt Damon, Michael Douglas, Will Ferrell, Mel Gibson, Hugh Grant, Tom Hanks, Jennifer

Love Hewitt, Elizabeth Hurley, Jennifer Lopez, Bill Murray, Julia Roberts, Kevin Spacey, Ben Stiller, and John Travolta.

Sometimes interviewing a big Hollywood star isn't all that it's cracked up to be. Harrison Ford was in Chicago promoting his movie about a Russian submarine. He was not only the star of the film, he was one of the producers. Yet, it was obvious from the moment he stepped into the interview room that he wanted to be a million miles away. Five or six people were granted access to this interview (roundtable) including representatives from the shows of both writers of this book. Ford scowled at the interviewers and often didn't even answer the questions. When he walked out of the room a few minutes later, not one person in the room had anything usable. It wasn't the questions. It was the interviewee. John Swanson found a creative way to use the interview anyway. By taking one comment out of context (Ford drank Vodka in Russia), Swanson poked a little fun at the ornery star. In the interview that aired, host Eric Ferguson asked all the questions he originally intended to ask, and Ford answered every question by talking about vodka.

▶ ▶ ▶

Sometimes with a little perseverance, a little creativity, and a lot of luck, a major movie star can appear on your show. John Travolta appeared on a few radio shows with John Landecker in the seventies when both of them were at the pinnacle of their respective businesses. They formed a friendship, but lost touch when Travolta's career went into a slump and Landecker moved to a different market. After Travolta's resurgence with *Pulp Fiction*, Rick Kaempfer (Landecker's producer) tried to book Travolta to appear on the show for a birthday surprise. He found out that Travolta was filming in Texas and talked to the unit publicist. Kaempfer sent her pictures of Travolta and Landecker together, and tapes of their previous interviews. It was obvious from all of these things that there was an actual friendship there. Still, the unit publicist wouldn't budge. Finally, Rick asked her to just mention the name Landecker to Travolta. If he said he didn't know Landecker, Rick promised to stop calling. She gave in. Travolta was excited to hear from Landecker and called in to the show on Landecker's fiftieth birthday as a surprise. After that, every time he came to Chicago he insisted that Landecker's name was put on the list of one-on-one interviews.

▶ ▶ ▶

Sometimes you have to bypass this movie monopoly all together to get a movie star on your show by appealing to one of the star's other interests. Russell Crowe does movie publicity, but also likes to talk about his music career. His band Thirty Odd Foot of Grunts appears at medium-sized venues throughout the country. John Swanson booked him on *The Eric and Kathy Show* on WTMX by promising to talk about his music, and by promising not to talk about his personal life. Of course he also talked about his movies, but he wasn't as guarded, and the interview was much better because of it.

TELEVISION PUBLICITY

It used to be virtually impossible to get television stars to do radio interviews. They work fifteen-hour days on the set, they get paid enormous amounts of money, and their free time is precious. Plus, if you live anywhere east of the Rocky Mountains, they won't want to get up early enough to call a morning show.

A few years ago the networks got smart. They started doing radio tours. They offer these via satellite or phone. Television stars are brought into a room in New York or Los Angeles. The PR people have lined up radio stations across the country and given each of them eight to ten minutes (lately they have cut this down to as little as four minutes). Now the stars can do interviews in ten or fifteen cities in America from one convenient place.

How do you get in on these tours? You can call your local TV reps and they should be able to give you the names and numbers of contacts. Or, you can call the networks in Los Angeles or New York directly and ask to be placed on their e-mail lists. (Again, when you call the network you are asking for the publicity department.) Remember to mention to the network if your radio station is part of the same company that owns the network (ABC and CBS both own radio networks), because you'll be given preferential treatment. If there is something else about your radio show or station that makes you attractive to the networks (like young demographics), be sure to mention that too. That may help you get preferential treatment as well. Otherwise, it's done largely on a first come, first served basis in each market.

These tours are offered sporadically, with only one or two days' notice, and the offers come via e-mail. If you check your e-mail often, you may get one of the biggest stars on television on your radio show. These include the hottest reality TV stars (like *The Bachelor* or the winner of *Survivor*), cable TV stars (like members of *The Sopranos* or *Sex in the City* casts or *Queer Eye for the Straight Guy*), and traditional network stars (like Dan Aykroyd, Jim Belushi, Drew Carey, Dan Castellaneta, Dick Clark, Ted Danson, Kelsey Grammer, Bonnie Hunt, John Mahoney, Regis Philbin, David Schwimmer, and Oprah Winfrey).

Movie and television stars also have their own publicists. By calling the Screen Actors Guild directory, you can obtain the phone number of any actor's agent. Once you get the actor's agent, you need to call his office and ask for the name of the actor's publicist. That person may be able to help you. You can try it. It has worked a few times in the past. However, we have found that you are more likely to book a celebrity if you go through someone else who has a merging of interests with you.

LOCAL TELEVISION PUBLICITY

Talking to a local TV news anchor or reporter about a big local or national news story he is covering can be a very memorable and topical interview. If you are interested in booking your local TV stars (usually news anchors and reporters), they can be reached through the publicity department of the television station. Treat this person the same way you treat all the other PR people you encounter. You are cultivating a relationship.

The truth of the matter is, however, that you can probably just call the local TV star directly. When you call the switchboard ask for him by name. You'll probably be put right through to his voice mail. You'll be shocked at how easy it is.

In some smaller markets, the local television station may not even have a publicity department. Try calling the stars directly first.

POLITICIANS

Even though a politician doesn't have a publicist, per se, he will have a press secretary and/or a scheduling secretary. This is another relationship to cultivate. If the politician is in Washington, you can get his office number by calling information. It's that easy. When you reach his office, ask for the press secretary, and away you go. During an election campaign, a simple call to information will find the local campaign headquarters. The same approach applies.

Unlike Hollywood-type stars, politicians move toward the microphone or telephone like moths to a flame. If it's an election season, it's even easier. The secret to getting a politician on your show is to somehow let him know that the show is on his side. Because of the way this country is split right now between conservatives and liberals, he may not want to appear on a show that disagrees with him. He probably realizes that he will never convert someone with an agenda. However, if you are bi-partisan, non-partisan, or you have the same affiliation as the politician, make sure you let the press secretary know that.

There are exceptions to that rule, of course. Any show that reaches a huge audience of his constituents will be too hard for him to pass up, even if the host disagrees with him. Also, some politicians actually revel in the debate, because they think they are more informed on the issues than a mere radio host. And, as we discussed earlier, sometimes politicians are out on book tours, and politics doesn't matter when you want to sell books. Some of the most famous names in the world will appear on your radio show to promote their books. Some examples from recent years include General Wesley Clark, Senator Hillary Clinton, former Vice President Al Gore, former Speaker of the House Newt Gingrich, former New York City Mayor Rudolph Giuliani, Secretary of State Colin Powell, and former President Jimmy Carter.

As with any other guest you are trying to get on the show, the key is to make sure there is a merging of interests. Can he reach people that will vote for him? Can he show a side of himself that other radio shows won't allow him to show? Have your angle prepared before you call the office.

ATHLETES

Athletes are at your mercy when they are on the road. All the professional teams stay at the same hotel. It's not too hard to find out which hotel that is. Your listeners will probably let you know. Sports radio producers use the hotel approach all the time. They call the front desk, ask for the athlete's room, and sometimes the front desk will actually put you through.

This isn't an approach that we like to use, but, then again, we haven't worked on shows that had a lot of athletes as guests. We prefer going through the publicity department of the team, just as we do with the other guests we try to book. You are showing the potential guest more respect this way, and when you do get them on your show, they won't be as irritated.

Many people think that athletes are not great guests, but they can be if handled correctly. Nearly everybody in your town follows the local team. If a member of that team became a regular contributor to your show, it could instantly make your show a part of the community. Some athletes could be persuaded to contribute regularly, especially if they have aspirations for a post-sports broadcasting career.

Even a female demographic station can have athletes on the show talking sports. How can you avoid it, especially if you are in a major market where passions run high? It's all about the angle. Many football teams now have clinics for women every year. Many athletes are involved in charities and have fundraisers. Keep an open mind, and it can be a win-win situation.

A FEW MORE WORDS ABOUT PR PEOPLE

A producer will deal with public relations professionals every day he is on the job. We gave you some tips from the producer perspective, but we also wanted to give you a glimpse of the other side. We asked a few public relations executives about what they liked or didn't like about dealing with radio producers. They had some good insights.

Nick Harkin is the vice president/public relations for Carol Fox & Associates. While he says that his dealings with radio producers have been wonderful for the most part, he does offer a few suggestions to improve long-term relations:

"If you want me to bring a guest to your show, I need to be able to make sure that they will have the opportunity to discuss what they are promoting. Celebrities rarely want to appear on radio shows 'just for fun.' They generally do interviews only when they are publicizing a new project or product. This does not mean that the interview has to be a non-stop sales pitch, but it does need to be a respectable portion of the conversation.

"The most successful producer/publicist relationships work because they have a strong foundation of mutual understanding. In the end, the clients pay my salary, so I will book them on radio shows where they will have fun, will be treated with respect, and will have the opportunity to communicate their messages. If, however, a radio producer misrepresents his show, and the client ends up feeling embarrassed or treated rudely, I will certainly hesitate before I bring another guest to that show. On the other hand, if I know that the interview will be a great experience for the client, I will bend over backwards to try and bring even the biggest celebrity to that station."

Lissy Peace is a partner with the public relations firm of Blanco & Peace Enterprises, Ltd. She has dealt with countless radio producers and celebrities in her career. She has further advice for the radio producer.

"Always get back to the public relations folks, whether it's an e-mail, note, or phone call. You never know who might bring you the next biggest celebrity or high-profile story. Many times, PR people will give those individuals that have responded to them over the years, *the* big interview. Also, always tell guests how long they are expected to be on the air, and always review the material before doing the interview."

That last statement is so basic, yet you'd be amazed how often an interviewer isn't prepared. That's the host's fault, right? No. The producer also has to prep the host, and that's a subject we'll explore at great length in the next chapter.

3

CRAFTING A GREAT INTERVIEW

AS WE ALLUDED TO AT THE END OF THE LAST CHAPTER, BOOKING THE celebrity guest is only the beginning of the interview process. You must still prepare the host for the interview. In this chapter, we'll break down an interview so that you understand the basic elements and types. Once you understand this, it will be easier to provide the kind of raw data the host can use to craft a great interview. We'll also show you where to get the raw data, how to present it to the host, and what you can do with an interview after it's complete.

Throughout the chapter, we'll give you real life stories and examples to illustrate our techniques. We're not saying that you have to do it the way we do, we're only showing you one way to do it. Each producer has his strengths and weaknesses and you might want to tailor your interview prep to your strengths.

ELEMENTS OF AN INTERVIEW

There are basically three different elements to an interview; the introduction, the body of the interview, and the close. To create a great interview you must have a basic idea of what to do in each of those elements. You are simply putting together a possible blueprint for the interview. Realize that once an interview begins, it may go in a totally different direction. That's absolutely fine. The host can choose to take your suggestions or not. It's his show.

Your job is to give him all the information he needs to make the choice that's best for him.

The Introduction

Remember the celebrity is coming on your show because she has something to promote. She will have her shtick rehearsed. If you let her say her rehearsed PR stuff unfiltered, it will be an interview of "blah, blah, blah." Avoid that at all costs.

The host needs to do something that she doesn't expect, something that will throw her off her "blah, blah, blah" game right out of the box. This will bring out the real person in the celebrity, and that's when the interview will be compelling. But how can you throw her off? You don't want to anger her or scare her, but it's not a bad thing to make her laugh, politely embarrass her, or start with something so strange she couldn't possibly have anticipated it. Once she has loosened up, she will be a better interviewee.

Marilu Henner was a guest on a show produced by Rick Kaempfer: *The John Landecker Show*. The first thing John said to her on the air was: "We'll be right back after these commercial announcements. Marilu and I are going down to Michigan Avenue in a taxi and we'll be conducting the interview from there." Marilu was completely thrown off, but went with the concept. She still got to plug the book she was promoting, but she also talked to a taxi driver about her show *Taxi* and had a wonderful time doing an interview that was completely different from the ten other interviews she had to do that day.

▶ ▶ ▶

Mary Tyler Moore was a guest on a show produced by Rick Kaempfer about five years ago. She was appearing via satellite on a television publicity tour. It was scheduled to be a ten-minute interview. Mary knew that she was going to be interviewed by a man and a woman, but that was all she knew. As soon as the interview started, the female interviewer started getting belligerent and questioned Mary Tyler Moore's sincerity. Mary got upset. She started to go after the woman, until she began to sense that something was going on. After a few more seconds, she recognized the voice. It was her good friend and former co-star Valerie Harper, who happened to be in town doing a play. The awkwardness of the first few seconds of the interview led to a truly special interview that Mary probably remembers to this day.

The Body of the Interview

In the introduction to this book we mentioned that one host used to tell his producer that he needed him to be the frosting and the cake. If the introduction to the interview is the frosting, then the body of the interview is the cake.

The host must know what he wants to accomplish in the interview, he must know what the guest wants to accomplish, and he must have a good idea how to make that happen as creatively as possible. The producer is an essential part of this equation. He does the research into the background of the guest to find questions that the celebrity hasn't been asked a million times. There are all sorts of places to conduct this research, but everything starts on the Internet.

Doing a simple Google search will land you countless Web sites with information about any celebrity guest. For example, let's get really obscure. We did a Google search on Scott Valentine, the actor who played Mallory's boyfriend Nick on the eighties sitcom *Family Ties*. Would you care to guess how many Google matches there were? Would you believe at this writing there were 5,450 matches? No offense to Scott Valentine, but 5,450? Of those, there were even a few very helpful sites.

Tvtome.com had a Scott Valentine bio (he was born in 1958 in Saratoga Springs, New York, by the way) and a complete list of his television acting appearances. Did you know that he's been doing voice-over work on cartoons lately? He did voice work for *Batman, Pinky & the Brain*, and *Phantom 2040*. He recently had a guest-starring role on *Jag*, too. The next match on the Google search was the ever-helpful Internet Movie Database (which is commonly referred to as IMDb). We found more information about Valentine at imdb.com. Did you know that he has been working pretty steadily in B-movies since *Family Ties* went off the air? He has had over thirty roles since the mid-eighties, and even worked as a director on a TV project named *Black Scorpion*.

All of that information about an obscure celebrity comes from two Web sites and one Google search. It took us about five minutes. Imagine what you'd find about bigger names if you spent a little more time and effort. You can find more extensive biographical information, old interviews, funny television or movie appearances, learn about private passions and causes, and really get a feel for what the guest will be like. You can even find Web sites that have audio clips you can download. That will save you a lot of legwork when you don't want to call video stores looking for *Black Scorpion*. (We'll get into a more in-depth discussion of how to accumulate and organize audio in chapter 18.)

Once you have finished your private research, remember what public relations executive Lissy Peace mentioned at the end of the last chapter. She said that the producer needs to make sure the host has at least reviewed the guest's material. This is what she meant. Give the celebrity the courtesy of knowing what she wants to talk about and incorporating some of that into the interview. It's the least you can do.

Now you are ready to put something together for the host to peruse. Since you probably aren't going to interview Scott Valentine (again—no offense, Scott), we chose another celebrity to give you a more realistic example. See appendix C for a sample celebrity interview prep sheet.

Once you give your suggestions to the host, it's his baby.

The Close

You know generally how long the interview is going to last. The length is nearly always set in advance because the guest is usually on a tight schedule. Therefore, you have to be prepared for the way you want the interview to end. The host will usually hold something in his back pocket to finish the interview with a flourish. It doesn't need to be anything outrageous or spectacular, it just needs to be something that can quickly change the subject and give the host an opportunity to say goodbye without sounding rude (and without making the celebrity sound like she is being rude because she has to leave in mid-interview).

There are many ways to tackle this and the techniques vary from host to host. Listen around and you'll hear all sorts of different approaches. It almost doesn't matter which approach the host chooses. As long as the interview begins with a bang and ends with a flourish, listeners will remember it fondly.

Michael Douglas was doing a satellite interview on *The John Landecker Show* from New York to promote a movie. To close the interview, Landecker played audio clips of the sex scenes from *Fatal Attraction*, *Disclosure*, and *Basic Instinct* and asked Douglas to identify who he was having sex with in each scene. Douglas got a kick out of the creative approach, correctly identified each woman, and the interview ended with a flourish.

▶ ▶ ▶

Matt Damon and Ben Affleck were appearing on a radio show to promote their participation in *Project Greenlight*. Affleck and Damon have a tendency to verbally spar with each other when they are on the air together. The host of the show realized this and told them he wanted to end the interview by playing a clip of each of their finest acting performances. When the host played a clip from *Reindeer Games* to playfully tease Affleck, Damon piled on to gently mock his buddy. When this clip was followed up by a toy horse whinnying, Affleck got to mock his buddy for being the voice of the animated horse in the movie *Spirit*. The interview ended with a flourish, and both actors left the studio laughing.

TYPES OF INTERVIEWS

For the purposes of this chapter, we're not identifying interviews by topic or tone. We're more concerned about setting. There are basically four different types of interviews and each one demands a different approach. A live in-studio interview is the pinnacle. If you can't get a live in-studio interview, however, you may accept a live phone interview. It's not quite the same as face to face, but at least it takes place live on the air. The third type of interview is a satellite interview. It can sound like an in-studio interview but may create technical issues. The fourth type is the recorded interview, and this kind of interview is taking place more and more.

We'll attempt to examine each type of interview and tell you the different concessions that may have to be made for each one. They each have their advantages and disadvantages, but as long as you are prepared for it, you can make the best of the situation.

Live In-Studio Interviews

If a guest is in town, the producer will always try to secure the in-studio interview. It doesn't make sense to settle for a phone interview when the guest is only a few minutes away. The in-studio interview gives all of the advantages to the interviewer. He can see the guest's facial expressions, can read her body language, and will have a chance to chat with her off the air before the interview and during commercials. The host will also feel comfortable because he has home field advantage. It's his studio, he is the boss, and the celebrity will have to follow. We've yet to meet a host who preferred phone interviews to studio interviews. There is something about the intimacy of being in the same room that contributes to an interview's success.

An in-studio interview is also the top choice for technical reasons. You have full access to your audio library, and the guest can hear everything perfectly. You can take calls from listeners if you so desire. You can have your picture taken with the celebrity to put on the station Web site. The in-studio interview isn't foolproof, but it's the closest thing to foolproof that you'll get in radio.

There are times when even an in-studio interview can derail for technical reasons. John Mahoney and Virginia Madsen were appearing live in John Landecker's studio to promote their film *Almost Salinas*. By a fluke of nature, the transmitter of the radio station malfunctioned about a minute after the interview began. The station was not on the air at all. However, the producer of the show (Rick Kaempfer) was the only person in the room who realized it. The headphones were not plugged into the on-air monitor because the show was in delay, and therefore, the host and the guests had no idea that something was wrong. Instead of telling everyone and ending the interview, Rick calmly walked out of the studio and called the chief engineer. While the engineer worked on getting the station back on the air, and Rick flop-sweated like Albert Brooks in *Broadcast News*, the interview was completed. None of it aired live because the transmitter wasn't fixed for another twenty minutes. However, the interview was recorded on a DAT (digital audiotape), and it was replayed on the air the following day, just as it originally occurred.

Phone Interviews

The advantage of the phone interview is obvious: flexibility. A celebrity can call from anywhere to be on the show. She can call from a movie or television set, she can call from vacation, she can call from her bedroom. Dick Clark admitted to us that when he does morning show phone interviews, he's not even dressed.

When someone is not in town, a phone interview is a necessary evil. There are precautions you must take, however. It's important to prep the guest on the phone as much as possible before the phone interview takes place. The guest should know the names of everyone who may be talking to her. There is nothing worse than listening to a host stop an interview in progress to explain who is talking to the guest and why they are talking to her. If you can give the guest an idea of what kind of a show she is appearing on, that would be helpful too. Most celebrities are pretty good at pretending to be good pals with the host. If you give them a few cues, it can make the interview warmer, friendlier, and take away one of the disadvantages of the phone interview, the fact that they can't see each other.

While prepping a guest on the phone, you should also make sure she is speaking on a landline and not a cellular phone or cordless phone (or heaven forbid—a speaker phone). The landline is your best technical phone option. The other types of phones have bad sound quality, can crap out at any time, and sometimes even pick up other conversations. If you have no choice but to conduct an interview by cellular phone, be prepared for the worst. Get the number so you can call back if it craps out. Also, scale back any audio options you may have prepared. The cellular phone user probably won't be able to hear the audio very well anyway.

Satellite Interviews

This is a relatively recent phenomenon. We mentioned it in the previous chapter about booking celebrity guests. Television networks make some of their stars available for satellite interview tours. The celebrity sits in a studio and does interview after interview.

The advantages of the satellite interview are that it sounds like your guest is live in your studio and she can hear you better than if she were on the phone. The disadvantages include a split second delay (unavoidable when doing it via satellite), the potential technical nightmares of hooking up via satellite, and the fact that the host can't see the guest.

The delay makes the host and the guest talk over each other, hesitate, and sound just a little off. With a satellite interview, you also have to dial up to the correct satellite position. The satellite setting is usually in another room, like engineering master control, and we've seen too many examples of someone else at the station unwittingly switching the setting for their own usage. This can leave the producer scrambling at the last second, trying to do something he thought he had done the day before.

Luckily, when you are offered a satellite interview these days, you are also given the choice of doing it on the phone. Take the phone. Believe it or not, it's less of a headache. They always have a reliable landline that the celebrity can use, and it usually works out better.

Joan Collins was doing a satellite tour from New York a few years ago. However, no one bothered to tell her in advance that she would be required to wear headphones. When she arrived, she refused to wear the headphones because it would mess up her hair. The studio engineer in New York had to set up a tiny speaker so that she could hear the interviewer when the microphones were turned on. Unfortunately, this made the delay problem even worse because now it wasn't just in the headphones—it was coming over the microphone. The interviewer heard all of his questions coming back to him a second or so after he asked them. Needless to say, every interview done with her that day was a complete technical nightmare.

RECORDED INTERVIEWS

Recorded interviews come in all shapes and sizes. You could record a face-to-face interview in your studio. You could record a phone or satellite interview at your studio, or you could record an interview from a remote site.

It wasn't too long ago that big-time hosts simply refused to record interviews (and some still do). That is changing. The competition for celebrity interviews is pretty intense in most cities, and you do what you have to do to fit someone in, even if that means more work for the host.

What sort of situations would lead to a recorded interview? If a celebrity is performing in a late-night play or concert and can't get up early, she may agree to come to the studio to record an interview in the afternoon. If the celebrity is big enough, you make the concessions. If she comes into the studio to record it, it will sound just as good as a live in-studio interview. Some people think it will sound better because you can edit it afterward. We won't go that far. It's hard to maintain the edge in a recorded interview. The host and the celebrity both know that something can be taken out if they screw up. The urgency isn't usually there. Nevertheless, it could come out sounding great.

Recording a phone interview would be appropriate if a guest is in a different country or time zone. During the war in Iraq, several radio stations recorded phone interviews at odd hours and played them back during the prime-time hours. During the Olympics, this is also often done. Lately, celebrities in Hollywood have started doing recorded phone interviews at more reasonable hours for them. If the host is willing to stick around or come back to the radio station, and if you have access to a studio, it's often worth the trouble.

In the last chapter, we told you about the movie star interview. This is a prime example of the remote-location recorded interview. The advantages are obvious. You can get a big name star (and let's face it—you probably won't go to the trouble unless it is), and the interview can sound very intimate. You can also edit out anything that didn't work, and therefore your finished product could end up sounding smoother than a live interview. Also, the host can re-record any questions that some other person might have asked so that it sounds like he conducted a longer interview than he really did. With the help of a talented editor, a recorded interview with a major star can sound very impressive—even if the host actually conducted that interview with a room full of other press people and didn't even ask the questions himself.

Recording phone interviews in studios that aren't normally used for recording interviews can present all sorts of logistical problems. Normally, you have to kick a production person out of his studio to do this, and he has everything set precisely the way he wants it. A few years ago, one of the writers of this book was attempting to tape a phone interview with Bob Newhart. The production director had no idea how to set up his control board to record a phone call. The first two times Newhart got on the line, the production director accidentally hung up on him. By the time the studio was properly set up, Newhart had been waiting on the line for twenty minutes. Luckily, he had a great sense of humor about it. He thought that they were trying to do a phone bit like the ones that made him famous.

AFTER THE INTERVIEW

You've done a great interview, it aired on the radio, and people enjoyed it. Now it's time to move on, right? Not yet. There are two more issues you should consider after the interview is over. Ask yourself this question: Did the guest reveal anything newsworthy during the interview? If the answer is yes, you should be contacting the press to let them know.

Getting Press

The person you call in the press will depend on what the celebrity said, and what kind of news it was. If this was just gossip-page fodder, a call to the local newspaper gossip columnist is in order. To give you an idea of what sort of information a gossip columnist might consider news, here's an example. When Carl Reiner and Mel Brooks appeared on one of our shows, they started riffing and did an entirely new two thousand-year-old-man bit. We sent a transcript to the gossip columnist and they printed it. Your gossip item may be more traditional like who is dating whom, and what the next project is for a certain star, but if you haven't heard the news before, it will probably be considered newsworthy by the gossip columnist.

Now, if the newsworthy item from your interview was a real news story (and let's face it, this is rare), you can go directly to the AP news wire or whichever wire service your station subscribes to. Once it appears on the news wire, it's a story. Once it's a story, you have something that money can't buy: free publicity. Keep an ear out for these stories every time you have a newsmaker or politician on your show.

Archiving the Interview

The second issue you need to consider is how you want to archive the interview. We suggest you save everything. You might want to separate a really entertaining part of the interview and put it somewhere it can be accessed easily, and put the entire interview into a more permanent storage area. Or you may have a different system in mind. It doesn't really matter what the system is, as long as you have a system. If you don't keep this audio organized, you are doomed. It's best to get it out of the way as soon as possible. It's one less thing to worry about. (Much more information about audio storage will be covered in chapter 18.)

Helpful Hint: When you have an item that you consider a story and you want to plant it with a newspaper columnist, never give it to more than one. The one you choose may decide not to run the item, but if she finds out that you have given the same item to another columnist (and she will, believe us), she may never run another item for you. It's the way newspaper people think. If it's not a scoop, it's not a story. If you are giving the story to more than one reporter, then you aren't a source, you're a PR person.

4

Coming Up with Ideas

WE MENTIONED A FEW CHAPTERS AGO THAT A PRODUCER IS JUDGED BY the number and quality of celebrity guests he books. It's the most easily measured part of a producer's job performance. However, it's really not the most important job. Coming up with ideas for a radio show is much more important.

How important? We'll be spending the next three chapters showing you where to come up with ideas and how you can help craft those ideas into radio segments. Next chapter we'll teach you how to create a great phone segment. In chapter 6 we'll teach you how to write for radio. This chapter will lay down the groundwork for both of those chapters.

The raw ideas have to come from somewhere. If coming up with ten to twenty new ideas every day sounds impossible to you, you need to expand your horizons. We've broken down the places you can find material into eight different sources: newspapers, magazines, television, the Internet, news wire services, prep services, press releases/mail, and your personal life. Within each of those sources are hundreds of more sources. You won't have time to check out all of them every day, but you will develop a few favorites that work for you and your show. Once you've done that, it will make this seemingly insurmountable task a little less intimidating.

NEWSPAPERS

A radio producer devours newspapers. It's really one of our favorite parts of the day. When we get those newspapers in our hands, we almost can't wait to go through them. Why? It's fresh meat. Inevitably you'll find brand new material every time you crack open a newspaper. It's a gold mine. This is especially true if you are working on a morning show. You'll be one of the first people in the city to read the paper. Everything you take out of the paper is new to the listeners—hence the first three letters of the word newspaper.

Depending on your market you could be reading up to ten newspapers a day. There is no way that a listener has read everything in every paper. Of course, you can't literally read every article in every paper, but it won't take you long to spot the articles you can transform into radio segments. You are looking for different angles on the big stories of the day, and offbeat stories that are unusual or strange. Those two areas will suffice for nearly every radio format.

Think about it for a moment. The big stories are self-evident. The same stories are on the front pages of every newspaper. You've been watching the news channels on television, and they have been covering the same stories too. For your purposes, a simple discussion of the top story isn't good enough. You need to come up with a new angle, a compelling new way of looking at the top stories. When you look at a newspaper, it will spark something. A columnist may have an angle. A headline may be written in a way that sparks an idea in your mind. A reporter may have covered an angle of the story that you hadn't yet considered. You can't avoid talking about the big story of the day. Your job is to make sure that your show doesn't talk about it in the same way as every other show. (In the next two chapters we'll give you the nuts and bolts of translating your angles on the big stories into radio segments.)

As for the offbeat stories, these provide the spice that further separates your show from everyone else's. This is where you can really make your mark. You'll find a few of these stories in every newspaper. Read the newspapers with a pair of scissors in your hand. You'll be clipping out anything that catches your eye. Because you've been keeping an eye on the news anyway, the stories you haven't seen before will jump off the page. You should also check out the local columnists, including the gossip columnists. They may have some information that will be particularly interesting to your audience.

What newspapers should you read? That depends on your town. You should be reading every local newspaper. For instance, in our hometown of Chicago we have four daily newspapers, the *Chicago Tribune*, the *Chicago Sun-Times*, the *Daily Herald*, and the *Daily Southtown*. If we expect to serve our entire audience, we have to look at all four of those papers every day. If you are working in a smaller market, you should read your local paper and the biggest paper in the region. You should also be reading *USA Today*, the *Wall Street Journal*, and at least one of the big New York newspapers (most likely, the *New York Times*).

Hopefully your radio station will subscribe to the key newspapers. If it doesn't, you can read most of these papers on-line. It's not as much fun (we like the smell of fresh newsprint), and it's not as convenient, but you can just as easily print a story from the Internet. Many of these papers make you register online now. They do this so they can get you on their mailing lists, but it's worth the spam and the junk mail you receive to have access to this kind of information.

THE WIRE SERVICES

Your radio station will certainly subscribe to a news wire service, whether it's AP, UPI, Reuters, or one of the new services created by the big networks specifically for their radio stations. This is even fresher meat than the newspapers.

When you get into work, check the wires. Every service has a summary page of headlines. Because you have followed the news so thoroughly, you will already know what the breaking news items are. These are the stories that will be leading all of the newscasts on your show. You better have an idea of how you want to handle them. You'll also see the stories that the newsperson will likely use as a kicker story (the humorous/off beat story at the end of a newscast). These come on a separate page, nicely sorted for the newscaster's convenience. Ask the newsperson if he has decided which kicker stories he's going to use. It may give you an idea of something the host can say or do when this story airs. Also, you may want to take a kicker story and expand it into a full-fledged radio segment.

Most wire services that radio stations subscribe to also have an audio service. Check the list of audio available. A written list will always accompany the audio. By looking over this list, you can tell if you need to listen to any of the audio. Again, something may really jump out at you. Maybe your sports team had a controversial game and the wire service has audio of the star player having a meltdown. Or maybe a figure in the news held a press conference and said something interesting or controversial. Having the audio to accompany a story like this makes all the difference in the world to a radio program. It's using your medium to its fullest.

If your station doesn't subscribe to a wire service, or you are unhappy with the service they have chosen, you can still find wire services on the Internet. Believe it or not, the Drudge Report has links to the AP, UPI, and Reuters. There are many other Web sites that also have direct links. Bookmark these Web sites and save yourself some time.

MAGAZINES

Magazines don't offer fresh news, but they do have all sorts of articles and features that can be used on the radio. Don't even know where to start with a list of magazines? Go to the local Borders (or local newsstand) and get some ideas. Think about the demographics of your audience and the types of magazines that are produced for them. Write down the names of the magazines. Ten is a nice round number. You probably won't have time to read any more than that.

You can probably get a free press copy of the magazine sent to your radio station if you call and ask for it. If not, maybe the station will pay for it. If not, and you think it can provide you with great show ideas, it might be worth your while to shell out the cash yourself. (Abbreviated versions of some magazines are available online too—but they usually don't give out the best stuff on-line for free.)

Believe us, there will be days you need ideas. There will be days when the well has run dry. That's when magazine articles come in handy. The great thing about magazines is that the information usually isn't time sensitive. You can read them at your leisure, at a time that is most convenient to you. And when you start adding up how much time it takes to accomplish all of your daily duties, you'll realize how precious your time really is.

The magazines most pertinent to your audience depend on your format and your station's demographics. Obviously, news/talk stations will be getting news magazines, but we recommend everyone get *Time, Newsweek,* and *U.S. News & World Report.* Other magazines that have great information and features include: *People, Entertainment Weekly, TV Guide, Us Weekly, Premiere, Cosmopolitan, Esquire, Glamour, GQ, Ladies Home Journal, Mademoiselle, Maxim, Men's Health, Redbook, Rolling Stone, Spin, Sports Illustrated,* and *Variety.*

TELEVISION

We like to think of television as our personal news department, covering the globe to bring us audio clips and actualities from the people making the news. If you tape at least one local newscast and one national news show every day, you'll more than likely have the crème de la crème of that day's audio (in addition to the audio we already discussed in the section about news wires).

Television does much more than give you news audio. Entertainment programs and network events are often news stories too. Sometimes they are culture-changing or flavor-of-the-month programs. These become water cooler fodder even for people who don't watch them. Some examples from recent years include shows like *Survivor, The Bachelor, American Idol, Joe Millionaire,* and *The Osbournes.*

Sometimes a news magazine will have an interview with someone on the front page of the newspapers. Shows like *20/20*, *Dateline*, and *60 Minutes* often have moments you shouldn't miss. The same is true of *Hardball* on MSNBC, *The O'Reilly Factor* on Fox News, *Larry King Live* on CNN, and *Meet the Press* on NBC.

Sometimes television carries events that are so huge that the entire country is watching them—shows like the Super Bowl, or the Oscars. These are no-brainers.

The bottom line is that you should be rolling tape on all of these shows. An audio clip from the biggest television event of the previous night will be a crucial part of your radio show. What's more effective and descriptive—simply talking about the show, or having an audio clip to play from the show while you discuss it? (Later in this chapter we'll tell you about a few prep services that cover nightly television for a fee.)

You'll be told, of course, that you aren't officially allowed to play these clips on the air. There are a few instances where this is true. For instance, David Letterman is very protective of his Top Ten List because it's nationally syndicated as a radio feature. Jay Leno cracks down on the use of his monologue for the same reason. Also, you've probably heard sportscasters warn you about "the unauthorized use of the pictures and accounts of this game."

Other than these examples, however, a simple attribution of where you got the clip will be enough. You are promoting their product. Something like, "Thanks to MSNBC for the audio clips of *Hardball*," will keep everyone happy. Believe us, even in markets like New York, Los Angeles, Chicago, and Washington, where most of the media people live, clips from television are played on the air on a daily basis. This isn't being done on the sly. In fact, in all our years of producing radio shows, we've only received two cease and desist orders, and neither of them were nasty or threatening. We simply stopped playing the clips and they stopped receiving the free publicity.

Think of the broadcasting world we live in today. After all, the same company that owns a television network may own your radio station. Those companies even have a name for using audio clips from the network that owns your station: synergy. For instance, if you are working for Viacom/Infinity (one of the two biggest radio companies in America), your network also owns Comedy Central, MTV, VH1, Nickelodeon, and CBS among others. If you are working for ABC/Disney, your station owns ABC, ESPN, Disney, etc. You get the picture. You're just promoting the company product.

All of the networks and all of your local stations are also online. Most of them are great at staying on top of the news and teasing what sort of shows they will be airing. Periodically check in on them and you'll find even more information. It's worth bookmarking CNN, ABC News, CBS News, MSNBC, Fox News, News Hour PBS, BBC-UK, Sky News-UK, CBC-Canada, and CNBC. They all have excellent Web sites.

THE INTERNET

We've already given you a lot of examples of Web sites that can help you come up with information and show ideas. After you've checked out Web sites for newspapers, wire services, and television stations, there are so many more places you can go on the Internet.

A few excellent Web sites accumulate links to places that will really help. We mentioned the Drudge Report earlier. While he does highlight stories with a slightly conservative bent, he also provides links to virtually every major newspaper, including all the big-name columnists. He provides links to international news-gathering operations, including European, Asian, Middle Eastern, and African wire services. He has links to the major magazines and public relations wire services. We highly recommend bookmarking this site: *www.drudgereport.com*.

Another Web site that accumulates useful links is *www.assignmenteditor.com*. Jim Lichtenstein was once a television producer in Chicago and has tailored his site for television newsrooms. However, it is just as helpful to radio shows. He does charge for some of the links, but others are free. Among them, Internet magazines like *Salon* and *Slate*, political sites like the U.S. Congress Briefing Room, Roll Call, C-SPAN, and Inside Beltway, and travel sites like Airport Directory and Zagat Online. Our favorite links, however, are the non-news sites. He has links to some of the greatest Web Sites on the Internet like *www.thesmokinggun.com*, the Library of Congress, and Gray's Anatomy.

What about places on the Internet to find wacky or offbeat stories? We like *www.ananova.com*, *www.bonehead.oddballs.com*, and *www.eonline.com*, but there are hundreds of them out there. Each of the wire services has an "odd news" section, for instance. Do some exploring and you'll find one that's right for your show.

If you can't find show material on the Internet, you aren't trying very hard. Of course, we should also warn you about using the station computer to do your searching. One false move on a Google or Yahoo search and you may end up on a Web site that you shouldn't be visiting on station time. It can be completely innocent, but you don't want to get in trouble and have to explain how a search for "Bush" or "Dick Armey" led you to a, shall we say, inappropriate Web site. Also, when you look up the White House, the Web address is *www.whitehouse.gov*. The last three letters are crucial. Just trust us.

For a complete listing of the Web sites mentioned in this chapter and the other chapters of the book, check appendix E. Those Web sites form a solid backbone of your favorite places on the Web. After you check them all out, we strongly recommend you bookmark them. You'll be going back to them over and over again.

PREP SERVICES

In a perfect world, you won't need to use any of these services to help you come up with material. Many shows don't use them at all, others rely on them heavily. It's a decision that you have to make along with your host and your program director. The bottom line about prep services is that they cost money.

There are hundreds of prep services in this country that compile the latest news, do wacky production bits and songs, and give you punch lines, phone numbers, and/or audio. They usually do this in exchange for commercial airtime (or "barter"). In other words, they give you the service, and your station airs the commercials that the service has sold. Some stations are simply not willing to give up the airtime so that you can have access to these services. On the other hand, many of these prep services also offer additional services to the program director (like research, ratings information, and information about competitors and other markets). Your program director might be more willing to agree to one of these services if she gets something out of it too.

We've sampled a few of these services over the years and can give you our opinions, but any of them will offer you a free trial period to check them out. The prep service that works best for you might not be the one that works best for us. These are the services that have worked best for us over the years.

Bitboard

This is a unique service, offered in exchange for airtime (barter). It's a Web site with contributions from producers and radio hosts from all over the country. Each member of Bitboard is required to contribute some material once a week. You'll see ideas that work in other markets that may work in yours. Or you may see a good germ of an idea that you can transform into your own idea. The best thing about this service is that everything is fresh, it's usually not generic, and people who have to come up with ideas just like you prepare it.

Wireless Flash

We'd love to know where the people who run this service find some of the stories they compile for Wireless Flash. A lot of prep services compile offbeat stories but, quite frankly, we've been doing this so long we rarely see something we haven't already found ourselves. The Wireless Flash is different. It has a collection of offbeat stories that we don't see anywhere else. The writers also do a little legwork and find the phone numbers of the people involved in these stories, including celebrities. That's a rare bonus for a prep service. Our only complaint about this service is that the price is a little steep. Program directors always roll their eyes when they hear it. (This is also a barter service.)

X-Radio

We just discovered this service recently. It can save you a lot of time because it provides a daily library of audio from the previous night's television. Sometimes it doesn't cover exactly what we want to cover, but it does a pretty good job. It's also a barter service.

Bit Exchange

This is another prep service that provides a daily library of audio from the previous night's television. This service also does a pretty good job of providing off-beat news stories that you won't find elsewhere. It's a barter service.

Other Prep Services

We've heard of many other services that might be right for you. Dan O'Day and Ross Britain have excellent reputations, but we've never actually tried their services. Also, a group of former producers from the West Coast have a service called The Complete Sheet. Other services that we have tried include Morning Sickness, Power Sheets, Premier, the American Comedy Network, TM Century, and Morning Mouth. Each of them has elements that are excellent. It doesn't hurt to check them out. Any and all of these services are available on the Internet and will give you a free trial period.

There are hundreds more that we've never heard of and never sampled. If you feel your show really needs the help, it's worth investigating a prep service. On the other hand, we've given you enough information in this chapter to create your own prep service. If you really love searching out ideas, a prep service can end up being redundant.

YOUR PERSONAL LIFE

Just by living your life you will come up with ideas if you know how to look for them. The simple act of going to a movie, or going to a restaurant, or a shopping mall, or a grocery store may spark an idea that you can turn into a topic of discussion. Go out with your family and you may learn more than you will watching eight hours of television. The more closely your life resembles that of the audience, the more material you can reap from this method.

We've noticed over the years that some hosts and programs get so caught up in the breaking story that they lose a connection with the listener. Many listeners don't care about the breaking story at all. They might be looking for something else—a personal connection, someone who can relate to them. Things are happening in your life every day that are also happening in the lives of your listeners. Share these with the host, and have the host share these with you. You'll be amazed at the great material that will come out.

Some programmers believe that listeners aren't interested in the lives of the people on the radio. We couldn't disagree more strongly. When a host shares details of his personal life, it humanizes him. He comes to life before the listener's eyes, moving from disembodied voice to flesh and blood. When a host shares details of his personal life, he becomes a friend to the listeners. They feel they know him. He is joining them every morning for breakfast. Or he is in the car with them every afternoon on the way home from work. If he shares the common travails and difficulties and mundane triumphs that every listener also experiences, he can make a personal connection. Examine the most popular shows in radio history and you'll see what we mean. The fans of popular shows can tell you all sorts of details about the person they listen to every day. It's one of the reasons they listen.

Some producers become personalities on the shows they produce. Rick Kaempfer shared all sorts of details about his personal life, including the birth of all three of his sons. The listeners followed the pregnancies, and Rick brought a tape recorder into the delivery room to record the actual births. As his sons grew up, a regular feature developed on the show called "My Three Sons." Rick would share humorous anecdotes, which would often lead to listener-participation phone segments. The boys would also make periodic appearances in the studio to tell jokes or answer funny questions. Art Linkletter didn't make a fortune on *Kids Say the Darndest Things* for nothing.

PRESS RELEASES/MAIL

Smart PR firms send out press releases with information that not only promotes whatever they are trying to promote, they also provide you with an angle of how to use it on the radio. A press release may have facts from a recent survey, or it may point out an issue that isn't getting enough attention. It's worth your while to read through your mail carefully. You never know what you'll find. That also includes correspondence from listeners, whether it's via snail mail or e-mail. A listener may inadvertently start up a firestorm with a criticism or an observation. Read all personal correspondence from the listeners. They are the people you are trying to reach. If they are contacting you directly, that means you're reaching them.

CRYSTALLIZING THE RAW MATERIAL

Now we've shown you the eight ways to accumulate the raw material you need, but you still need to know what to do with this information to convert them into radio segments. Over the next few chapters we'll show you a couple of ways to do it.

5

CRAFTING A GREAT PHONE SEGMENT

WE ALREADY DISCUSSED ONE OF THE COMMON FEATURES OF ALL BIG-time radio shows: celebrity guests. There is another common link, and this is arguably more important than having lots of guests on a show. A radio show isn't a radio show if it doesn't involve the listeners.

Talking to the listeners on the air is important for so many reasons. They give you immediate feedback much like a theater audience gives an actor immediate feedback. They will let you know when you have gone over the line, when you are doing something that relates to them, and what is or isn't connecting.

But they also do something else. They do your show for you. If you craft the right phone segment, get the right listeners on the air to discuss the topic of the day, and properly direct the flow of their calls, you have the kind of segment that makes a successful radio show. A news/talk, sports/talk, or personality/talk radio show that executes phone segments well will be a popular show. It's as simple as that.

In this chapter we'll discuss how to turn your raw show material into a phone topic. We'll break down the phone segment into elements and walk you through each of those elements. If you want to be a producer, it behooves you to pay close attention to this chapter. After all, the phone segment is dependent on the producer. He may or may not come up with the topic, but he will definitely be responsible for getting the right callers on the air. This is a crucial skill. Even the best topic with a perfectly executed introduction will be a complete failure if the callers aren't right.

That's where we come in. In this chapter we'll install an internal alarm system for dealing with a phone segment. We call it the "Red Alert System." It is the best system on the market for avoiding a complete phone meltdown. And it's completely free of charge . . . other than the very reasonable cost of this book. If you avoid the bad callers by using the Red Alert System, find and coach the good callers, communicate to the host which callers are the best, and then get them on the air, you will have crafted a great phone segment.

TURNING MATERIAL INTO A PHONE TOPIC

Depending on the format of your show, the phone topic is the lifeblood of the show. This is especially true of news/talk, sports/talk, and personality/talk shows. It really isn't a complicated process, either. Find a story that will relate to the listeners, frame the story in a way that will encourage the listeners to contribute, and then put the listeners on the air to talk about it.

Some shows handle these phone topics matter-of-factly. They look for a controversial topic about which listeners have a very strong opinion. Then the host will take either the popular position or play devil's advocate. Of course it isn't quite that simple. There are only so many controversial or compelling topics, so a host must be able to approach each of these topics in many different ways. That is a challenge unto itself. The listeners will respond to the topic based upon its presentation and delivery. Shows that handle phone topics like this are usually serious news-talk shows.

Maybe it's better if we give you a specific example. Health insurance is a controversial topic these days. Nearly every political campaign involves a discussion of the nation's healthcare crisis. Here are just a few different generic angles on the same topic. Remember that a specific news story will probably come up on a daily or weekly basis that allows you to take even more approaches.

- The insurance companies are fleecing consumers: Stories of outrageous insurance company rejections
- The pharmaceutical companies are fleecing consumers: Stories of outrageous prescription drug prices
- The doctors are fleecing consumers: Stories of outrageous doctor charges
- The insurance companies are forced to charge outrageous fees: Stories of outrageous legal decisions against insurance companies
- The insurance companies are forced to charge outrageous fees: Stories of doctors performing completely unnecessary procedures

- The insurance companies are forced to charge outrageous fees: Stories of pharmaceutical companies fleecing insurance companies
- The pharmaceutical companies are forced to charge outrageous fees: Stories of pharmaceutical research and development

That sort of approach is really only appropriate for serious-minded programs. We've worked on personality/talk shows, and they tend to have a slightly different approach. A personality/talk host most often turns a phone topic into a more lighthearted lifestyle issue. He usually ends up asking some variation of the question: Has anything like this ever happened to you? Just as the examples listed above, when the listeners call in with stories from their daily lives, they humanize a story in the news. That will give the show a much more personal connection with its audience. The difference in this case is that the angle is usually light, cute, or funny.

Having trouble understanding exactly what we mean? Last chapter, we told you the eight places you can find your raw material for a show. Any of those sources may provide you with a more lighthearted phone segment.

News Item: The man who coined the phrase "Keep on Truckin," passed away. That's a phrase that was popular in the early seventies. Depending on the age of your listeners, it may or may not have a personal connection with them. But it might have had a connection with their parents. A slight twist on the news item can give you the following phone topic: What phrase or saying from the past do your parents like to say?

You get the picture. That may not sound like a great topic to you, but you'll be amazed at the phone calls that come in for a set up like that. Take a news item, add a little creativity, and turn it over to the listeners to do your show for you. It's not difficult. You'll get the hang of it pretty quickly. Here are a few examples of what we mean:

News Item: A nasty celebrity divorce has both celebrities ripping each other mercilessly in public. Phone Topic: What song should Celebrity A dedicate to Celebrity B?

News Item: A politician's sex scandal has introduced a whole new group of "notorious celebrities" to America. Phone Topic: Cast the TV movie of the scandal.

News Item: A woman punches a man talking on his cellular phone at the movies. Phone Topic: What is your pet peeve?

News Item: A child vomits on the President during a photo opportunity. Phone Topic: What is the most embarrassing thing your child has ever done in public?

News Item: The Fighting Irish of Notre Dame win the national championship. Phone Topic: What is the most unusual school mascot you've ever seen?

News Item: A famous impersonator does a public appearance with the President he impersonates. Phone Topic: What famous celebrity can you impersonate?

These are just a few examples to show that even the most innocuous news story can lead to a phone segment. Last chapter we also mentioned that events in your personal life can also be good sources of material. In fact, we've found them to be particularly good sources of phone topics. Think about the things that have happened to you, and you'll see what we mean.

- Things you've hit with your car
- Vacation disaster stories
- Stupid things you and your spouse argue about
- The most embarrassing CD in your collection
- Caught with no clothes on
- Misunderstood lyrics
- Proposal stories
- Useless parental advice
- Strangest place you fell asleep
- The biggest prank you ever pulled
- The secrets you keep from your mate
- Brushes with celebrities
- Things your mother used to make you eat
- Your mate's most annoying trait
- Words or expressions that drive you crazy

Just about everything that happens in the news or your daily life can be turned into a phone topic. It's a matter of paying attention and thinking in these terms when you read the newspaper, watch TV, surf the Internet, or live life. The best phone topics are humorous, relatable, and engaging.

THE PHONE SET UP

Having the phone topic isn't enough. There are several more steps before you have crafted a great phone segment. Program directors tend to obsess about the set up. They want the host to say it as quickly as possible, get great callers on the air right away, and get out after a few calls.

We've never actually seen it work that way in real life. A set up should be brief, but you still have to paint a picture with words before you can frame it. By that, we mean that you have to suck the listeners in to the topic and get them thinking about it for a few moments before you state the angle and ask for telephone calls.

If the host is using a news story as a launching pad to the phone segment, he has to get into some of the details of the story. He has to tell the story and set the stage. If he skips this part, it's like telling the punch line of a joke without the set up (something a program director actually told one of us to do once). To illustrate what we mean, let's look at an example news story we mentioned earlier in this chapter; a child vomits on the President during a photo opportunity. First we'll do it the brief way favored by some program directors.

"Last night at the Kennedy Center in Washington, the President was having his picture taken with six-year-old Tiffany Murphy. Tiffany vomited on his lap. That's embarrassing for the parents, isn't it? Ever been embarrassed like that by your kids? Call 591-SHOW."

You may get calls. You may get some really good calls. But you also missed an opportunity to tell the funny story. Here is the way we would suggest. It may take a few seconds longer, but nobody will be turning off the radio listening to this story.

"Last night at the Kennedy Center in Washington, the President was having his picture taken with six-year-old Tiffany Murphy. Tiffany looked a little pale, but was cute as a button in her little pink dress. When the throng of photographers gathered around the President and the cute little girl, she seemed to get uncomfortable with all of the attention. The President was doing all he could to reassure her, but she was looking around wildly for her mom. When she saw her mom, she waved to her. The TV cameras got a close-up of the mother waving nervously back to her little girl. When the cameras returned to the cute photo opportunity, Tiffany looked at the President and said 'I think I'm going to throw up.'

"And she did, right on his lap, seconds before he was scheduled to go into the Kennedy Center for an awards ceremony. When the camera returned to the mother, she looked like she was trying to melt into the sidewalk. I found myself feeling sorrier for the mother than the kid or the President. I've been there, although not to that extent. I remember one time my son went up to an older woman at K-mart and said 'My dad loves to fart.' Just like that—out of the blue for no reason. I didn't see my face, but I'll bet it looked exactly like that poor mother in Washington yesterday. Has anything like that ever happened to you?

We want to hear your stories. Let's make this poor mother feel better by showing her she isn't alone. Call us now at 591-SHOW."

See what we mean? We guarantee the second example will get more calls and better calls. Plus, this story was worth telling. If you tell the story well in the set up, you are entertaining the people who will call and the people who won't call. (They tell us that only about 5 percent of your listeners will ever call.) That is an essential part of crafting the phone segment.

A set up can be written like our example above, or the host can improvise it, but it should be given great thought before the host cracks the microphone. The producer may or may not get involved with the set up of a phone segment. Many hosts would rather handle this duty themselves. We include this information just in case you are ever called upon to do it.

Sometimes radio shows have phone segments at the same time every day. The daily feature may even have a name like "The Feedback Patrol." This is called a benchmark bit. (We'll explain this concept further next chapter.) If a show has a benchmark phone bit, the listeners will know they are supposed to call the show when the bit begins. By doing the same bit at the same time every day they have trained the listeners like Pavlov's dogs. In that case, a very quick set up may be sufficient.

INSTALLING YOUR RED ALERT SYSTEM

The producer's main role in crafting a great phone segment is getting the best possible calls on the air. He is looking for callers that sound articulate, have a good story to tell, and can tell their story quickly and concisely. He also needs to find these callers in mere seconds.

In order to do this task in a short amount of time, it's essential to get rid of the bad callers as quickly and nicely as possible. There are really seven types of callers to avoid at all costs. To identify them instantaneously, you have two choices. You can learn through trial and error like we did. Or, you can install our patented Red Alert System—designed after years of screening calls. It's your choice whether you want to use our experience or not. For those of you who don't want to personally experience phone segments blowing up in your face, please read on.

The Red Alert System is the internal gut feeling that tells you immediately whether or not a caller will be good on the air. We're hoping that with the following suggestions you can install yours in a much shorter amount of time. The one important thing to remember is to never disregard the Red Alert. You will regret it.

The Inside Caller

Caller #1: "Hi, I'm a friend of Larry's. We met at the blood bank benefit."

Red Alert! Red Alert! Red Alert!

Why? Because the host's (Larry) friends don't call on the request line. Because he isn't really a friend if they just met at the blood bank benefit. Larry's "friend" is about to say something that 99.9 percent of the listeners won't care about, something "inside." He will get on the air and mention the blood bank benefit along with whatever details of his personal conversation he can remember. That will only be interesting to one person—this particular caller.

The Red Alert System has just saved the show from having a boring call.

Of course, knowing that a caller won't get on the air isn't enough. You still have to get rid of him quickly without angering or irritating him. After all, he's a big fan of the show and you need all the listeners you can get. We have developed a few friendly kiss-offs that can accomplish this task in just a few seconds. Let's try that call again.

Caller #1: "Hi, I'm a friend of Larry's. We met at the blood bank benefit."

Friendly kiss off: "Larry is really busy during the show, but I'm sure he'd love to hear from his friend. Why don't you give him a call after the show on his private line?"

You haven't insulted the listener, but you also haven't brought the show to a screeching halt by allowing him to go on the air. If he really is Larry's friend, you are also covered, because Larry's friend will undoubtedly have the private line number to call him after the show. If he isn't really Larry's friend, no harm, no foul.

The Long-Winded Caller

Caller #2: "Oh man, I have a great story. One time a friend of mine and I were going to the show with these two guys we met at the store. They were at the store shopping for jewelry and Marcy and I were just looking at some earrings, and we sort of hit it off. Anyway, while I was sitting in the theatre, which had a really sticky floor, you know the kind of floor that sticks to your feet, and my shoes were expensive, they were those new pink-laced kind from . . ."

Red Alert! Red Alert! Red Alert!

Why? Because you need a scorecard to follow what she is talking about. We've already heard five or six completely unnecessary details of the story. Anybody who takes that long before getting to the point is going to be even worse when she gets on the air. She thinks the host will want the "full story." Trust us—some people just can't tell a story.

Friendly kiss off: "I'm sorry, can I put you on hold for a second? It's crazy here right now and I have ten phone lines ringing. I'll be right back."

You don't have time to kiss her off quickly. She may not even stop talking when you try to cut her off. Don't waste your time even trying. Simply put her on hold and write something really obvious on the phone screener. We suggest "Don't take this call!" It doesn't leave any room for misinterpretation. If your studio set up doesn't have a phone screener, you might want to accidentally hang up on this caller. That may anger her, but if she calls back you've already set the scene by telling her how crazy it was. A simple "I'm sorry" will suffice. You cannot let her on the air. She will cause people to tune out. That's a guarantee.

The Daily Caller

Caller #3: "Hi, Joe. How's your wife doing? Listen, I have another great story to tell Larry. If he loved my story about Chico, he'll love this story."

Red Alert! Red Alert! Red Alert!

Why? This is the daily caller. Every show has daily callers. Sometimes they are excellent callers, too. You just don't want to have the same people on the air every day. It will seem like your show only has five listeners. You want a variety of voices of all different ages, sexes, and accents. You don't want the same guy every day. The daily caller calls so often that you'll recognize his voice right away. In this case, our Red Alert siren went off with "Hi, Joe." Remember the quote from the movie *Jerry Maguire*. It's not show friends. It's show business.

Friendly kiss off: "Hey there, Rocco! It's crazy on the phones this morning. I've got a bunch of people ahead of you, and I don't want to make you hold on the phone all day again. Talk to you soon and thanks for listening."

The daily caller needs a little longer kiss off at first because he is the most loyal listener you have. After awhile, the daily caller won't even care about getting on the air—he'll just want to chat. When he does that he won't mind getting an even shorter kiss off. ("Hey, Rocco—Gotta Go! Go Hawks!) He just wants to feel like he is a part of the show. If you refer to him by name and show that you know something about him, mission accomplished.

The Foul-Mouthed Caller

Caller #4: "Hey great show! This has been some pretty funny s***. I had some f***** do the same thing to me."

Red Alert! Red Alert! Red Alert!

Why? This one is pretty obvious, but some producers make the mistake of putting the foul-mouthed caller on the air because he is enthusiastic. Unfortunately, simply warning the foul-mouthed caller to watch his language won't be enough. Anybody who swears that regularly can't help himself. Even if your station has a delay system, why put someone on the air that will force you to use it?

Friendly kiss off: "Thanks for calling and thanks for listening." (Hang up.)

You got rid of him before he could tell you his story, and if he calls back you can tell him that you are now out of time. Apologize profusely for hanging up on him. If he doesn't call back, it didn't bother him or he realizes that his bad language got him the hook. He probably won't call back.

The B.S. Caller

Caller #5: "I met Mother Teresa at a K-Mart about two years before she died."

Red Alert! Red Alert! Red Alert!

The B.S. caller will say absolutely anything to get on the air. In fact, what he says to you when you screen his call may not even be what he says on the air. It's not worth having the B.S. caller on the air even to make fun of him.

Every kind of show needs to worry about the B.S. caller. Think of all the stories you've heard about phony calls making it on the air during a crisis situation only to say something like "Howard Stern." If a phone call seems too good to be true, it probably is. The brother of a victim wouldn't be taking time to call you during a crisis. The father of a "close personal young friend" of Michael Jackson wouldn't be calling. George Clooney wouldn't be calling you on the request line.

We wish this sort of ruse had never burned us. Ask one of the authors of this book what Michael Dukakis sounds like on the phone and watch the flop-sweat form on his forehead. Nothing is more embarrassing. Nothing. Ever. We're having nightmares just writing about it.

Friendly kiss off: "Wow! I bet it was thrilling meeting Mother Teresa, but I have guy on the line here who had a double cheeseburger with the Pope. Thanks for calling." (Hang up.)

He knows you aren't telling the truth, but he won't care.

Depending on the number of shows on your station, the secret in-studio phone number (commonly called the hotline) may not exactly be a secret. In that case, you may have to install a hotline Red Alert System. During the 1988 presidential election, Michael Dukakis was in Chicago attending a fundraiser. One of the writers of this book (OK—it was Rick) had unsuccessfully attempted to get him on the show he was producing. As the traffic reporter was discussing the traffic created by the Dukakis motorcade, the hotline rang. It was someone claiming to be in the limo with Dukakis. He said that Dukakis wanted to get on the air to let Chicago know he was sorry for the traffic delay. Because the producer had made several calls to the Dukakis campaign, he believed the caller. The host was pleasantly flattered that a presidential candidate would be calling the show, and he believed it too. However, about three seconds into the Dukakis call it became obvious that isn't wasn't Dukakis. It was a hoax. If the producer had insisted on speaking to Dukakis himself on the phone before he told the host, the entire situation could have been avoided because the producer would have realized it wasn't Dukakis. However, his Red Alert System was turned off because the call came in on the hotline. After that, the Red Alert System was never turned off again.

The Crackly Phone Line Caller

Caller #6: "Hey, I have the greatest (static). You (static) him until (static). I laughed (static) all (static).

Red Alert! Red Alert! Red Alert!

Why? Even if you think the material will be good, the sub-par quality of the phone line will negate anything the caller says. This could be a cellular phone, a portable phone, or a speakerphone. The last one is a no-brainer. A speakerphone caller should be asked to get off the speaker. Otherwise he will never ever be allowed on the air. The portable phone caller can be asked to go to a landline. The cellular phone caller can be put on hold until he gets in a better cell, but it's probably best to ask him to call back. If you are in a hurry and you have to get a call on the air, it's best not to mess with the crackly phone line caller.

Friendly kiss off: "It sounds like a great story, but the connection is really bad. Try calling back when you get in a better cell (or on a different phone)."

The Slow Caller

Caller #7: "I . . . have . . . a . . . great . . . story . . . . Um . . . it . . . happened . . . about . . . a . . . week . . . ago."

Red Alert! Red Alert! Red Alert!

Why? This is what we call the sloooooow caller. He isn't taking a long time getting to the point. He's taking a long time, period. Pacing is important. If your host isn't a slow talker (and not many of them are), then your caller shouldn't be a slow talker. It will sound like the show is slamming on the brakes. It will kill the pace and tempo of the show.

Friendly kiss off: "I hate to do this to you, but the phones are ringing off the hook here. Can I put you on hold for a second?" (Hang up.)

Whoops. You hung up on him. We've already used this technique a few times, but it really is the most effective way to handle the slow caller. If he calls back you can apologize and say that there are too many calls ahead of him now.

> If you are producing a minor market show or a brand new show at a medium or major market station that has never had a "call-in" show before, you may run into hurdles that hinder the installation of your Red Alert System. For instance, you may have to overcome technical issues like learning how to answer phones quietly because your station doesn't have a producer's booth and you are in the same room as the host. Or you may have to coach listeners who are not accustomed to being part of a radio show. The Red Alert System won't really work until you begin to establish the show. Never fear. The listeners will get the hang of it pretty quickly, you will learn how to overcome technical obstacles, and the Red Alert System can still be installed. It will never fail you.

BEYOND THE FRIENDLY KISS-OFF

Sometimes a friendly kiss-off isn't necessary. A certain type of caller doesn't even deserve the twenty seconds it would take to get rid of him in a friendly way. We call him the "abusive caller." Every show has abusive callers. A few sample comments from the abusive caller?

- ▶ Tell Larry that bit sucked
- ▶ Tell Larry that he couldn't ad-lib his way out of a paper bag
- ▶ Tell Larry that we don't give damn about his mother

There are people that actually call every day with helpful comments like these. You don't even need to give them the friendly kiss off. We suggest a simple "thanks for calling" followed by a hang up.

The abusive caller is such a strange phenomenon we can't even begin to explain it. These are the same people calling day in and day out. Obviously, despite their hatred of the host and the show, they are still listening every day. Don't let the abusive caller get to you. Remember that they call every show, especially the most popular shows. Just ask the producer of the Rush Limbaugh show or the Howard Stern show if he ever gets abusive callers. It will make you feel a little better.

COACHING THE GOOD CALLERS

Now that you've used your Red Alert System to filter through the bad calls, what do you do with the good calls? Is it enough to put them on hold and let the host know they are there? No.

When you get a good caller on hold, remember to say two things every single time. First of all, tell her to turn off her radio. If your station is using a delay system and she doesn't turn the radio off, she will be hearing everything coming back to her a few seconds after it was originally said. This will throw off anybody, and it sounds terrible on the air. If your station isn't using a delay system and she doesn't turn her radio off, she will get feedback. Don't forget to tell her. It's important.

The second thing you need to tell the good caller is what will happen next. Tell her that she will be on the air soon and that you are putting her on hold. Tell her that the next person she will be talking to is the host. (The host only speaks to callers on the air, so if she hears the host talking to her, she can assume she will be on the air.) Tell her that she will hear a slight static noise and that will be the signal that her phone line is on the air. (The phone line will make a pfffffft noise when it's put on the air. Only the caller will hear this.)

That should be sufficient information. You may not have time for much more than that. If you do have extra time for some reason, and there is something about her story that is particularly amusing or interesting, be sure to tell her not to omit that part when she tells the story to the host. There is nothing wrong with coaching a good caller. The caller will appreciate it, the host will appreciate it, and the audience will appreciate it.

If a good caller gets on the air and really hits it off with the host, she may be on the air for a long time. If that happens, make sure you constantly talk to everyone on hold to make sure each of them is still on the line, still paying attention, and still have their radios turned off. (They should still be hearing what is happening on the air while they are on hold. If they aren't, something is wrong with the phone line.) If no one is there when you pick up one of the calls on hold, dump it. Don't take a chance that they will be back when the host comes to that line. It's not worth it.

PREPARING THE HOST FOR THE CALLER

The set up of the radio studio doesn't allow for in-depth communication between the producer and the host while the show is in progress. (For more details about this, see chapter 16.) The producer is probably sitting in a producer's booth on the other side of the glass from the host. He has to communicate via a computer screen. We call this computer device the phone screener. Because the host doesn't really have time to read lengthy notes, a producer must develop a sort of shorthand that the host can understand.

Each phone line on the phone screener computer only has a line or two of space on the screen for comments. You have no choice but to communicate with few words.

For instance, you can't write: "Francesca has a great story about the first time she and her boyfriend made out in the backseat of her car and her father caught them." The lack of space and time will confine you to a shorthand version like this: "Francesca: caught making out by Dad." All of the juicy details are there, the host can figure it out instantly, and he can take the call as it fits into what he is trying to do. If it's a home-run call, the producer may put a few asterisks next to the name or message too. Whatever the method, keep it consistent and make sure the host understands what you are trying to communicate.

Some hosts prefer knowing the town of the caller. Some hosts like knowing the approximate age of the caller. Some hosts prefer being surprised by the caller. Talk to your host and ask him what he thinks is the most important information. Tailor your approach to make it the most convenient for him. It's his show, he's the one that has to pull off the phone segment on the air, and his needs are the most important.

You may or may not realize that many shows record phone calls. This is typical of personality shows that also play music. The host may do a phone set up as a tease going to a song or commercial, asking people to call just as the song or commercial begins. Instead of asking people to hold for five or ten minutes while the commercials and/or songs play on the air, he is busy behind the scenes recording the calls. There are many advantages to doing this. The biggest advantage is that you know what the phone call will say—the risk is removed. Another advantage is that you can edit out the extraneous parts. Another advantage is saving the "home-run call" to close out the segment. There is nothing quite as comforting as knowing you have a very funny or compelling way to go to commercials.

FINISHING UP WITH THE HOME RUN

The phone segment has been going well, but the clock is ticking and you still have to go to commercials. How do you end a segment when you are relying on the phone calls of people you don't know?

There are really two ways to do it. The best way is the home-run call. If the host has any skills at all in handling these segments, he is looking for the home run call right from the beginning. He looks at the screen and saves what he thinks will be the best call for last. As soon as he begins speaking to that home-run caller, he is looking for a great line with which to end it. It may be his own line or it may be the listener's line, but he'll know the line when he hears it. It's really an honor to see this in action. The truly skilled host is like a magician at working the phones.

If the host is not quite as skilled with phone calls, or he picks the wrong home-run call, he must have another way of ending the segment strongly. In this case, much like a baseball pitcher, he must have an out pitch. It might be an observation, a one-liner, or a piece of audio. Much like the conclusion of a celebrity interview, he has to hold this in his back pocket and save it for the last moment. If he uses this correctly, he can segue out of a phone call smoothly with his out pitch and end the phone segment in style.

A PHONE SEGMENT CANNOT BE FOOLPROOF

Sometimes you do everything right and it still doesn't work out. The topic is great. The set up is smooth and well delivered. While screening calls, you follow the Red Alert System, pick the best callers, put them on hold, tell them to turn off their radios, communicate to the host what they will say, and the host has chosen a great home-run call. Nothing can go wrong now, right?

Wrong. Sometimes callers just choke. They get on the air, get nervous, and suddenly an articulate person becomes tongue-tied. Or the articulate caller thinks of a better story while he is on hold, and the host is totally thrown off by the call.

There is nothing you can do about these calls. Don't beat yourself up about it. Don't sit up at night trying to figure out ways to avoid it. You can't. It happens. Move on. Like a great baseball closer, you can't get gun-shy. Next phone segment, you'll still get the ball. And next time you'll be firing strikes.

6

WRITING FOR RADIO

PRODUCERS ARE ASKED TO PERFORM DUTIES THAT VARY WIDELY, AND very few people in the world excel at all of these things. It's important to remember that a producer isn't expected to excel at everything. To be a well-rounded producer, he is merely expected to become competent in all of these areas. For instance, a producer must have some technical abilities if he expects to edit audio. He must have some sales abilities if he expects to book celebrity guests. He must have some resourcefulness if he expects to find show material. And he must have some writing ability if he expects to transform that raw show material into radio segments.

We mention this because writing is something that scares many producers. If you think you don't have writing ability, don't worry. We'll show you how you can contribute in this area even if you aren't gifted as a writer. We'll also show the producers who want to contribute as writers the many different ways they can. The sky is the limit, and for those of us who enjoy writing, there is nothing more satisfying or exciting.

RADIO SEGMENTS

We keep referring to radio segments, and if you haven't looked it up in appendix A, you might be a little confused. A radio segment is the on-air material between commercial breaks. Let's say your show runs six commercial breaks an hour at :00, :10, :20, :30, :40, and :50. That would leave you with six segments an hour. (The time between the :00–:10 breaks, the time between the :10–:20 breaks, etc).

If you are working on a full-service show, at least two of those segments every hour will be reserved for news, traffic, and/or sports. That leaves four segments an hour under the control of the host and the producer. For the purposes of this book, those four segments are what we're talking about when we refer to "radio segments."

Between the producer and the host, you have to come up with something to fill those four segments every hour. We've already talked about a few possibilities: celebrity interviews and phone segments. In each of those examples we discussed how writing plays an important part. For instance, a producer or host will write an introduction, questions, and a close to an interview. For a phone segment, he will write the topic, the set up, and possibly the close. In this chapter we'll give you a few more examples of how writing plays a part in each of those types of segments.

However, our main focus will be on the other types of segments we haven't yet discussed. There are all sorts of radio segments that can be created (and written) out of the raw material you accumulate on a daily basis. For instance, there are feature stories, produced bits, parody songs, contests, stunts, and long-form specials. We'll take a look at each kind, provide some examples, and hopefully expand the way you think about the possibilities of radio.

FEATURE STORIES

In chapter 4 we discussed the two types of stories you look for when you accumulate raw material for a radio show. There is the big news story of the day, and the offbeat story. In many cases these stories are converted into phone segments. When they aren't, they fall under the category of feature stories.

Most shows that do feature stories use them as fillers. These are segments that are thrown in to give the show some texture and variety. It's a nice little change of pace and a chance for the host to show his sense of humor.

To convert a big news story or an offbeat story into a feature story, writing will be required. No matter how compelling or funny a story may be on its own, it doesn't make sense to read it or discuss it on the air if you don't have an angle. This is the way it usually works: the host reads the story, makes comments and observations about the story as he reads it, and then ends it with a punch line.

Offbeat Feature Story

It's easier to understand if we provide an example. The news headline reads: "Winner of Wife-Carrying Championship Crowned Over the Weekend." As he reads this story, the host will be making observations and comments. He may say something like "Can you imagine the wife on the husband's back as he runs in the race saying 'Honey, do I feel fat in this outfit?'" He may add "My wife would be saying 'This is only fair. I've been carrying you for years.'"

Comments like this add spice to the story while he reads it, and although they sound off-the-cuff, they are usually prepared written remarks. When the host gets to the end of the story, he has to have a way to get to the commercial break and leave the listeners smiling. This story screams for a closing punch line. The producer or host will have to write one. Here are a few possibilities:

Punch line #1: Congratulations to the winner, although he won't repeat as champion. Next year Harrison Ford and Calista Flockhart are getting married the day before the race.

Punch line #2: Congratulations to the winner, and please send all cards and letters to Memorial Hospital for the last-place finisher... George Jefferson.

Offbeat Guests

Sometimes the best way to handle an offbeat story is to get the person in the news on the show. If the newsmaker is an average Joe, he may even be listed in the phone book. It's worth a shot to call information for his town and see. If not, check for other names in the article that may be listed. Sometimes you can't immediately get the newsmaker's number, but you can get the number of a friend who is quoted in the article. That friend may give you his number.

While getting an offbeat guest isn't technically writing for the show, it is creating a segment. When you get the story straight from the horse's mouth, it can be very entertaining. This segment will go beyond the information in the news story and give the listeners something to remember.

Headline Feature Stories

It's just as easy to turn the big news story of the day into a feature story. For instance, during the glorious Bill Clinton years, a host of characters came to the forefront. What show in America wasn't turning Linda Tripp, Paula Jones, or Monica Lewinsky into some sort of a feature story? When the story is so big that it dominates the headlines for days, weeks, and months, you have to find little nuggets and turn them into feature stories. You can't make that story the focus of your show every day or people will get bored. A little creative writing will keep the biggest story of the day on the show, without turning people off.

When we point out these offbeat stories and headline stories to producers who claim they can't write, they start seeing what we mean by the various degrees of radio writing. This isn't writing in the way they think of it. But it's more than handing over a story to the host. It's giving him an angle. It's giving him a way out. It's essentially writing an entire segment of the show.

PRODUCED BITS

On the other end of the spectrum, some shows take writing to the next level. They write scripts and produce pre-recorded bits. Sometimes the host has a character who comments on the events of the day, or he does an impersonation of a celebrity. Or he may have supporting players on the show who do that. The pre-produced bit might be a good way of showcasing those talents.

The Don Imus show in New York is a great example of a show that has lots of pre-recorded bits. The Dick Purtan show in Detroit is another. These are scripted bits, recorded in a production studio before the show, and fully produced with music and sound effects. The producer may or may not be writing the script but, rest assured, he is definitely involved in the creative process.

The produced bit is actually an excellent way of bringing together all of the talents of a producer. He can write it, help voice it, and use his technical skills in putting it together. (In part 4 of this book we'll get into all of the nitty-gritty technical knowledge necessary to produce a radio show.)

A famous example of the produced bit is the Dickie Goodman record. Dickie Goodman invented the bit that interspersed quotes from a reporter with clips from records. The reporter would ask a question of supposed celebrities, and the answer would be a line from a famous hit record of the day. It all started with his *Flying Saucer* record in the fifties. He actually released a few of these that made the pop charts. His *Mr. Jaws* in 1975 went up to #4 in the nation. Radio performers have imitated the Dickie Goodman approach for many years.

▶ ▶ ▶

For the twentieth anniversary of *The Empire Strikes Back*, George Lucas re-released the movie into theaters across the country. *The John Landecker Show* created a produced bit mocking that. A famous television commercial character in Chicago is the Empire Carpet Man. Landecker and his producer Rick Kaempfer wrote a script that interspersed actual clips of the characters from the movie with the re-written lines by the Empire Carpet Man. They convinced the actual Empire Carpet Man to record those lines, their technical producer Vince Argento produced it with Star Wars music, and the show unveiled "The Empire Carpet Man Strikes Back."

PARODY SONGS

There are a few things that have to exist before you can create a parody song. You must have a news story with legs—that is, a news story that will be around for a long time. You must have a host, co-host, or producer who can sing. And you must have a karaoke CD of the original song, or a band that is willing to re-record an instrumental version. If all of those elements are in place on the show you produce, parody songs are a lot of fun, and listeners seem to respond to them.

Why do you want stories that will be around for a while? Because with the effort that goes into creating a parody song, you want to be able to play it more than a few times. If it's good, and the story allows you to play it relatively often, you may have a hit on your hands.

What stories over the past twenty years have had the kind of staying power required for a parody song? The best stories are the scandals where no one was killed or seriously injured. Scandals like the ones that befell Jim and Tammy Bakker, Jimmy Swaggert, the Michael Jackson/Lisa Marie Presley marriage, Tonya Harding/Nancy Kerrigan, Bill Clinton/Monica Lewinsky, Monica Lewinsky/Linda Tripp, John Wayne Bobbitt, and Martha Stewart. Other good targets include celebrities that become caricatures of themselves like Marlon Brando, Teddy Kennedy, Jesse Jackson, Dan Quayle, and George W. Bush (before 9/11). If you handle everyone the same—offering no special treatment to people with the same political beliefs as you, no one will be offended (except, of course, the target).

That's the first part of the equation. The second part of the equation is who will sing the song. The best person is the host of the show. He's the one who people are tuning in to hear. If he can sing, you'd be amazed at how wildly popular a parody song can become. If the host does a lot of these, he can form a band and go on tour. During the summer season, nearly every community has festivals and carnivals where live bands perform. The station would love to have something like that promoting them for free. If the host can't sing, someone else on the show is the next best choice.

When you write a parody song, the choice of song is crucial. It should be up-tempo, it should fit the news story (especially the chorus), and it should match the format of your radio station. Which brings us to the third part of the equation—acquiring the karaoke version of the song you choose to parody. These are easier to find than ever before. With the exploding popularity of karaoke nights across the globe, karaoke versions of nearly every song are available on the Internet. Check places like the Karaoke Warehouse (*www.karaokewh.com*), or Karaoke Galore (*www.karaokegalore.com*). You may even have a store in your town that sells them. The only complaint we have about karaoke CDs is that they aren't really created with the radio guy in mind. They are for karaoke singers. Therefore, many of them have very noticeable back-up vocals. There are ways of stripping these with editing software, but it adds a lot of time to the process. (For more technical information about editing software, see part 5.)

Now it's time to write. A few tips we learned from writing hundreds of parody songs over the past two decades: It behooves you to keep the original rhyming scheme. It just sounds right. On the other hand, do whatever you can to make sure you don't keep any of the original lines. That's just lazy parody writing.

You'll want to listen to the original song many times to get a good feel for it. (Caution: As the writer of a parody song, you'll end up hating the original because you have to listen to it so many times to get the cadence correct.) Once you have a good feel for the song, think of the punch lines in advance to use as the last line of each stanza and work backwards. You don't have to write the whole song, just a verse or two. If you go on tour with the song, then you can write all of it. For the purposes of the radio show, a minute or so will get the message across.

It's a time-consuming process, but it's a lot of fun. It's hard to explain the thrill you'll feel when listeners respond to it. It's even more difficult to explain the thrill you'll feel if the song is actually performed live on stage.

The Michael Jackson/Lisa Marie Presley marriage was the big news story of 1994. *The John Landecker Show* wrote a parody of Elvis' *Burning Love* with John Landecker playing the part of Elvis as he sang. The marriage didn't last, but the lyrics still work ten years later. Lyrics reprinted courtesy of John Landecker and Rick Kaempfer.

Use Your Glove (Landecker/Kaempfer)
Lord almighty, Lisa Marie's so surprisin',
Just like Priscilla, she gave her old man the heave ho,
But girl, girl, girl, this new husband that you've acquired,
Is a llama owning, crotch grabbing, monkey loving, scary freak show,
So tonight when it's time to retire,

And he's wearing your dress he admired,
Say not tonight, Michael I'm tired.
Use your glove
Ooh ooh ooh, Michael is so mesmerizing,
He plays with the kids and pretends to be Frankenstein,
He comforts them when it's raining and the sun ain't shining,
That's OK—as long as they ain't no kin of mine,
So tonight when it's time to retire,
Surround the kids with barbwire,
Put a damper on his desire,
Spurn his love.

CONTESTS

This is another example of writing that producers do without even thinking about it. Producers are constantly called upon to create contests. They may be simple trivia questions, or they may be more elaborate contests to help give away big prizes.

We have a few words of warning about writing trivia questions. Be absolutely sure that you have the correct answer. If you have any doubt at all, don't do it. Someone will call to correct you if you are wrong. That's a guarantee. And if they catch the mistake, you technically owe them the prize. The way around this is to word the question so specifically that only your answer is correct and make sure the host reads it verbatim. Some hosts also get around this by saying that the listener has to match the answer he has in mind. That gets you out of the obligation of giving away the prize, but it doesn't stop the picky phone calls.

Also, if it's possible at all, try to create a contest that won't attract the prize pigs. If you've never worked at a radio station before, you probably aren't familiar with the contest prize pig. If you have worked at a radio station, no matter what type of format it is, you know them all too well. These are the kind of people who call whatever station is doing the best giveaway. If you listen to a lot of stations, and you're a savvy listener, you will begin to recognize the same contest winner names over and over again. Those are the prize pigs. They may be good people, but they aren't good winners. A contest that requires extended listening is most likely to scare off the prize pig.

While the Internet is a gold mine for all sorts of research, sometimes it simply isn't convenient to log online. A producer will need to look things up on a daily basis in the preparation of his show material, especially while preparing contest questions. Make sure that you have a fully stocked reference library at your disposal. In the bibliography of this book we've included a list of the basics. These books will give you answers to the kinds of questions you'll face every day. Instead of signing online every single time, it may be more convenient to look it up in one of the books in your library.

STUNTS

There are radio shows all over the country that participate in stunts. Usually the producer is sent out with a cellular phone and asked to do these stunts. If you are quick on your feet, and you enjoy being on the air, you may suggest a stunt to tie into a news story of the day. Or you may suggest a stunt to tie-in to a contest or giveaway.

The shows that do stunts are almost exclusively personality morning shows. Some stunts go way over the line. Former New York personalities Opie and Anthony were fired after their offensive church sex stunt. Stunts can go too far if they aren't considered carefully, but they can also be a memorable and effective way of painting an audio picture. As the person executing the stunt, you are essentially writing the material as you go along.

John Swanson was sent out with a cellular phone while dressed in a giant chicken suit. As "Swany the Love Chicken" he delivered a Valentine to a listener's husband. Another time he was sent out in a giant bunny suit as "The Reluctant Easter Bunny" and passed out plastic eggs filled with $1 coins. These were harmless stunts, but they painted an audio picture for the listeners.

LONG-FORM RADIO SPECIALS

So far we've really only discussed comedy writing for radio. There is another level that is considered the Holy Grail of radio writing. This is the kind of long-form special that is part of a radio show like "This American Life" on NPR. Several of the National Public Radio programs offer an opportunity for writing that simply doesn't exist in commercial radio.

A producer for "This American Life" is really more of a traditional writer than a traditional producer. It's journalism, but it's not really news. These writers tell stories in a narrative form, told in a personal style. You choose the topic, you research it, and you tell it with the help of audio vignettes. The host of the show will voice it, but the producer really creates the piece.

As for the equivalent in commercial radio, the closest thing a commercial radio station producer will experience is the opportunity to put together a one-time special. These may be on music stations (Rick Kaempfer wrote several specials for Westwood One radio network and his radio station in Chicago), or they may be on sports stations (a look back at the team's season), or they may be on a news station (a look back at the election or a major local news event). If you get an opportunity to write a long-form special, jump at it. It's a great experience.

BENCHMARK BITS

Throughout this book we've mentioned the concept of a benchmark bit. This is the type of bit that a producer is most often asked to write. A benchmark bit is a regular feature of the show that appears at the same time every day or every week. Most of the types of radio segments we've talked about in this chapter and previous chapters can be turned into benchmark bits.

Benchmark Celebrity Bits

These are often contests like "Mystery Guest" or "Mystery Voice," but celebrities are also asked to be "Guest DJs" or "Guest Co-Hosts." When they are, they very often need help with writing. You will end up writing one-liners, writing angles, and helping them come up with material.

Benchmark Phone Bits

If you do a phone segment at the same time every day, and the segment has a name, you will probably be asked to write and produce an introduction for this segment. Some examples from shows we have worked on include Eric and Kathy's "Anybody Listening Who" phone segment, which simply asks a different "Anybody Listening Who" question and asks listeners to respond, and Jonathon Brandmeier's "Crack Me Up Line," where listeners were asked to call in jokes, or

"The Shove It Line," where listeners were asked to call in and tell their bosses to shove it. All of these examples had a pre-produced opening and a signature music bed. The listeners were trained to call when they heard that music.

Benchmark Feature Stories

When you peruse several newspapers a day and read everything else you can get your hands on, you start to see certain trends about what kind of stories make it to the press. Sometimes you group these stories together and make them into a benchmark bit. Larry Lujack and Tommy Edwards of WLS Radio did one of the most famous benchmark bits with feature stories. They called it "Animal Stories" and it featured various different funny stories about animals in the news. Other types of stories you'll see a lot of are dumb crook stories, outrageous lawsuit stories, and medical abnormalities. Each of these can be turned into a benchmark bit. When it is, however, the producer will most likely be responsible for accumulating the stories and helping the host come up with the punch lines.

Benchmark Contests

Music stations all over the country have music trivia contests at the same time every day. Many stations also mimic game shows and convert them into "radio games." On stations like this the producer is asked to write the questions. This becomes almost like second nature. You will develop sources on the Internet and put your resource library to extensive use. That makes it a very simple task.

A TOP-TEN LIST

We asked one of Chicago's best radio writers, former Jonathon Brandmeier producer and writer Brendan Sullivan, to give us a few of his writing tips. He gave us ten.

1. Don't listen to other similar radio shows. It will drive you nuts thinking "Did I just think of this cool idea, or did I hear it somewhere else?"
2. Run a concept by the host before you spend five hours writing, editing, and producing a bit the host has no interest in.
3. Save all of your writing in a file somewhere. The Oscars will come around every year. You'll want to make sure you are able to recreate last year's successful segment without repeating the same material.

4. Read everything you can get your hands on. Inspiration is everywhere. Especially in the age of the Internet, there is no such thing as "There's nothing going on."
5. Lose your ego. As brilliant as a written piece is, most listeners will figure that the host wrote it. Sometimes the host will give you credit, sometimes he won't.
6. If a particular bit that you wrote kills on the air, get an audio copy of the bit with the on-air reaction. It's nice to have for a number of professional and personal reasons.
7. Steal a bit structure (I mean, come on, the *Match Game* has been around forever), but never steal a bit. There is nothing worse than having a listener call in and say "That was funny. It was even funnier when I heard it last week on Letterman."
8. Never give the host something to read you wouldn't read if it was your show. If you and your host aren't on the same wavelength, you're on the wrong show.
9. Kerblooey is a funny word.
10. Don't force yourself to write a list of ten when you run out of gas after eight.

Write Here, Write Now

You won't ever hear a host say "Hey Shakespeare, write me a sonnet." But the host will constantly lean on you for ideas and ways to convert those ideas into usable radio segments. If it's a skill you don't have, don't worry—you can develop it. We've given you enough tips in this chapter to get you started. If you really want to improve, you may find a writing class offered at a local community college. You may even be as lucky as we are in Chicago to have an improv school (Second City, etc.) in your area. Improvisation is a great teaching tool for comedy writing.

If you do have the writing skill, radio is a great medium for you. It offers the kind of creativity that simply doesn't exist in local television. Take full advantage of it and find your voice. You may be able to create something truly special.

7

PITCHING MATERIAL AND PLANNING A SHOW

NOW THAT YOU KNOW ALL OF THE PLACES TO FIND MATERIAL, AND YOU know all of the different possibilities for transforming that material into radio segments, you have to convince the host to use that material on the show. We call this "pitching" material. It's not unlike what goes on in Hollywood when they pitch movie or television ideas, hoping to get them "green-lighted." The only difference is that you have to get ten or fifteen ideas green-lighted every day.

In this chapter we'll tell you how to pitch the material you've accumulated, and then we'll tell you what to do with the material once it is green-lighted. By the time you finish this chapter, you'll understand how to put together a radio show.

PITCHING MATERIAL—WHEN AND WHERE?

The answer to those questions depends on the time slot of your show, the host of the show, the relationship of the producer and the host, and possibly "the way we've always done things around here."

You have to adjust yourself to the show. In all of our discussions of how to produce a show, we've only scratched the surface of the host/producer relationship. When it comes time to pitch material for the show, you'll be reminded very quickly who the boss is. It's the host. Ask the host when he wants to hear your pitch, and where he wants to hear your pitch. It's his show. It's his call.

For morning shows, the pitching of material usually occurs the evening before—on the phone. Or, it may even occur the morning of the show. We've worked on both kinds of shows. For afternoon shows, the pitching may occur first thing in the morning, giving you the whole day to put the show together. Or, it may occur the evening after the previous show, to give you even more time. Regardless of when and where it happens, the bottom line is that the producer has to constantly be searching for material, because there is always another show coming up.

PITCHING MATERIAL—WHAT?

You have a pile of news stories and ideas in front of you. These should be broken down into the types of radio segments the show does. You will be pitching celebrity guests, guests that you've tracked down from news stories, phone segments, contests, recorded bits, parody songs, feature stories, and material for the show's benchmark bits.

If you always keep in mind that your ideas should fit into these various categories, it helps you fully form your concepts. You can see a funny story and look at the options before you, and then decide which category it would fit in. That's how the host does it. That's how you should do it too.

PITCHING MATERIAL—HOW?

The most important trait of someone pitching ideas is confidence. This is crucial. You must project that you know what you are talking about. Writers and directors in Hollywood have to do the same thing when they pitch ideas. Don't waste time pitching an idea if you know full well that the host won't want to hear it. Don't waste time pitching ideas that are not right for your audience. Don't waste time pitching ideas that are not completely thought out and refined by you.

This is important. You have to be absolutely sure that you have considered any objections the host may have to the material before you pitch it. There are really only a few you need to think about.

- How do we get into the bit?
- What's the punch line?
- What's the payoff?
- What's the angle?
- How do we involve the callers or co-hosts?
- Why would our listeners care?
- What sort of audio do we have to dress it up?

That should cover it. With your mental prep work done, now you are ready to pitch.

You should pitch your fully formed ideas first. These are the ideas that have a beginning, middle, and end. We gave a few good examples of this in the chapters about celebrity guests and phone segments.

Think to yourself how you would do the segment if you had to do it on the air. Thinking like a host will help you discard the mediocre ideas and let you know which ideas are the best before you pitch them. Then, when you pitch them, pitch the entire segment—what the beginning could be, what the middle could be, and how you could end it. These ideas, along with the host's ideas, will form the basis of the show.

If you have a germ of an idea that may blossom into something with the help of the host's insight, make sure you are getting him at the right time. Don't waste your time if he is crabby or not paying attention. Don't present an idea with an opening line like "This probably isn't anything, but . . . ." The host wants ideas. In the crucial trust-building era of your relationship, you want to show him how much he can count on you for help in this area.

Pitch bits, not fits. What do we mean by this? It's simple. Some, if not many, if not all of your ideas will be rejected at first. Even with the help of this book, you must make allowances for your lack of experience. If the host doesn't like your best ideas, get over it. This happens to all of us at one time or another. It's not the host's fault. You either didn't pitch the bit correctly, the host didn't think he could perform it correctly, or it just isn't good enough. You don't want the host doing a bit or topic that he won't feel completely comfortable doing on the air. If you have to push too hard, or you use guilt to make him try it when he doesn't want to, it most likely won't turn out well anyway. Move on.

One of us pitched material to a host who decided what he wanted by saying "naaaaaaah" or "aaaaaaah" to the ideas he didn't like. It may seem a little harsh, and you may be a little taken aback by this, but it certainly doesn't do any good to pout about it. You'll never gain his trust that way. Instead, work on toughening yourself up. Work on improving your pitches. Work on improving your material. It's not technically your job to come up with a show—it's his. He will welcome any help he can get (most of the time), but until you can do it well enough, you just have to keep working at improving.

You can only do your best, and over time your best will get better and better. Don't expect it to happen overnight.

PLANNING THE SHOW

Once you have pitched your ideas, and the host has chosen which ideas he likes and combined those ideas with his own ideas, it's time to start planning the show.

Remember the segments we discussed in the last chapter? Now is the time when you fill in every segment for the show. Some hosts like to have this wrapped up the night before the show. Others do it in the moments before the show begins. The point is, every show does it. The unscripted fly-by-the-seat-of-your-pants shows have virtually disappeared from the radio dial. They all have a game plan, a blueprint, a show breakdown.

We call this the "prep sheet." It's similar to a musician's set list. When the show begins, the host has every intention of sticking to that prep sheet and performing the show as planned. Of course, other things come up. Some segments work better than planned and get extended. Other segments don't work as well as planned, and get shortened. A guest may show up late or not at all. A breaking news story may cause you to shelve the less timely material. A technical snafu may make you alter your plans. We'll get into those issues in chapter 10.

For the purposes of this chapter, we're simply talking about planning the show. It's usually a three-step process: decide what you want to do, how you want to do it, and when you want to do it.

The Rundown Sheet

Most shows take one more step before they put together a more comprehensive prep sheet. They have a blank rundown sheet with the times of each segment, and they start placing the ideas into time slots. In the sample rundown sheet below, we've shown you how it would look for a morning show that has four segments an hour.

We're assuming that the segments at the top and bottom of each hour are filled with a news/traffic/weather/sports package. That's why you don't see any listings at :00 or :30. The host usually doesn't involve himself in those segments, so he must only fill the rest of the show— four segments an hour. The 6:10 segment, for instance, runs from approximately 6:10—6:20. The 6:20 segment runs approximately from 6:20—6:30, etc.

SAMPLE SHOW RUNDOWN SHEET

6:10 _____

6:20 _____

6:40 _____

6:50 _____

7:10 _____

7:20 _____

7:40 _____

7:50 _____

8:10 _____

8:20 _____

8:40 _____

8:50 _____

9:10 _____

9:20 _____

9:40 _____

9:50 _____

Filling in the Show Rundown Sheet

There are many different factors that go into planning what time of the show is best for a particular segment. First of all, you want to put your best material at the time you have the most listeners. (For morning shows that's typically the 7 A.M. hour. For afternoon shows that's the 5 P.M. hour). You are also trying to space out similar material so that the show provides a nice balance for the different types of preferences your different listeners may have.

If you have two phone segments, for instance, you probably don't want to do these back to back. If you have two celebrity guests, you probably don't want to have them on back to back. If you have two segments about the host's personal life, you want to space those out too. The plan is to have the most balanced show possible. You want to cover the top story of the day, the offbeat news stories, and you want to reveal a part of yourself (the host). You want to do all three of those things in as many different ways as possible. It's a difficult balancing act.

Different formats have different ways of filling in their rundown sheets. However, they all want to accomplish essentially the same thing. News/talk formats may not be looking for the humorous angle of a story, but they are still looking for an angle. They may not be spacing out the phone topics because they do more of them, but they are spacing out the types of phone topics. Sports/talk shows are the same way. The purpose of balancing the show is to appeal to the different kinds of listeners every show may have. Some news/talk fans like local politics, some like national politics, some like policy discussions, some like strong opinions, etc. A sports/talk show won't want to talk about one team or sport for the whole show. Different topics and different approaches bring in different listeners. And the goal, after all, is to get the biggest audience you can.

The Prep Sheet

The prep sheet is the final step of the planning process. This is what the host has in his hand when the show begins. It's not enough to look at the filled-in rundown sheet and go from there (although some hosts can and do).

The producer prepares the prep sheet. He takes the filled-in rundown sheet and goes into more detail. If an introduction needs to be written, the producer does it on the prep sheet. If a punch line needs to be written, the producer does it on the prep sheet. If additional research needs to be done, the producer summarizes it on the prep sheet. If there is audio that can accompany a segment, the producer notes it on the prep sheet. If an article needs to be summarized, the producer does this on the prep sheet.

The prep sheet is stapled to the top of the articles being used on that particular day. Any additional material that the producer has found since the show was planned will also be attached and highlighted to the prep sheet (like any new articles in the morning paper).

With the prep sheet and the packet attached to it, the host has all the tools he will need to perform a top-notch radio program.

PLANNING A SAMPLE SHOW

It's probably easier to see what we mean if we provide you specific examples. For the purposes of this chapter, we'll show you how to produce a prep sheet for *The Larry & Mary Show*. The host is named Larry. He's forty-two years old and has been in the market for over ten years. He has a co-host/sidekick named Mary. She is thirty-five years old, and the mother of two young girls. Larry runs the flow of the show, and Mary chimes in when she has something to add. They do a lighthearted personality morning show that appeals to soccer moms in their twenties, thirties, and early forties.

After discussing the possibilities with their producer, Larry and Mary have decided on which ideas they want to use. They have transformed those ideas into the types of segments they want to do, and they end up with the following list.

- Off-Beat News Story: Dog eats man's paycheck/Phone Topic: Things your pet has eaten
- Off-Beat News Story: Nude man climbs skyscraper/Feature-Punch line
- Top Story: The President misspeaks in India/Parody song

- Top Story: Governor paid same amount in taxes as sanitation worker/Feature-Punch line
- Personal Story: Mary's daughter has been given the nickname Snotty Dottie/Phone Topic: Childhood nicknames
- Benchmark Bit: "Monday Movie Mania"/Contest
- Benchmark Bit: "The Dumb Crook File"/Feature
- Benchmark Bit: "Mary's Daily Inspiration"/Feature
- Celebrity Guest: Richard Simmons/In Studio
- Celebrity Guest: Mayor Meisterberger (on his sixtieth birthday)/Phoner
- Newsmaker Guest: Hog-calling champion from state fair/Phoner
- Personal Story: Larry is doing an appearance at the blood bank/Feature

Filling in the Larry & Mary Rundown Sheet

Some things are easy to fill in on the Larry & Mary rundown sheet. For instance, they have several benchmark bits. Remember that benchmark bits are always at the same time. Mary does her words of inspiration at 6:10 every day. Larry and Mary do "The Dumb Crook File" at 8:20 every Monday morning. They also do the "Monday Movie Mania" contest at 9:20. Those cannot be moved (because they are probably sponsored).

Some of the ideas they have will take up two segments: the phone segments and the celebrity interview. Phone segments usually take up two slots on the rundown sheet because the first slot will be the setup story (with a few calls to get the bit going). The second slot will be more calls and the home run call. An in-studio celebrity interview will usually merit two segments (although this isn't always true). In this case, Richard Simmons is a bundle of energy and will be difficult to hold to one segment.

The producer has had the foresight to book the celebrity guests in different hours. For instance, the hog-calling champion will be on the air in the 7 A.M. hour (on the phone). Richard Simmons is the in-studio guest at 8:30. Mayor Meisterberger will be called at his office after 9:30.

That leaves a couple of topics that are similar. Three topics are about the hosts of the show: the phone segment about Mary's daughter, "Mary's Daily Inspiration," and Larry's appearance at the blood bank. Three topics are about offbeat stories: the hog-calling champion, the dog that ate the paycheck, and the nude man crawling up the skyscraper. Two topics are about the big stories of the day: the President's slip of the tongue and the governor's taxes. You want to separate these as much as possible.

Look at the following filled-in rundown sheet. See how Larry and Mary (and their producer) have managed to take their list of ideas and transform them into a well-balanced show? In chapter 10, we'll actually show you what this show would be like for the producer in the studio.

LARRY & MARY RUNDOWN SHEET—MAY 21

6:10—"Mary's Daily Inspiration"
6:20—Governor Story
6:40—Phone Segment: Things your pets have eaten
6:50—Phone Segment/Part 2
7:10—President Misspeaks/Parody song
7:20—The Hog-Calling Champion
7:40—Phone Segment: Childhood nicknames
7:50—Phone Segment/Part 2
8:10—Larry at the Blood Bank
8:20—"The Dumb Crook File"
8:40—Richard Simmons in the Studio
8:50—Richard Simmons/Part 2
9:10—Nude Man Story
9:20—"Monday Movie Mania"
9:40—Call to Mayor Meisterberger
9:50—Sign Off/Tease of tomorrow's show

Creating the Larry & Mary Prep Sheet

To create the prep sheet, the producer examines every single segment and tries to imagine what will be necessary. He is looking at what needs to be written, what needs to summarized, and what sort of audio is available to spice up the show.

Break it down segment by segment, starting with the 6 A.M. hour. For the 6:10 segment, he needs to have the audio introduction and music bed (instrumental music that plays underneath the segment) ready to go. For the 6:20 segment, he has to have the article summarized and a punch line. For the 6:40 segment, a summary of the news story is necessary, along with an introduction to the phones.

The 7 A.M. hour includes a parody song, an interview, and a phone topic. Let's assume that the parody song has already been written and recorded previously by the show (because the President often has slips of the tongue). This hour's prep sheet will still need a summary of the President story, a fact sheet about the hog-calling champion, and an introduction to the phone segment.

The 8 A.M. hour will need the summary and punch line of the nude climber story, the elements of the dumb crooks benchmark, and the interview prep sheet for Richard Simmons.

The 9 A.M. hour will need the details of Larry's appearance, a contest question for Monday Movie Mania, and a fact sheet for the call to the mayor. The call to the mayor doesn't require an entire interview prep sheet because this is only a short birthday call.

After the producer sketches out what will be necessary, it's time to sit down and put it all on paper. The completed product is waiting for Larry and Mary when they walk in the door the next morning. (See appendix D for the completed product. See chapter 10 for this show in action.)

FLEXIBILITY WITHIN PLANNING

We've taken the planning of *The Larry & Mary Show* to its logical extreme just to show you how much planning can take place before a show. It pays to plan as much as possible, even for a show like *The Larry & Mary Show*—which is admittedly breezy and light. Not every show plans to the extent that we have planned this fictional show, but all shows plan something. It may just be a rundown sheet, or a list of possible topics, but when the show goes on the air, the host has a very good idea of what is going to happen.

On the other hand, it's crucial that a show remains flexible. There are so many things that could go wrong or better than expected that the show can change while it's in progress. In the sample show we created, all sorts of things can go wrong. For instance, Richard Simmons may have been late. Or the mayor may have been late getting to his office, or had to deal with an emergency of some kind. The hog caller might have been a dud—and his segment might have been cut short. Either of the phone segments might not have gotten good enough callers. The tape of the parody song could have been corrupted and/or damaged. Mary might have called in sick and caused the phone segment about her daughter to be scrapped.

Prepare for the unexpected even if it means having a backup plan. There are a million things that can happen that you can't possibly foresee.

Ask any show host or producer that was on the air on the morning of September 11, 2001.

The John Landecker Show had a "Mystery Guest" segment scheduled during the 8 A.M. hour (central time) on September 11, 2001. Rick Kaempfer was speaking with Butch Patrick (Eddie Munster) on the phone, prepping him for the mystery guest segment, when he was alerted about the first tower being hit. He politely said goodbye to Butch Patrick, turned on the television in the studio, and the show became a full-service news program. The newscaster Richard Cantu told all of the details that had been confirmed. As the show members tried to make sense of what was happening, the second tower was hit. Landecker and his co-host Leslie Keiling saw it happening and described it to the listeners. The listeners that normally would have turned on the news/talk station stayed with the program. Even today people who were listening to the show that day stop Landecker. They thank him for handling the situation so professionally and feel a personal connection to him because of the real emotion he and the rest of the show members displayed on the air.

8

MAXIMIZING YOUR TIME

NOW THAT WE HAVE TOLD YOU THE DUTIES YOU ARE EXPECTED TO PERFORM, YOU may find yourself wondering how in the world you will manage to find the time to do them all. It's really up to you whether you want to work eighteen hours a day or ten. If you chose eighteen, move on to the next chapter. If you chose ten, you really need to get organized.

Get an idea, write it down. Remember a show you need to tape, write it down. See that a celebrity signed a book deal, write it down. Voice mails you need to return, write them down. Any and everything you need to do needs to be written down so that you always have it in front of you. Write it down, write it down, and write it down. What do you need to do? Write it down. Not following us? Write it down. The very act of writing something down reinforces your memory. This job is too big to trust your memory all the time. If you have something written down to remind you, you'll save time.

In this chapter we'll tell you what to write down and where to write it. We'll help you organize your office, your briefcase, your phonebook, and your studio. When you are organized, you will be able to perform all your duties while managing to also live your life. You don't want to be one of those workaholics who can't see the forest for the trees.

After we organize everything for you, this chapter will also help you try to plan out your day. If you try to live by a schedule you will be more efficient. And after all, being an organized and efficient producer should be your goal.

ORGANIZING YOUR PHONE BOOK

The longer you produce, the more impressive your phone book will become. As it grows in size, the more unmanageable it becomes. Whether you use a computer database like Microsoft Excel or Microsoft Works to keep track of your phone book, or you use a Palm Pilot, or you keep a Rolodex with handwritten names and numbers, the key is to stay on top of it. With the volume of names and numbers you deal with on a daily basis, it's much too easy to misplace a stray piece of paper with some scribbled details.

Don't fall into this trap. It's so tempting. You'll tell yourself that you won't need a number again, or that you'll put it in your book some other time. Before you know it you'll have a big pile of scrap paper falling out of your book. Then, when you really need that number you'll waste time trying to find it. If you book someone on your show, take the five seconds to write or type the name directly into your book. It will save you tons of time in the future—and that's what this chapter is all about.

A producer's phone book is an essential tool of the trade. Like a tradesman who pampers his tools, you should do the same with yours. Keep it neat and tidy and it will perform for you when you need it.

Producers are often guilty of keeping incomplete information in their phone books. They may just write the celebrity's name and not the publicist's. That's an obvious mistake. You'll be dealing with the publicist, not the celebrity. The publicist may also give you her cellular number, home number, fax number, or e-mail address. You need to keep track of all of them, and that's not all you need to record. If the celebrity is booked through a one-time source like a local event, keep that person's name too. If she had the power to book the celebrity once, she will know who you need to contact if you want her on again. If a celebrity is staying at a local hotel and you are given the phone number, make a notation of the hotel in your Rolodex. Celebrities like to stay in the same hotels. If you are unable to book her the next time she comes to town, but you know what hotel she prefers, you may be able to track her down directly.

Keeping Track of Voice Mails

We suggest using a separate notebook to keep track of the calls you get on your voice mail. Let's call this the voice mail log. The number of voice mails you receive will preclude you from entering all of them into your phone book right away. You may average more than twenty calls a day if your show is popular. These unsolicited callers may not even understand what kind of program they are calling. You'll want to return as many as possible anyway.

Even if you realize right away that you won't use the guest the PR person is suggesting, write down her number in your voice mail log anyway. If you take the time to call her back and let her know what kind of a show you produce, she won't bother calling you the next time, unless it's someone that fits your show. Also, you can ask her what kind of guests she generally publicizes. There's no need to embarrass her if she is offering a lung cancer expert for your wacky morning show, or a juggling clown for your hard news/talk show. Publicists handle all sorts of guests. Just because she was way off the mark this time doesn't mean that she won't be able to help you sometime in the future. Remember that your interests are bound to intersect someday.

We don't recommend you transfer her number into your phone book until you actually book a guest through her, but you can keep her number in your voice mail log. Make a notation next to her name and number if she may publicize guests you can use in the future. We know it sounds like wasted time and effort, but in the long run, you are saving time. You are eliminating the unnecessary voice mail calls from publicists, which will save you time in the future. You are keeping all of the numbers you retrieved from voice mail in one place, which will also save you time in the future. Most importantly, you are writing everything down. Have we mentioned yet how important that is?

ORGANIZING YOUR IDEAS

The hunt for ideas is a never-ending quest. You are constantly reading, watching, searching. The hunt for ideas will add two more items to your briefcase: a folder and another notebook.

The folder holds ideas for future shows. It's for any newspaper or magazine article you run across in your daily reading. Sometimes you'll see something for an upcoming holiday, or something you need to save for an upcoming benchmark bit. Clip the article and put it in your folder. You may see something about a celebrity signing a book deal or going on a concert tour. You may find something that sparks a contest idea or remote broadcast idea. Clip the article and put it in your folder. You may find something good on a day you have more than enough material for the next day's show. Clip the article and put it in your folder. If you get a press release for a future event, or you see an article about a television show coming up in a few days or weeks, you know where to put it, don't you? The future shows folder will save you hours and hours of time.

The notebook is for a running tally of ideas you want to pitch for the next day's show. This notebook should be around you all the time. If the host says something during the show that sparks an idea, write it down. If you think of an idea while reading the newspapers, watching TV, or surfing the Internet, write it down. If something happens to you or the host that you think can be used on the air, write it down. If you keep a running tally of the material you accumulate on a daily basis, it will save you lots of time. When it comes time to pitch your ideas to the host, you can do it right from the notebook. When the host approves the ideas, you can write your prep sheet right from the notebook. Plus, the idea of having a running tally also lets you see how often you are pitching the same ideas, and what kind of ideas the host likes better than others. That will also save you time.

ORGANIZING YOUR STUDIO

We're going to get into this a little more in the next few chapters, but the time you spend at the radio station has to be used to it's fullest. You must have your production area as organized as possible. (We mention some good ideas about organizing your audio in chapter 18). You must also have the air studio as organized as possible. You only have a few minutes before and after the show to get everything set in place. If you lollygag or you aren't completely ready to go when your time is up, the show has to start anyway. Take it from us—that's no way to begin a broadcast.

Next chapter we'll introduce you to a very powerful organizing tool: the studio checklist. It will save you time during the crucial moments before and after a show.

CREATING A TO-DO LIST

In addition to your phonebook, the voice mail log, the future shows folder, and your ideas notebook, we're going to introduce one more thing to add to your briefcase. This is the granddaddy of them all: the to-do list notebook.

In this notebook you'll be writing down everything you need to do. Is there a PR person you need to call about a guest? Write it down. Is there a show you need to tape on television? Write it down. A tape you need to archive? Write it down. A guest you need to research? Write it down. A thank you card you need to send to someone? Write it down.

Once you complete a task, you can cross it off your list. This will make you realize you are actually accomplishing something. Also, the things you haven't done yet will jump off the page because they aren't yet crossed off the list. You'll avoid procrastinating just so you don't have to keep looking at the constant reminder. That will make you more efficient.

There are some electronic devices that will help you do some of the things we suggest to organize yourself. A Palm Pilot, a laptop, an electronic planner, or sales software can help, but none of them can do all of the things we suggest with the proper flexibility. That's why we went with the old-fashioned paper and pen. At the risk of being so "twentieth century," we also suggested the old-fashioned technique because not every producer can afford the electronic devices we listed above. The bottom line is that it doesn't matter how you organize yourself—as long you do something. A producer who doesn't work on keeping himself organized will not last long.

SCHEDULING YOUR DAY

Now that you have your many duties organized in a manageable order, you need to know when to do all of these things. Of course, it depends on the timeslot of your show. For the purposes of this book, we're going to plot out the day of a morning producer because it's the most common type of producer, and he has the most complex job of organizing his day.

The morning producer is waking up around 3 A.M. If his show begins at 5:30, that doesn't leave him much time to prepare for a radio show. Getting up any earlier will throw his day off so badly it's not worth it. That means a producer must go to bed at night with most of his preparation work done. In the next two chapters we'll get into what a producer must do in the ninety minutes or so before the show, and what he must do during the show. For the purposes of this chapter, we're more concerned about what a producer must do to plan tomorrow's show.

The following is a sample work schedule for a morning show producer, starting when today's show ends.

- 10:00—1:00—Meeting with the host, daily production, phone calls
- 1:00—4:00—Idea search, writing, keep an ear and eye on news
- 4:00—6:00—Family time

- 6:00—7:00—Pitch/planning call, writing prep sheet
- 7:00—9:00—Watch/tape TV

That schedule is just a sample. The afternoon hours vary widely. Some producers work all afternoon writing and working the phones. Other producers take the afternoon off because they prefer preparing at night (say, after the kids go to bed).

The good news is that very few producers today are expected to do all the writing, all the production, all the taping, and all the idea gathering we've talked about in this book. We have done all of them in our careers, but it's not like that anymore.

Nevertheless, the schedule we lay out in this chapter is a very realistic work schedule for top-notch producers. And it's not as taxing as it seems. Yes, you are working for many hours, but you aren't exactly doing strenuous manual labor. You're reading, calling, and watching TV. The untrained observer may even think you are a couch potato.

We have to remind our wives that we're getting paid for our work.

Meeting with the Host

The host rarely stays at the station more than an hour after the show. Since the producer is going to stay there longer, he has to make talking to the host his top priority before he attends to his other duties. What should he be asking the host? These questions should cover it. It shouldn't take more than ten or fifteen minutes (which may be all that you have).

- Which of our unused ideas from today are worth saving?
- Do you have any ideas that came to you during today's show?
- Do you need anything for a segment scheduled for tomorrow? (For instance: Audio or research for a guest or benchmark bit.)
- What segments from today's show are worth archiving?
- Are there any segments from today's show that we might want to try again in the future?
- The following celebrities are coming to town. Are there any that you are interested in?
- What time are we going to discuss the rundown sheet for tomorrow?
- If I need to get in touch with you for an emergency, where will you be?

Phone Calls

The quest for the guest begins as soon as you finish meeting with the host. Once the host has green-lighted the celebrities he wants, you can make the calls. Plan your time at the radio station around the best time to call whichever time zone you need to reach. If you are in the Midwest and need to reach a New York publicist, you better get on the phone right after you talk to the host. It's already 11:30 Eastern time, and the publicist may be going to lunch at any minute.

If you are talking to the West Coast, you might want to do production first, before going to the phones. Depending on your time zone and the time zone of the people you need to reach, you can adjust your schedule accordingly.

Regardless of how you time it, you really should try to make as many calls as possible from the station before you go home. You can always check your voice mail from home later to see if someone called you back, but you'll rack up a pretty hefty long-distance phone bill if you make all your calls from home. Plus, at the radio station you have a receptionist answering your calls for you, you can get answers to questions by walking down the hall, and you are getting valuable face time in the office. Everyone sees the last person in the office. Nobody sees the first person in the office, and that's you. It doesn't hurt to let everybody know that you work hard—after all, you do.

The thing about making phone calls and trying to book guests is that you can't define when and where you have to make those calls. You have to adjust to the situation. You may spend two minutes on the phone and get everything accomplished. Or, you may spend two hours on the phone and get nothing accomplished. It's hard to plan for it. Just assume that you'll make the bulk of your calls in the morning. After that, you'll just be doing a stray call here and a stray call there to tie up some loose ends.

Production Work

The amount of production work required varies widely from one producer to another. It depends on the format, the host, the skills of the producer, and the facilities. If there is production work required, there are usually three basic duties: prepare the promo, create production bits for tomorrow's show, and archive material from today's show. Again, not every show will require their producer to do all three. Some shows have technical producers that handle all of these duties. (For a much more detailed examination and explanation of technical skills required by the producer, see part 5 of this book. Each of the following examples is explained more thoroughly.)

SHOW PROMO

Some stations don't run promos for the morning show. Most do, but this isn't a difficult production assignment. During the show the producer is listening for the "promo moment." This is usually nothing more than a well-delivered one-liner. Promos are never longer than about forty seconds, so if you hear a good one-liner, you know you have a promo. The producer makes a notation of the time, takes the tape of the show into the production studio, cues up the one-liner quickly (because he made a notation of the time), and then re-records it into the editing software. He edits the segment slightly so it sounds perfect, cuts and pastes the audio into the promo template, and saves his work. He then lets the production director know it's done, and he washes his hand of the promo.

Note: The production director usually creates the promo template. This usually consists of a pre-produced promo open and close (voiced by the "voice" of the station). The promo template also usually has a music bed to be placed under the content of that day's promo. It sounds complicated, but it's really just another example of the kind of cutting and pasting any computer-savvy person does on a daily basis. (In chapter 17, we'll explain exactly how to do this and all other digital editing.)

PRODUCTION BITS

Not every show does production bits either. These are usually time-consuming projects, so the producer knows he has to get it out of the way. On days when elaborate production bits are required, the producer's whole schedule can be thrown off. To avoid this, some producers do part of the project the day before and come into the station an hour or so early to finish the project the following morning.

ARCHIVING THE SHOW

As for archiving the show, it's very important that this is done at least once a week, if not every day. When the material is fresh in your mind, you are better able to recognize what was worth keeping and what wasn't. You should obviously save every interview, but the other segments need to be very strong to be worthy of archiving. It depends on whether or not your show has regular "best of" shows. If they do, you'll need to archive more. If they don't, you won't need to archive as much.

Some shows take archiving to another level: releasing CDs every year or every few years of the "Best of" show highlights. If your show does this, you could become an official record producer, a member of NARAS (National Academy of Recording Arts and Sciences), and end up voting for the Grammy Awards. Rick Kaempfer did this after he produced "Steve & Garry's Decade of Service" in 1989.

Idea Search

The idea searching process is also thankfully flexible. In the morning before the show you are really only skimming a few newspapers. Plus you are checking the news wires for the most up-to-date stories. You don't have time for much more than that. The rest of your reading occurs after the show.

Many producers have a leisurely lunch as they read the papers they didn't have time for before the show. Or they'll talk on the phone while surfing their favorite Web sites looking for material. They usually have a few ideas left over from that day's show already, or they have a guest booked already, greatly relieving the stress of the search.

Once you get a routine down, idea searching can take place anywhere, anytime. There is a lot of downtime in the afternoon if you do a morning show. Producers may go through magazines as they wait for return phone calls. Or they go through their mail, reading the press releases, as they jot down a few notes for that night's prep sheet. This is a multi-tasking skill even a man can handle.

If you have any curiosity about the world around you, searching for ideas is fun. It really doesn't seem like work unless you are bone dry of ideas. That happens occasionally, but if you maintain your future shows file, and read whenever you get a moment of downtime, it won't happen enough to make it feel like work.

Writing

The producer that waits for full approval of every idea by the host is the producer that spends all night writing. Once you know the likes and dislikes of the host, it isn't hard to figure out what he will choose to do on a given day. Even if you haven't gotten him figured out yet, you may have a guest scheduled. Putting together an interview prep sheet can be done before the pitch meeting. Benchmark bits can also be prepared before the pitch meeting.

If you are doing your job right, the writing of the show prep sheet will take no more than thirty minutes after everything on the show is approved. And once that is written, you will no longer feel like a giant anvil is hovering over your head.

TV Taping

You have set the VCR or TiVo before you left the station, but you still need to watch the shows. Even on nights you haven't set the recorder, it pays to roll tape whenever you watch TV. You never know when you'll witness something that would make a great piece of audio. (For an explanation of how to extract this audio and convert it into something that can played back on the air, see part 5 of this book.) Nothing is as frustrating as missing something not because you didn't see it, but because you didn't have tape rolling. Just roll it when you watch. Trust us.

Do we need to point out that watching television at night for the big highlights is hardly backbreaking work? There always is something that needs to be taped almost every night. If you haven't subscribed to a prep service that handles this part of the job, or you don't have an assistant or intern that can help with this, you must choose your shows wisely.

On a busy night, pick two or three. Think of what your audience will be watching and cover those programs. You might get nothing, but you might end up with something better than the segments on the prep sheet. Don't forget, the prep sheet is never etched in stone.

THE PRODUCER'S WORKDAY

The best thing about the work schedule of a producer is the flexibility. It's perfectly acceptable to work less if you figure out a way to get your work done well in a short amount of time. As you progress through your producing career, your workday won't increase, it will decrease. That's because you will become more efficient, more organized, and more aware of your skills and liabilities. Guests will begin calling you, listeners will begin giving you ideas, and you will slowly but surely adjust to the hours.

At first the long list of duties will seem overwhelming. It may take a new producer a few months to get the hang of things. But one day a light bulb will go on. And the same producer who had been walking around like a zombie (because he was working eighteen hours a day) will be living a typical American life. And he will probably love his job.

In the next part of this book we'll examine what a producer does while a show is in progress. That's when everything you've learned is put to the test. It's exciting, it's terrifying, and it's the reason why all of us do this for a living.

PART THREE

IN THE HEAT OF THE BATTLE

Ask any NFL player about the difference between a practice and a game, and he'll tell you that the speed of a game is impossible to recreate. You can prepare, you can practice, you can simulate, you can even run a scout team, but until you get on the field you don't really know what you'll face.

The same is true of a radio show. In part 3, we'll do our best to simulate real game experience. It won't do it justice, but it may give you an idea of what you will be up against.

9

PRE-GAME SHOW

AFTER THE FIRST HORRIBLE JOLT OF THE ALARM CLOCK AT 3 A.M., AND those first twenty minutes of bleary-eyed fuzziness, there's something oddly comforting about being the only person awake. There's no traffic on the way in, nobody to talk to except the overnight guy, and the phone in your office won't ring. It's a deceivingly blissful way to start your day. It's also a blessing because you have a lot of work to cram into the ninety minutes before the show begins, and you don't have time for interruptions.

Such is the life of the morning show producer. While we'll be concentrating on the morning show producer in this chapter, the principals apply to producers of every day-part. Every producer has the same question running through his mind over and over again as he prepares for the show: What can go wrong? Answering that question as fully as possible is the producer's primary duty before the show begins. It is the most effective way to avoid disasters.

One of the tools you'll use to accomplish this task is the checklist. We'll get into a rather thorough discussion of checklists soon enough. We'll also help you see the potential trouble spots on a prep sheet. But first, the producer has to do any last-second production work, and he has to find out if anything has happened in the world since he put the prep sheet to bed.

PRODUCTION

If you have planned out your day correctly, you won't have a lot of production work to do in the minutes you have before the show. You may have a few audio clips from the previous night's television, or you may have to download audio from a wire service or prep service, but this process shouldn't take too long. (See part 5 of this book for more details on how to do all of your technical duties.)

Adjust your start time to the amount of production you will be required to perform on a given day. If you have more than usual, start earlier. On a normal day with about fifteen to thirty minutes of pre-show production, you'll be arriving ninety minutes before the show. Don't make the mistake of not allowing enough time. You'll understand what we mean when you see everything else you still need to do before showtime.

THE LATEST INFORMATION

In chapter 4 we went over eight different places a producer can find show material. In the minutes before the show begins, these places are cut down to three. You are looking at the news wires, skimming the papers, and checking e-mail. That's all you will have time for. This entire process should take no more than thirty minutes. That leaves you with approximately forty-five minutes before the show begins.

The News Wires

The news wires have a headline section and a section for kicker stories. If you have a competent newsperson, he should already be at the station putting together his newscast. Ask him what he is using for his kicker stories, and what his lead stories are. There shouldn't be any surprises about the lead story because you have been following the news so closely, but make sure you take a copy of the kicker stories with you and give them some thought. If you can't think of an angle, at the very least you should give them to the host when he walks in the door.

You will also need to check the audio that came in via your news wire. The wire service will send a list of all the available audio, and a simple perusal of this list will usually be enough. If nothing jumps out at you, ask the newsperson if he has heard anything spectacular. If he has, you'll want to make sure that you can also make this available to the host. Luckily, with everything being transmitted via computers these days, it may be a simple matter of transferring the audio from one computer to another.

The Newspapers

You are only skimming the newspapers because you already know what the big stories are. Check for interesting angles on the news stories that you hadn't considered. Also, look at the various columnists and see if they have new angles that you can also use. As you skim, the stories you don't already know about will nearly jump off the page. If you think they could be of interest to the host or the audience, clip them out. You aren't really going to have time to do anything more than make photo copies of the articles for everyone on the show and highlight a few facts in the articles that caught your eye. Staple these to the back of the prep sheet.

E-mail

Before you put the full packet together, get online and see if there are any e-mails from listeners that you may be able to use on the air. Someone may have a comment on a topic you will be addressing. Or someone may have a suggestion for a segment that is better than what you have already prepared. If so, print them out and staple these to the back of the packet too.

You should now have your complete packet ready to go. Hand one to every member of the show (or more likely, put the packets in their empty chairs, awaiting their arrivals).

THE MAINTENANCE CHECKLIST

The maintenance checklist was created to help you avoid any big problems that may occur. This list should cover just about anything that could go wrong aside from show content and studio equipment. (We'll address those a little later in this chapter.) Every show has a different maintenance checklist, but this sample may give you some ideas. Checking every item on this checklist should take no more than fifteen minutes. After you read it, we'll explain.

- Commercial log checked for live copy
- Music log and commercial log copied for everyone that needs it
- Contest book checked
- Coffee machine turned on, coffee brewing
- Fax machine turned on and full of paper
- Voice mail checked
- Mailbox emptied

The Commercial Log

The commercial log is just what it sounds like. It's a log of all the commercials that will be played on the radio station for that day, along with the times they will air. These are listed in order by time (i.e., 6:10, 6:20, etc.). The traffic and continuity department will have them divided up by commercial breaks. The person running the board usually follows the commercial log, but if that person isn't the host, he should have a copy too.

What can go wrong with the commercial log? If the commercial log isn't there, you'll really find out what's important at a radio station. After all, commercials may be missed. If that happens, heads will roll. Nothing gets people hopping at a radio station like a missed commercial. You'll have to make a phone call right away. Trust us. Don't delay. Make that call and save your fanny.

For our pre-show purposes there is another reason for checking the commercial log: live commercials. If the host has live commercials scheduled, he usually doesn't know about it in advance. He will have to be warned, and you are responsible for making sure he has seen the live copy and pre-read it before he does it on the air. That takes a little planning. The live copy is usually located in a book labeled "live copy" or something else equally obvious. Thanks to the maintenance checklist, the producer will remember to pull out the copy in advance. That will lead to a better live commercial, which will lead to a happier client, which will lead to a happier boss. Happy boss equals happy producer.

The Music Log

The music log is also self-explanatory. Every music station in the country has a computer printout of the songs that are expected to be played. These are usually broken down by hour and put in a highly researched order. Program directors don't take kindly to hosts who don't follow the music log correctly. The host and the producer should both have copies of the music log.

If the music log isn't there, people won't be fired, but the program director will be extremely upset. A call would have to be placed right away. The days when a host could pick his own music have been gone for about twenty years now. Most hosts have never picked their own music. They would be lost without the music log.

The Contest Book

Every station has a contest book in the studio. This book contains all the details about the giveaways and has empty prize sheets to fill in the winner's name and address. What can go wrong if you don't check this before the show? A prize may have been yanked out of the book by a salesperson or the promotion director because a client didn't provide the prize as promised. Or, a prize may have been added at the last second. If you have prepared a contest and don't discover there isn't a prize until the contest begins, you will have egg on your face. If there is a prize that you didn't anticipate and the show ends without you giving it away, you will be in trouble. Check the contest book every morning. It can't hurt, and it could avoid disaster.

Coffee Machine

What can really go wrong if the coffee machine isn't working? If you are doing a morning show, the coffee machine is no small matter. The host will not be firing on all cylinders until he gets his jolt of coffee. A host without coffee will probably be cranky, fuzzy, and slow. That's not a good combination for someone trying to do a radio show. Get him his coffee. It's not beneath you. It's essential.

Fax Machine

Between the times the business day ends and the morning show begins, the fax machine has been pouring out faxes for twelve hours. Most stations only have one or two fax machines and they receive a tremendous volume of faxes. Nearly every morning the fax machine will be out of paper. At least once a week the fax machine will be out of toner. If you give out the fax number to your listeners for contests or comments, or you expect faxes from potential guests, the fax machine has to be working. It won't be if you don't check it every morning.

Voice Mail and Mailbox

What can go wrong if you don't check your voice mail or mailbox before every show? Someone may have left you instructions about that morning's show. Often a promotion director will leave details about a contest in your mailbox. An account executive (salesperson) may have left you information or updated copy for a live spot. A guest may have called and cancelled on your voice mail.

We've both been victimized at one time or another by not checking our mailboxes or voice mail before a show. That's why we put them on the checklist.

STUDIO CHECKLIST

After you've checked off everything on the maintenance list, you still have between fifteen to thirty minutes to make sure the studio is prepped properly. The studio checklist will be the tool that prevents as many potential technical problems as possible. Again, every show has a different studio checklist. This sample may give you some ideas.

- Headphones
- Microphones
- Tape Rolling
- Harmonizer
- Reverb
- Delay System
- Phone Screener
- Operating Log
- Special Requests

Headphones

What can go wrong with headphones? You would be amazed at how often these break or short out. If the headphones aren't working properly, the host will be distracted during the entire show. The producer should check everyone's headphones before the show begins just to make sure. If there is a problem, a replacement set should be brought into the studio. Because radio performers are very picky about their headphones, make sure that the extra sets are exact duplicates of the "first stringers." Every show should have at least two extra sets of quality headphones in case of emergency.

Because each person can adjust the headphone volume, the headphone mix must also be checked before the show begins. Each host will have a preference about which mix he wants in his headphones. For example, the overnight host may listen to the air-mix and your host has to listen to the program-mix because he uses the delay system. It better be on the right setting for the host. Otherwise, he may hear himself in delay. And that will be a disaster.

Microphones

What can go wrong with microphones? Previous shows may have unplugged a microphone because they didn't need it. A production director may have switched microphones to record a commercial. A microphone may have shorted out. A guest microphone that hasn't been used in awhile may not be working properly.

You've probably been to a concert and seen the roadie check each microphone on stage. In radio, the producer performs the same task. If you do it before the show, disaster may be averted.

Tape Rolling

Most producers like to roll multiple tapes on every show to make sure that nothing is missed. Even shows that don't run highlights or "best of" features make sure to tape the show. Clients may ask for a tape of a live commercial or contest. Listeners may ask for tapes of themselves on the air. The FCC (Federal Communications Commission) may ask for tapes of something considered to be a violation.

Don't let the show start unless you are sure tape is rolling. It may be a DAT (digital audiotape), it may be a videotape (some stations record audio on videotape), it may be a CD, or a mini-disc, or it may be a cassette or reel-to-reel tape. Whatever format you choose, start the tape, and check to make sure the levels on the VU (volume units) meters are correct and it's recording at the correct speed. What can go wrong if you don't thoroughly check each part of this equation? The tape may run out if it's recorded at the wrong speed, or the tape may be distorted or not record at all if you don't check the levels.

Harmonizer

Not every show uses a harmonizer. This is a device that alters someone's voice. In our fictional *Larry & Mary Show*, let's say that Larry has a character named "Spiffy" who has a very high-pitched cartoon-like voice. He creates this effect by using a harmonizer set on high. What can go wrong if you don't make sure the harmonizer is set to the correct position for Spiffy? He may end up sounding like Barry White instead. That would kill the bit pretty quickly, wouldn't it?

Reverb

Like the harmonizer, the reverb has all sorts of different settings. If the host calls for reverb, he must know that it's set exactly the way he likes it. If he expects the reverb to sound like he is in a large hall but it sounds like he's inside a barrel instead, that might throw him off a bit. If he presses the reverb button and it's turned all the way down, he may not get any reverb at all. It only takes a few seconds to make sure it's correct. Check it every day.

Delay System

What can go wrong if the delay isn't on? We don't really need to spell that out, do we? With the way the FCC has been cracking down lately, it's more essential than ever. The FCC is radio's governing body, and any infraction of its rules can lead to a fine or the loss of your station's license. This is something every radio station takes extremely seriously. The host should have a good idea of what's against the FCC rules, but the listeners don't. (See the accompanying box for a full explanation of the FCC indecency rules.) Any infraction by a caller is still an infraction by the station in the eyes of the FCC. The delay system is the device that eliminates any chance of that happening. It only takes a second to make sure the delay is on. Usually you just need to press the button that says "delay." If your show doesn't use the delay system, but it's turned on, make sure it's turned off. It's simple, but important enough that it needs to be placed on the studio checklist.

The rules regarding obscene or indecent speech are a little vague. There are really three different definitions of what is considered obscene material by the Supreme Court.

1. An average person, applying contemporary community standards would find the material, as a whole, appeals to the prurient interest.
2. The material depicts or describes, in a patently offensive manner as measured by community standards, sexual or excretory conduct.
3. The material, taken as a whole, lacks serious literary, artistic, political, or scientific value.

The way the FCC has chosen to enforce these rules has focused on "graphically depicting a sex act or excretory function." Virtually every fine for obscenity has involved those two no-nos. If you are clever with your word choice and you don't get graphic, you can still talk about sex or going to the bathroom. However, there are some specific words that you simply cannot say. You've probably heard about the "seven dirty words" from a George Carlin routine. These expletives should never be said on the radio for any reason. We'd rather not spell them out for you, but we'll give you a few hints. The F word, the SH word, the P word (urinate), the C word (female body part), the MF word, the T word (female body part), and the C-sucker word, are all off limits. Of course, it doesn't take a genius to realize you shouldn't be saying those words on the radio. We don't even feel comfortable writing them in a book. The bottom line about indecent or obscene speech is that you should avoid it all times. We know there are hosts that push the envelope, but you should never allow yourself to be sucked into one of these conversations on the air. Your station will sacrifice a producer in a heartbeat before they risk being fined by the FCC.

Phone Screener

What can go wrong if the phone screener isn't working properly? The producer may be cut off from his only means of communicating with the host while the show is in progress. There are so many different settings on a phone screener computer that a different show on the station may have slightly altered something. Check it every day. Make sure the settings are just the way you like them. This only takes a few seconds but it could prevent a crisis.

Also, check to make sure the phone is working in the studio. If for some reason the phones or the phone screener isn't working and you can't fix it yourself, you must call the engineer right away. Otherwise, you may have to drastically alter your show plans that day.

The Operating Log

The FCC is most concerned about the operating log (also sometimes known as the transmitter log or the program log). This is the sign-on/sign-off sheet with the transmitter readings. The person that signs this varies from show to show. Usually it's the host or the producer. If it's the host, it should be put somewhere where he won't forget to sign it.

The operating log is an FCC requirement, but there is one more reason a producer concerns himself with it. He looks at the transmitter readings to see if there have been any transmitter problems. If there were any emergency warnings overnight, that information will also be contained on the operating log. What can go wrong if you start the show without knowing about transmitter problems or emergency bulletins? You may not be on the air at all. It's hard to imagine a bigger impediment than that.

Special Requests

This is where every show will be different. We've worked for shows that asked for the phone to be placed in a particular spot. We've worked for shows that put up a curtain between the host and the co-host. And we've worked for shows that needed a guitar, a set of bongos, a megaphone, a stool, and/or a vacuum cleaner. Other shows have special requests like a certain chilled beverage or a special scent. You'll be amazed. Whatever the host needs every day will have to be put on the studio checklist. Otherwise, there will be problems—and you don't want to have any problems if you can avoid them.

RECHECK THE PREP SHEET

After you've done the maintenance checklist and the studio checklist, it's time to take one last look at your prep sheet in the fifteen minutes or so before the show begins. Again, you must answer the question: What can go wrong? You'll answer that question by answering the following questions.

▶ Do you have everything you'll need for every segment?

▶ If you are relying on someone else in a segment (like a guest or the callers), do you have a backup plan in case something doesn't work as planned?

▶ Is the host properly prepared to handle each segment on the prep sheet?

▶ Is the co-host prepared?

▶ Have you found something better while you skimmed this morning's papers and news wires?

If you have answered all of those questions to your satisfaction, you've done everything in your power to avoid problems with the prep sheet.

FASTER THAN A SPEEDING BULLET

As you'll discover in the next chapter, there are still many things that can go wrong once a show is in progress. We wish we could tell you that the show in chapter 10 is an aberration or an exaggeration. Unfortunately, it's pretty typical. You'll be trying to stay one step ahead of the host to avoid each and every thing that can go wrong, but you won't be able to avoid them all. However, if you've done everything we suggest in this chapter, at least you'll be able to hand over the keys to the host without trepidation.

Go into your producer's booth and strap in. It's showtime. In the next chapter we'll try to show you how hectic a show can be even with a maintenance list, a studio checklist, and a comprehensive prep sheet (we'll be working from *The Larry & Mary Show* in appendix D). In the 1950s, the television show *Superman* opened with an announcer saying these immortal words: "Faster than a speeding bullet." That's what a show in progress can feel like to a producer. We probably won't be doing justice to the feeling, but we'll try in chapter 10.

10

SHOWTIME: A DAY IN A LIFE

THE FOLLOWING RUNDOWN SHEET IS TAPED TO EVERY MICROPHONE stand of *The Larry & Mary Show.*

MAY 21

6:10—"Mary's Daily Inspiration"
6:20—Governor Story
6:40—Phone Segment: Things your pets have eaten
6:50—Phone Segment/Part 2
7:10—President Misspeaks/Parody song
7:20—The Hog-Calling Champion
7:40—Phone Segment: Childhood nicknames
7:50—Phone Segment/Part 2
8:10—Larry at the Blood Bank
8:20—"The Dumb Crook File"
8:40—Richard Simmons in the studio
8:50—Richard Simmons/Part 2
9:10—Nude Man Story
9:20—"Monday Movie Mania"
9:40—Call to Mayor Meisterberger
9:50—Sign Off/Tease of tomorrow's show

The more comprehensive prep sheet (appendix D) is stapled to the top of the packet producer Sean Harrison has placed in front of each microphone position.

The clock ticks down to 6 A.M. Newscaster Charlie Stern looks at the clock as he frantically slams the side of his computer screen. Because of massive computer problems this morning, he is unable to access the newscasts he wrote. This first newscast will have to be a rip-and-read newscast instead. He has no choice. He grabs a few headlines from the morning paper, jots some notes in the margins, and nods to Larry as the song ends. Larry hits the news theme.

"It's 6:00, and here's Charlie Stern with this morning's first look at the news," Larry says.

As Charlie does his newscast, Larry motions for his producer. Sean comes bounding into the studio.

"Sean, I'm changing a few things around," Larry says.

"OK," Sean answers, pen in hand.

"I'm dropping the governor story unless you can get me a sanitation worker to deliver that punch line," Larry says.

"But that's in twenty minutes," Sean answers.

"That's all you got. I'll assume we're staying with the bit unless you give me thumbs down," Larry says. "And take a look at Charlie's news computer. It crashed again after you printed out these kicker stories."

"Got it," Sean answers.

"Sean," Mary asks sweetly. "Can you get me another cup of coffee too?"

"No problem," Sean replies.

He grabs the coffee cup and heads out of the studio. The coffee machine is right around the corner. As he pours Mary another cup, he hears the end of Charlie's newscast and watches the on-air light go on over the main studio door. Pushing the heavy door with his backside as he carefully holds the full cup of coffee, Sean quietly walks across the studio to Mary's microphone position. Mary has just begun her daily inspiration for this morning. He quietly places the piping hot cup of coffee to her left, so he doesn't disturb her as she speaks.

Larry makes eye contact with Sean and waves him over.

"Tell Mary after the show that she shouldn't do any more daily inspirations about smiling," Larry whispers. "This is like the fourth one. It's getting old."

Sean nods and quietly pushes the heavy door open, closing it quickly behind him. He opens the door to the producer's booth, and grabs his to-do list notebook out of his briefcase. He writes "Talk to Mary" at the end of the list. The door to his booth opens again.

"Sean," Charlie Stern says, poking his head through the cracked door, "take a look at my computer. It's completely screwed."

"Reboot it," Sean advises.

"I already did," Charlie answers. "It's not working. I have three newscasts already written on that damn thing, and my next one is in fifteen minutes."

"I'll be right there," Sean says.

The door closes and Sean grabs his phone book. He finds the main number for the sanitation department and dials it. After one ring, a recording begins.

"You've reached the sanitation department," the pleasant female voice says. "If you know your party's extension, please dial it now. To report a. . . ."

Sean presses zero, hoping to reach a person. The phone begins to ring again.

"You've reached the sanitation department," the same pleasant female voice says after one more ring. "If you know your party's extension, please dial it now."

Sean hangs up the phone and heads into the news booth.

"This @$#* thing," Charlie screams as he slaps the side of his computer.

"What's the problem here?"

"It's broken, that's what," Charlie answers.

"Did you save your files?" Sean asks.

"Why the @#$% would I do that?" Charlie answers.

Sean reboots the computer one more time. Charlie is lucky this time. The documents are still there.

"Sometimes you just have to shut it down for a few extra seconds," Sean tells him as he walks out of the news booth.

Sean hears commercials in the hallway and realizes he only has a few minutes to track down a sanitation worker. Larry waves him into the studio.

"Did you get one yet?" Larry asks.

"Not yet," Sean answers.

"Call the Sanitation department," Larry advises. "They should be open already."

"I already did, but I got a recording," Sean replies.

"Call Rocco," Larry suggests. "Doesn't he work for the sanitation department?"

"Yeah, but I don't have his number," Sean replies.

"He wins contests every other week. Look at an old contest form," Larry says as one commercial ends and another begins.

"Did you look at the live copy for the Mattress King?" Sean asks.

"Get me a sanitation worker," Larry snaps. "I'll worry about Mattress King."

Sean leaves the studio and walks down the hall to the promotion department. The door to the promotion director's office is locked, but Sean has a key. He distinctly remembers that Rocco won last week, but he has no idea where the promotion director keeps the old forms.

The radio on her desk is turned off, so Sean reaches over to turn it on. He hears Larry reading the live spot for Mattress King and realizes that he has less than sixty seconds to find Rocco's number. He spots a three ring binder labeled "Winner Sheets," grabs it off the book shelf, and runs back into the producer's booth.

Larry sees him out of the corner of his eye as he finishes up the Mattress King commercial. Sean holds the book in the air, Larry gives him thumbs up, and Sean starts leafing through the winner sheets looking for Rocco's name and number. It doesn't take long to find the name and number of their favorite contest pig. Sean looks at the clock. It's 6:20 and Larry has launched into the story about the governor.

The phone rings once. No answer at Rocco's house. It rings again. Larry is getting to the end of the Governor story and Rocco isn't on the line yet. Finally, a voice is heard on the other end of the line.

"Yeah," a groggy voice answers.

"Rocco?" Sean asks.

"Yeah," he replies.

"This is Sean from *The Larry and Mary Show.* Can you do me a favor?"

"What?"

"Can you say the punch line to this bit we're doing right now? Larry thinks it would be funnier if we get a sanitation worker to say it."

"No problem," Rocco answers, getting excited. "What's the line?"

"Say 'It's only fair, we both do the same thing—deliver garbage.'"

"Got it," Rocco replies. "Hey Sean, I never got my tickets to *The Vagina Monologues.* Would you check into that for me?"

"Yeah," Sean says. "I'm putting you on hold."

"Is that our good friend Rocco the sanitation worker on the line?" Larry asks on the air.

"Line three," Sean says over his intercom.

"Rocco!"

"Hey Larry," Rocco says.

"I had a feeling we would hear from you this morning. What do you think about this story? The Governor pays the same amount as taxes as you do."

"I guess it's only fair, we both do the same thing—deliver garbage." (Rimshot sound effect.)

"Thanks for putting it in perspective, Rocco. It's 6:27. Charlie Stern will be right up with the latest news. Don't go away"

The commercials begin and Sean picks up the line to thank Rocco. As he is doing that, Larry talks over the intercom.

"Get in here!" Larry orders.

The commercials are playing loudly over the speakers. Larry turns down the monitors when Sean enters the room.

"I don't know about this 'things my dog ate' phoner," Larry says. "People are eating breakfast. I don't think a sausage link is going to taste so great when you're listening to someone talking about rifling through dog crap. Why don't we switch the phoners around and do the nicknames now, and save the dog thing for later?"

"Won't some people still be eating breakfast at 7:40?" Sean asks.

"I'm having second thoughts about the nicknames phoner," Mary adds.

"Why?" Sean asks.

The commercial ends. Mary and Sean stop talking.

"And here's Charlie Stern with this morning's news," Larry says into the microphone. He turns it off, takes off his headphones, and looks at Sean.

"I told you that she would change her mind about it," Larry says.

"I don't think Dottie will be too happy if everybody in the school hears that her new nickname is Snotty," Mary snaps.

"They already know it," Larry answers.

"Not everybody."

"Fine, drop the nicknames phoner, we'll do the pet thing. But make sure the callers use euphemisms and don't get too graphic." Larry says. "What else do we have for 7:40?"

"What about that story from the Herald about men going to spas?" Sean replies. "That could be a phoner."

"What's the angle?"

"We could. . . ."

His sentence is stopped cold by the voice of Charlie Stern coming through the speakers.

"And that's the news, I'm Charlie Stern."

"Thanks, Charlie," Larry says. "Did you see this story on the news last night? Willie Nordstrum of South Bend brought home his paycheck last Friday and left it on the coffee table so he could change his clothes before going to the bank."

"I saw this one," Mary laughs.

Sean quietly leaves the studio and returns to his producer's booth as Larry and Mary go over the funny details of the dog eating the man's paycheck. Sean starts to look over the men going to spas story.

"Buster isn't the first pet to eat something he shouldn't have," Larry's voice says through the speaker. Gabe Kaplan's voice follows immediately.

"Please excuse Juan," Kaplan's voice says on the audio clip. "The dog ate his homework. And it will eat his homework tonight and tomorrow night too. Signed, Epstein's Mother."

Sean puts the spa article down on the counter and picks up the phone receiver anticipating the barrage of phone calls.

"Give us a call at 591-SHOW and tell us your story. We'll be back with your phone calls right after this."

The on-air light turns off, the intercom turns on.

"Tell them to keep it clean," Larry advises over the intercom.

"Larry and Mary show," Sean says to the first caller.

"Sean, this is Rocco. My dog ate a toad once."

"Rocco, we already had you on this morning," Sean answers.

"I know, but this story is hilarious."

"Next time, Rocco. Hello, Larry and Mary show."

"Are you taking requests for songs?"

"Not really."

"Hello, Larry and Mary show."

"My dog ate a rope once," the caller on line four says.

"Really? What happened?" Sean asks.

"I didn't even know he ate it until I saw something sticking out of his butt the next day."

"Does this story get gross?"

"Not really. I yanked on it a little, but when he started yelping I knew I had to take him to the vet."

"Great. Turn off your radio. Larry and Mary will be with you in a few minutes. When you hear a pffffft sound that means you're on the air. What's your name?"

"Brent."

"Hold on, Brent."

"Thanks."

Sean types the name "Brent" on the phone screener. He also types "dog ate rope" as he answers the next line.

"Larry and Mary show."

"My cat ate crepe paper once."

"What happened?"

"Her litter box was psychedelic the next morning."

"That's great. You told it perfectly. Tell it the same way when you get on with Larry and Mary. What's your name?"

"Vanessa."

"Vanessa, hold on the line, and turn off your radio. When you hear a pffffft sound that means you're on the air."

Sean types the name "Vanessa" on the phone screener. He also types "cat ate crepe paper" as he reaches to answer the next line. Larry's voice on the intercom interrupts him.

"Hotline is ringing," Larry says.

"Larry and Mary show," Sean answers the hotline.

"This is Mark from Richard Simmons' office."

"Hi Mark."

"Sean, I'm sorry to do this to you, but the producer at Fox is now telling us that Richard won't be done here until 9 A.M. Does that cause a big problem for you?"

"Uh . . . no, I guess not. We'll rearrange."

"Thanks, Sean. I appreciate it. We'll see you at 9 A.M."

"Who was that on the hotline?" Larry asks through the intercom as Sean hangs up.

"Richard Simmons is going to be a half hour late."

"Forget it. Tell him forget it," Larry snaps.

"But I just told him that . . ." Sean starts to reply into his intercom.

"I got thirty seconds left in the spot and only two calls screened," Larry interrupts. "Let's Go!"

Sean goes back to the phone lines. He looks up at the clock and sees that it's already 6:53. The psychedelic cat crap call will be the last one they have time for. Sean picks up the story about spas again. He sees a funny story about a man who fell asleep during a pedicure only to awaken with his toenails painted red. Sean highlights that paragraph and jots down the angle "Is it manly for men to go to a spa?"

The cat lady tells about the psychedelic litter box and Larry goes right to commercials. The intercom goes off again.

"Why is he going to be a half hour late?"

"Fox is keeping him longer than they originally agreed," Sean explains.

"Cancel him," Larry barks over the intercom. "We're not waiting around all morning for Richard Simmons to show up."

Sean walks into the studio, hoping to calm down the irate host.

"What's the big deal?" Mary asks Larry as Sean enters the room.

"The big deal is that we have to send a message to these PR people," Larry says.

"Fine," Sean answers. He and Mary make eye contact. Mary shakes her head gently. She knows they have two hours to calm Larry down.

"Did you change the mix on the backup vocals for the President parody song?" Larry asks.

"No. Do you want to me change it?" Sean asks.

"Yeah. You got ten minutes. See what you can do."

Sean makes a mad rush down the hall to the production studio. He finds the file for the parody song in the editing software and listens back to the first thirty seconds. He listens to it again, trying to decide how he can remix it, save the file, and still have it ready to go in time. He looks at the clock. It's 7:05. It might be possible, but if he's wrong, and the file is still being updated when Larry goes to it, it won't play on the air at all.

He closes the file, leaving the song exactly as it is. He runs back to the producer's booth. Larry is in the middle of the story about the President and sees Sean out of the corner of his eye. Sean gives him the thumbs up. Larry starts the song.

As the parody song is playing, Sean is on the phone getting the hog-calling champion on the phone.

"Hello, is this Chester?" Sean asks.

"Yes sir."

"Chester, this is Sean from the Larry and Mary show. We're finishing up a segment here and then we'll go to commercials. Do you mind waiting on the phone for a few minutes, or should I call you back in a few minutes."

"I s'pose I can wait. Gladys is fixin' me some flapjacks. Mind if I eat while I wait?"

"Not at all," Sean says, putting Chester on hold.

The parody song ends, the commercial begins, and Sean goes into the studio to prep Larry and Mary for the hog-calling segment.

"That was way better," Larry says. "I could barely even hear the backup vocals."

"Thanks," Sean says. "Do you have everything you need for the hog-calling champ?"

"Why don't we move Chester into the Richard Simmons slot," Larry suggests.

"Let's just do Chester now," Sean says. "He's on the phone already. I'm more worried about the 7:40 slot."

Sean hands Larry and Mary the spa article. Mary laughs out loud when she reads the portion Sean highlighted. Larry never goes against something that gets Mary to laugh out loud.

"Fine," Larry says, "Now what about that Richard Simmons slot?"

"Larry, why don't we just move Richard Simmons to 9:00?" Mary asks. "That way we can mention your blood bank appearance at 8:40. That's a bigger story than Richard Simmons anyway. People need to know that they can meet you today."

The end of the commercial stops Larry from answering, but he seems to be loosening up a little. Sean heads back to the producer's booth, and Larry puts Chester the hog-calling champion on the air.

"Chester, how is it down in Arkansas this morning?" Larry asks cheerfully.

"You the feller that sang that song before the commercials?" Chester asks.

"Not exactly Merle Haggard, am I Chester?" Larry asks with his trademark self-deprecating humor.

"Did you write them words too?" Chester asks.

"Sure did," Larry lies.

"Around these parts we're a little more respectful of our president," Chester scolds.

Larry is temporarily stunned. Sean says "go right to hog calling" in his headphones.

"Chester," Larry says, recovering quickly, "I understand you are the champion hog caller in Arkansas. Is that true?"

"Yes sir."

"Prove it."

"Soooooooo-eeeeeeeeeeee. Su-heee. Su-heeee."

"Chester, it's an honor to have a champion on our show. We're not accustomed to that around here."

Larry goes right to commercials. Sean thanks Chester off the air, and runs into the studio to make sure that Larry is all right. Because they ended the phone call so early, and they have four minutes to fill, Larry is getting ready to play a song out of the commercials.

"All set with the spa phoner?" Sean asks, hoping a change of subject will help.

"Yeah, but I want that clip of Chester isolated. Go into the production studio and put it in the gadget for me."

"What about screening the calls?" Sean asks.

"Mary is right. We need to move the blood bank benefit to a better time. Let's do it now, and then we'll do the spa phoner in the old Richard Simmons slot."

"What about Richard Simmons? Should I un-cancel him?"

"Fine, but make sure you tell his people that we'll only do one segment with him now. We have 'Monday Movie Mania' at 9:20."

Mary and Sean exchange smiles and Sean leaves for the production studio down the hall. He pulls the DAT out of the machine, rewinds it about ten minutes or so and rolls the entire Chester interview into Pro Tools. He not only isolates the actual hog calling, he isolates Chester saying "Around these parts we're more respectful of our president."

He transfers the files into the audio vault, making them available for airplay.

At 7:57 Sean walks back into his producer's booth, having missed both the 7:40 and the 7:50 segments.

"It's filed under Chester," Sean explains in the intercom.

Larry locates each clip, sees the quote from Chester, and uses it to introduce the news with Charlie Stern.

"Charlie, I know you are going to report on what the President said to the Prime Minister of India. Before you do that story," Larry teases, "there is something else I want you keep in mind." He presses the button and the audio plays.

"Around these parts we're more respectful of our president," says Chester. Charlie gets a laugh and the news begins.

Sean goes into the studio as soon as the on-air light turns off.

"Hey, we moved the nude man story to 7:50, so we have an opening now for Richard Simmons," Larry explains. "Is everything all set with that?"

"Yeah, no problem," Sean says.

"One segment with Richard—no more, right?"

"Right," Sean agrees.

"For 8:10, Mary and I are going to do the nickname phoner."

"School started at 8:00," Mary explains. "It should be fine now."

"But we can't take calls now because we have 'The Dumb Crook File' at 8:20 and that's sponsored," Sean says.

"Can we do the nicknames bit as a phoner after 8 A.M. tomorrow?" Larry asks Mary.

"That would be fine," Mary says sweetly, handing Sean a note, "would you mind running downstairs and getting this at Starbucks for me? Get some Evian too. Richard Simmons may want some."

"Larry, do you have everything you need for these next two segments?" Sean asks.

Larry nods as he puts on his headphones. He waves Sean out of the studio indicating his approval with the coffee run. Sean goes back to his briefcase, pulls out his idea notebook and writes down "Phoner: Nicknames."

He leaves the radio station, heads over to the elevator, and takes it down to the basement of the building. The Starbucks there is always jam-packed at this time of day.

He looks at his watch and tries to judge whether or not he will have time to get back upstairs in time for the 8:40 phoner. The line seems to be moving pretty quickly, so he makes the decision to go for it. The time keeps ticking away as he slowly makes his way to the front of the line. It's 8:20 and Sean takes Mary's note out of his pocket. His heart sinks as he realizes Mary's picky order has just added another five minutes to his wait.

"I'll have a Grande Skim Soy Latte with cinnamon and three Evians please," Sean says as he looks at his watch.

He gets the Grande Skim Soy Latte with cinnamon at 8:33, and runs back to the elevator. Now Sean is waiting with hundreds of other people who are just arriving for work. The elevator is packed as he hits the button for the seventeenth floor. The clock on the Elevator News Network says 8:42 when the door finally opens at seventeen.

Sean races into the producer's booth, and hears Larry and Mary discussing the spa article on the air. He quietly slips into the studio, gives Mary her frou-frou drink which she accepts with a smile, and Larry asks the question about whether or not it's manly for men to go to the spa.

"I don't see anything wrong with it," Mary says.

"What man really needs a pedicure?" Larry asks.

"Every single man on earth," Mary answers with a laugh.

"I want to hear from the kind of man who likes going to the spa. Defend yourselves."

By the time the first commercial starts, it's already 8:46. They barely have time for phone calls. Sean reaches over to start screening calls when the warm line rings. It's the receptionist calling say that Richard Simmons has arrived.

"Get the phones," Larry bellows into the intercom.

"Richard Simmons is here," Sean answers back.

"Perfect," Larry says over the intercom. "Send him in. I bet he's been to a spa before."

Sean greets Richard Simmons and his entourage, gives them each an Evian, and brings them into the studio. There is one minute of commercials left when Sean introduces Richard to Larry and Mary.

"Sorry we're a few minutes late," Richard apologizes.

"No problem at all," Larry says.

"But I've got good news for you," Richard says.

"What's that?"

"You're the last stop on my schedule this morning. I can stay until 10 A.M."

"Fantastic," says Larry.

Sean starts to step in to explain that they only have time for one segment, but Larry shoos him away. He has changed his mind.

Richard Simmons steals the show. Richard shows Larry his latest pedicure in the first segment. Richard talks about his doll collection in the second segment. Richard agrees to do the Monday Movie Mania contest with them in the third segment. For the fourth segment, Richard sings "Happy Birthday" to Mayor Meisterburger with such sultry style that it makes the mayor extremely uncomfortable.

When the show ends at 10 A.M., it barely resembles the show they put together on the prep sheet. But it was a show to remember.

11

REMOTE BROADCASTS

HOPEFULLY THE PREVIOUS CHAPTER GAVE YOU AN IDEA OF HOW HECTIC a normal pre-planned show can be. Now multiply that by twenty. That's a remote broadcast.

Producing a remote broadcast is like producing a totally different radio show. The entire show is out of its element. Most hosts find sanctuary in the studio. It's home-field advantage. When you're on the road, you're the visiting team.

In this chapter we'll teach you how to adjust to the road. You'll have slightly different content, different technical issues, and you'll have to speak a totally different language: remote. (We'll get into a more comprehensive technical discussion in part 5 of this book.) Unfortunately, you can't really appreciate the remote broadcast without experiencing it firsthand. Don't worry. Despite the difficulties, remote broadcasts can be very rewarding.

TECHNICAL ISSUES

If possible, set up a meeting with the broadcast team (host, co-host, newsperson, etc.), engineers, promotion department, and programming department to do a dry run of the show. If you can't all meet at one time, meet with them all individually. Here you'll be able to spot possible snags and concerns and ways to remedy them. Ask questions about what will be done if particular things go wrong. The execution of the remote is everything.

Obviously the technical adaptations are the most difficult for remote broadcasts. You aren't just worried about the usual things on your checklist. In fact, you're going to create an entirely different checklist. Before you create it, you need to ask your engineer a few questions.

- Wireless or wired microphones?
- Will there be a computer with an Internet hookup?
- Will there be a fax machine?

You need to know what kind of microphones you'll be using because it may limit the number of things you can do. For instance, if you don't have wireless microphones, the length of the microphone cable will limit the number of places the host can roam during the broadcast. A wireless microphone will allow for much more flexibility.

You need to know if you will have a computer with an Internet hookup to find out if you can access news wires from the remote location. If you don't have one, it might mean the newsperson can't come along. If you don't have a fax machine, then you need to make sure you have brought all the paperwork you need (i.e., commercial log, music log, contest sheets, etc.). For local remotes, this may require a trip to the radio station before you get to the remote location. If there is a fax machine at the remote, the board operator can simply fax this stuff to you (more about the board operator later).

More Technical Issues—Local Remotes

The checklist will be slightly different based on the questions we asked already, but there are a few more things to consider.

You may be having a bigger-than-life extravaganza that requires extra technical support. You may have a live band performing or a live audience. You need to know in advance what technical requirements the band will have. Who is doing the sound reinforcement? How many extra microphones will they need? Is there a microphone for the audience? Are there enough people setting up the equipment to make sure everything is ready to go by showtime?

More Technical Issues—Out-of-Town Remotes

When you are broadcasting out of town, you probably won't see the broadcast site until just before showtime. Find out who your contact is at the location. Call and ask him questions so that you understand the potential problems you might face. For instance, the location may cause unforeseen problems. Anticipate what those problems might be. Some examples of potential problems from a remote location include no shelter from the elements (this is electrical equipment after all), sound that will interfere with your show (like street noises or music being played nearby), no place to hide the wires (which will cause people to trip over them), or cramped space.

As for equipment, that will never be more important. Remember, if something is forgotten when you are out of town, you can't just send someone back to the station to get it like you can for a local remote. Check and double check with your engineer to make sure you have everything you need.

More Technical Issues—Out-of-Country Remotes

If you are broadcasting out of the country, your checklist expands further. Now you need to worry about what kind of equipment will cause problems with customs. For instance, some countries are so protective of their markets that they count the number of batteries you bring into the country. When you leave, if you don't have the exact same number of batteries, they will assume you sold them on the black market. You could be detained or fined. Make sure your engineer calls the consulate to find out which potential problems you may face.

A typical local remote will have more radio station staff available than an ordinary show. In addition to the show staff, the promotion director, a promotions coordinator, the engineer, the sales rep, and probably a representative of management will be on hand. An out-of-town remote will at least have an engineer and a promotions person. Despite the bigger staff, you are still your own biggest insurance policy at a remote. Be proactive. When in doubt, do it yourself. Not sure there will be a laptop there? Bring yours. Not sure there will be enough headphones? Bring them yourself. Not sure there will be essentials like paper, pens, water, sharpies, coffee, and clocks? Bring them yourself. We even recommend that you help the engineer loading and unloading the equipment. He will appreciate the help, and you will gain the peace of mind that comes from knowing everything you need is there.

LEARNING TO SPEAK REMOTE

There are two other questions you must answer before you prepare your remote technical checklist. We haven't taught you how to speak remote yet. Let's begin now, because you'll need to speak it in order to understand these last two questions.

▸ Are we doing the remote via ISDN? Marti? Satellite?
  Or Vector?
▸ Will the IFB be hooked up?

ISDN? Marti? Satellite? Vector? IFB? These five terms will allow you to speak "Remote" fluently. We should get that out of the way before we do anything else in this chapter.

ISDN, Marti, Satellite, or Vector?

Despite the technical terms, this question is really only asking: "How are we sending the remote broadcast back to the station?"

There are basically four different ways this can happen. An ISDN line is a digital phone line that transmits your show back to the studio. (It stands for Integrated Services Digital Network). The Vector is the same as an ISDN line, in that it basically transmits the show via phone line; however the Vector is analog (or non-digital). The Marti unit transmits your show directly to the transmitter tower. The Satellite transmits the show to a satellite in space, which then bounces it back to the studio.

It sounds intimidating, but you really don't need to understand how they work. You only need to recognize what method is being used to transmit the show and what challenges each of those methods will bring to your job on the day of the broadcast.

For instance, the ISDN line is not available everywhere, and it has to be ordered from the phone company well in advance. You and the engineer better be absolutely certain you can use this (especially true for remotes out of the country). Normally a remote using an ISDN line will also have a backup analog phone line just to make sure. If you are doing a live remote with a Marti Unit, you have to make sure that you are broadcasting from a location with a direct shot at your transmitter tower. If you've ever seen a TV crew doing a live shot in your town, they are using the same technology. The tip-off is the gigantic antenna sticking out of the roof of the station van. (Obviously, this can only be used for local remotes and isn't often used in cities with lots of big buildings blocking the path.) If you are doing a live remote via satellite, you are going to be experiencing a slight delay if you need to communicate on the air with someone back at the studio.

IFB

What in the world is that? The technical definition is interrupted fold-back. Don't worry about the technical term. The actual question you are asking is: "How are we communicating with the person running the controls in the studio?"

The layman's explanation is that IFB is used to communicate back to the station from a live remote through the microphone. Even during commercials and music, the host can talk to the studio through his microphone if the IFB is hooked up, and the studio can talk to the host in his headphones. That's why it's also commonly referred to as "talkback." The reason the producer needs to ask if the IFB is hooked up or not is that the producer will need to have a phone line dedicated exclusively for communicating back to the person running the controls at the station if IFB is not hooked up. It would behoove you to have a phone line with constant communication back to the studio anyway. It's a great contingency plan.

Working without IFB or a separate phone line is not an option. Once you lose communication with the board operator at the studio, you are flying blind. Trust us when we tell you that is a very unpleasant experience.

Once you have considered all of the questions we raise, you can make your own personal technical checklist. We can't do it for you. Each remote is different.

The Eric and Kathy Show on WTMX in Chicago was recently doing a morning show remote with John Mayer performing live. During the remote, they lost the IFB. Luckily, their producer John Swanson had a phone line backup, and the remote went off seamlessly, despite the potential for catastrophe.

CREATING A CHECKLIST FOR THE BOARD OPERATOR

Now that you have considered all of the technical issues you face, you have to think about the issues that the board operator will face. Put yourself in his place. He probably doesn't know exactly the way your show works. No question is too small to answer.

- Does he know when the news and traffic reports come?
- Does he know where outside elements come up on the board?
- Does he know where the broadcast comes up on the board?
- Does he know where you keep the intros/extros for regular features?
- Does he know how to put a phone call on the air?
- Does he know how to record something off the air?
- Does he know where you keep the tapes to tape the show?
- Does he have a key to your office if there is an emergency?

- Does he know about the special bumpers going in and out of spots?
- Does he know about the produced "show open?"
- Does he know about the special music you need for a specific segment?
- And most importantly . . . Does he know what to do if the remote goes off the air?

Depending on the experience of the board operator, there may be a few more or a few less questions you need to answer for him. Try to make your list as basic as possible. Give him your regular studio checklist (see chapter 9) and cross off the things he doesn't need to worry about, and then add the other things that he does need to worry about. During the show itself, use the commercial breaks to fill in the board operator about the upcoming segment.

Remember, if the board operator isn't prepared, it's the producer's fault—not the board operator's. Don't blame him. Blame yourself.

REMOTE SHOW CONTENT

Sometimes doing remotes can be a trap. You assume that there will be a plethora of material arising naturally out of the different location. That isn't always the case. Do research in advance. Prepare as much material as you possibly can.

This is especially true for out-of-town remotes. Over the years, we've heard some of the worst broadcasts by great hosts spending the week somewhere tropical. After two days, they are out of location material. Then what? It's natural to get in vacation mode and phone it in. Don't allow the host to fall into that trap. Make sure he has plenty of material.

Whether you are doing a local or out-of-town remote, you still need a show rundown sheet or prep sheet. You still want to balance the material so that you don't do too many of the same types of segments in a row. You want a show that contains all of the elements that your show usually contains. Even if you have more guests than you normally do, you still want to prep for each one. You may need help with the actual execution of these interviews (like finding the guests, getting them to the right place, keeping them happy before and after they go on the air, etc.), but you should handle them in the same way you normally do once they get on the air.

For out-of-town remote broadcasts make sure you also have an Internet hookup that allows you to check the Web sites of the hometown newspapers before each show. If that isn't possible, have the board operator fax the articles about the big stories happening back at home. When you are in touch with what is happening on the home front, you are more likely to do a good show for the people listening on their radios. After all, that's the vast majority of your audience—not the people watching your show in progress.

THE LIVE AUDIENCE

With a live audience you face the challenge of making the show interesting and entertaining to the people watching it, while making sure you keep in mind the bigger audience listening on the radio. It's very easy to get caught in the trap of playing exclusively to the audience. Remember, you aren't working in a visual medium. Sight gags may get laughs from the live audience, but unless you paint a picture with your words, the rest of the audience will be lost. On the other hand, a digital camera may help with this. Many shows now take pictures while the show is going on and post the pictures on the station Web site. If it's possible to set up a Web cam, that's one step better.

For out-of-town broadcasts, the show will most likely bring listeners along (usually they are prize winners). Often these listeners are an untapped source of material. Get to know each and every one of them. You'll be staying at the same hotel as them, and you'll see them all the time. Find out their quirks and their talents. Everybody can be entertaining for one segment if coached and guided correctly. By the end of the week (if you are doing a whole week of shows), you will have engaged the live audience by making them stars, and engaged the listening audience by giving them a parade of characters. But don't get carried away. It takes discipline to use the audience correctly.

Having discipline doesn't mean being serious. Don't lose your sense of fun, either. On the other end of the "playing to the live audience" spectrum, some hosts are militant about not altering their show at all in front of live audiences. That's not something we recommend either. A live audience is wasted if you don't keep them engaged. They can provide the show with extra texture. They can make a show sound bigger than it actually is. If you can somehow manage the correct balance, your remote may be a show that people talk about for years to come.

The John Landecker Show did a week of live broadcasts from the Dominican Republic. Every morning there were huge technical issues to overcome, but the shows were quite memorable. Rick Kaempfer and his wife renewed their vows live on the air (for their tenth anniversary). The ceremony was perfect for the radio. It was a surprise for Rick's wife, but every element of it was pre-approved by Rick and John. There were visual elements (the bride arrived on horseback) and audio elements (music, crowd reaction, and an audio play-by-play provided by John), plus it was all captured by the digital camera and instantaneously placed on the station's Web site. The live audience felt like they were involved in something special. The show ended with Rick and his wife, each holding one of their young sons, slow dancing to their wedding song. There wasn't a dry eye in the audience, and the listeners at home got to listen to the song, and see the pictures on the Web site—a truly multi-media experience.

YOU ARE NOT ALONE

The remote is a scary broadcast for a producer, but there are some advantages that you shouldn't ignore. For instance, you will probably have more people helping you than you've ever had before. The promotion department will undoubtedly have someone there. Use that person to help you get guests ready, keep listeners happy, coordinate the next segment, etc.

Also, despite the many technical issues we've put into your head, its wonderful doing a radio show with an actual engineer standing alongside you. Any technical thing that goes wrong won't fall into your lap, it will fall into his. You can help him, and we recommend that you do, but ultimately he will know how to fix just about any problem that occurs. If you have confidence in your engineer, you can concentrate on making the show as good as possible.

Who else will be at a remote broadcast? Salespeople, management, colleagues, clients, and listeners will all be willing to help. The crazier the show, the more people that are likely to show up and help out.

WTMX in Chicago did a special remote broadcast on Halloween. They were able to get Jon Bon Jovi and Richie Sambora to do an acoustical show during morning drive. They had about 200 listeners, clients, and guests come to a local haunted venue. The listeners provided some show material by dressing up and doing various things that won them tickets to the broadcast. When Bon Jovi and Sambora got on stage, the arena football team cheerleaders introduced them. (Ironically, Bon Jovi is now the owner of an arena football team.) Other highlights from that show included a keyboard accompanist introducing each segment, and an eight-foot alligator, and twelve-foot albino python on stage. It was a memorable show for the live audience, the listeners, the radio station personnel, and the entertainers. Bon Jovi called it the best radio show he's ever done.

MURPHY'S LAW

Remember the most important fact about remote broadcasts—they never, ever, go exactly as planned. The main question will always remain the same: What can go wrong? The only difference is that the answer is much longer. There are so many technical and logistical things that can go wrong, something ultimately will. It's nearly unavoidable.

That doesn't mean you shouldn't try. You can't anticipate everything, but if you are as prepared as possible, you will be able to think on your feet to avert a crisis. If you are unprepared, or you think everything will go perfectly, you may become overwhelmed by the instability of the situation. If that's the case, you'll be helpless when the inevitable occurs. Don't let that happen.

After you've done your first remote, you'll be battle tested. Make a list of the things that went right, things that went wrong, and things that could have gone better. Learn from your mistakes. When a remote goes well, there is nothing like it. It's nice to see you are pleasing the management, the sales department, and the clients. Plus, it's nice to get out of the studio once in awhile.

PART FOUR

GETTING YOUR FIRST JOB

The Radio Producer's Handbook is written as an educational
resource. But it doesn't come without a price to the
authors. We are revealing things in part 4 that we
shouldn't be. There's no telling what will happen
to us when this information becomes public.

This is the stuff of spy novels. Passwords will be given. Secrets
will be revealed. Before you finish part 4, you'll be able to
infiltrate the radio business. Please make sure your
papers are in order in case you get stopped
at a checkpoint.

12

LAYING DOWN AN EDUCATIONAL BASE

OVER THE PAST TWENTY YEARS WE'VE BEEN ASKED THE SAME QUESTION hundreds of times. Whether we are speaking to a group of high school students, college students, or just some friends and acquaintances at a cocktail party, they all want to know the same thing. Where do you go to school to become a producer?

The real answer is that no one goes to school to become a radio producer. You can't get a degree in producing radio shows. You can, however, acquire the right kind of education to better succeed as a producer. To put it in terms that college students will understand, it's like preparing for a Saturday night out. You have to lay down a base. That's why we call this chapter "Laying Down an Educational Base."

Technically, you don't have to attend college at all. Later in this chapter, we'll explain how people without a college education should proceed. But, we highly recommend attending some sort of institution of higher learning.

When you attend college you learn how to study, how to research, how to take notes, and how to do it all on a deadline. Any producer who develops these skills will be way ahead of the curve. When you attend college you learn how to live on very little money and how to ignore distractions. This will also help in your first few years as a producer.

College is a great training ground for life in general, and for life as a producer specifically. Of course, some majors are more helpful than others. We've tried to suggest some majors that would provide you with the kind of education you'd find most helpful in your producing career. You may decide to choose one, or you may decide not to choose a major at all. That's what a lot of students do today. They take courses in a variety of subjects and wait until they find one they really like before choosing a major. If you go to a school that offers any courses in the areas we suggest, it would behoove you to at least check out a class or two. You might find something you really like.

Peruse the information contained in the following sections, but please keep something in mind. After we break down each major we will reveal the secret weapon of the college-educated, producer candidate. It's one of the main reasons we're grateful we attended college, and it has nothing to do with picking a major at all.

After you decide on a major, we strongly recommend you go to the Web site *www.princetonreview.com*. You'll have to register on their Web site, but they don't charge a fee. This is the best place to find which schools offer particular majors. The search engine on their database will enable you to pinpoint the best school, the closest school, and the most reasonably priced school with your chosen major. It's a must if you are serious about finding the right school for you.

COMMUNICATIONS MAJORS

Depending on the university or college, the option of majoring in radio is probably not available. Some very prestigious universities like Columbia College in Chicago do offer this major but, for the most part, you'll have to choose something similar. We recommend that you do.

A communications school of a university may offer courses in journalism, broadcast journalism, advertising, and/or public relations. Getting a degree in any of these fields will give you an excellent base of information.

Journalism and Broadcast Journalism

Needless to say, journalism is helpful if you want to go into news producing. Despite what you see on the television talk shows, journalism is still a distinguished and noble profession. Journalism majors learn how to write, how to track down a story, how to research, and how to tell when something is a big story or not.

If you take broadcast journalism, you'll learn even more applicable producer skills. For one thing, you'll learn how to edit. (We'll spend an entire chapter later in this book explaining how to do that.) A broadcast journalism major will really be able to use that knowledge to his advantage when he tries to become a producer. It's the kind of knowledge you don't get in any other major, unless you discover our secret weapon (be patient, it's coming).

Advertising

Advertising is another good choice for a college major. (Rick Kaempfer got his degree in advertising.) If you only knew how much advertising controls radio, you'd understand the wisdom of pursuing this major. Coming into the job with a working knowledge of cost per point, gross impressions, cume ratings, quarter-hour ratings, time spent listening, and other advertising terms gives you a huge advantage over the producer candidates who have to learn everything from scratch. (For explanations of these and other radio terms, see appendix A.)

There are basically three areas of advertising: research, media, and creative. All three will give you knowledge that will be helpful in your radio career. In research you'll learn about the techniques used to obtain ratings and lifestyle data, and you'll learn how to conduct and interpret focus groups. In media you'll learn the industry terms we mentioned above and how to crunch the numbers that will one day decide your fate. In creative you'll learn valuable techniques that will translate well when you are asked to come up with ideas for a radio show. Plus, advertising offers one more thing that the other media majors don't offer. It sounds like a real "business-like" major to your parents. That's what tipped it in for Rick.

Public Relations

Majoring in public relations will also offer many of the same advantages as advertising. As a producer you will essentially be in charge of publicity for the program you're producing. A producer with knowledge of public relations will be a godsend. You will learn to write. You will learn how to manipulate the media. And you will be making friendships with the people who may eventually help you score the big guest.

There is one more major point in favor of pursuing a degree in public relations, but it might only be a selling point to our male readers. The world of public relations is something like 80 percent female. We don't know why, but it's absolutely true.

LIBERAL ARTS MAJORS

There is a school of thought that says only a person with a liberal arts education will become the kind of well-rounded person able to converse intelligently on any subject matter. While that is an oversimplification, a liberal arts major does get a tremendously broad education.

Therefore, we must concede there is some merit to this liberal arts argument. And there is an argument to be made that this sort of well-rounded education is perfect for a producer. As a producer, you'll have to possess something we call "tip of the iceberg" knowledge. Although you may have one or two areas of expertise, you'll need to know at least a little bit about every subject you can imagine. Among our top choices are political science, history, theater, speech communications, and literature. Possessing knowledge in each of these areas will be extremely helpful in your producing career.

Political Science/History

Every single radio show in the world is at the mercy of current events. Majoring in political science will give you the kind of knowledge necessary to make sense of the events within our country and overseas. One of the authors of this book took a heavy load of political science courses in college, including several about Eastern European governments. This was in the early eighties, when communism still dominated the region. Later in his producing career, the Berlin Wall came down and the Soviet Union was dismantled. Many Americans didn't understand the ramifications of the events, including the host of the show he was producing. He was able to explain it to the host, and through the host, the listeners.

A graduate with a degree in political science will be able to understand virtually every region in the world. In the complicated world we live in today, that kind of knowledge is like gold. History is another excellent choice. History won't teach you current events, but it will give you the kind of background that is necessary to understand current events.

Theater

Nearly every part of the theater department offers insights into your future career. A person who studies theater is forced to study the classics and will inevitably become well read. A well-read person makes a good producer. A person who studies acting will learn how to perform. Understanding what it takes to perform will help the producer when he deals with another performer, the radio host. Understanding the actor's mindset will also be invaluable while preparing your host for an interview with an actor.

Plus, getting to know the local theater scene will give you a leg up on landing guests. You'll know which theaters are likely to have actors well known enough to appear on your show. If you're lucky enough to get the opportunity to direct a play, you'll really get great experience. But there is one more reason to consider majoring in theater— it's fun (although much harder work than you might imagine).

Speech Communications

For some reason, this major is usually a part of the liberal arts school and not the communications school. Nevertheless, it's a useful major for future producers. In speech communications you will learn how to speak in front of people, you'll learn how to put together persuasive arguments, and you'll learn what it takes to become a great communicator. These are skills that obviously translate well into radio.

English/Literature

Some will argue that the true liberal arts education must possess a focus on literature and art. If you don't understand the place of art in society the argument goes, you are unable to appreciate the finer things in life. That's a bit heavy-handed for us, but we certainly see the merits of being well read and appreciating great art. Anything that gets your creative juices flowing is a positive prelude to a producing career.

BUSINESS MAJORS

There is one thing you must never forget about radio. It's a business just like any other business. Major corporations own most radio stations. They are publicly traded. The concerns of the investors are more important than the concerns of the employees. The pressure is constantly on to reach earnings projections, and those projections are often unrealistic and unattainable.

Every decision made by a radio station has those series of facts as a backdrop. If you can think like a corporate decision maker, you can better understand what they are looking for in a radio show. Therefore, we must suggest the following possibilities.

Marketing

The radio show is a product. It is marketed to a particular target audience in an effort to attract the most attractive demographics. The more attractive the demographics, the more money the radio station can charge for advertising. The more money that can be charged for the commercials on the radio show you produce, the more money you will make. Having a good head for business can never hurt a radio producer. Majoring in marketing may be just the ticket to thrive in the radio business today.

Business Administration

We know several producers who have gone back to school and gotten their MBAs. For producers eventually considering a career in management, having a degree in business administration is the first step. Also, some radio experts believe that an all-financial talk format will be one of the hot new formats. It already exists in many markets in America. Those shows need producers too. Why not you?

THE SECRET WEAPON OF THE COLLEGE-EDUCATED PRODUCER CANDIDATE

This discussion of education background is important because we are firm supporters of getting a college degree. However, when it comes right down to it, it really doesn't matter what degree you get as long you go to a school that has the secret weapon of the college-educated producer candidate. This weapon will give you a huge head start on people that don't go to college, and it has nothing at all to do with majors or curriculum.

Go to a school with a college radio station. That's it. That's the secret. Anyone who wants to be a radio producer and is attending a college that doesn't have a student-run station is going to the wrong school.

What schools have college radio stations? This is very difficult information to find. Luckily for you, we have done the legwork and found 415 schools that do have student-run stations (appendix B). We don't claim this is a comprehensive list, because with Internet radio stations, and dorm radio stations, and cable radio stations, we couldn't possibly find them all. But this is a good start. For your ease, we've divided them geographically by region. This list includes some of the finest universities in the country (Harvard and Yale, for instance) as well as local community colleges. The college that has a college radio in addition to your choice of major will be the perfect school for you. You will graduate as the producer candidate of a radio station's dreams.

WHAT CAN YOU LEARN AT A COLLEGE RADIO STATION?

A college radio station provides you with an empty canvas to learn all about radio. Working there, you will encounter every imaginable circumstance that you will experience at real radio stations.

On the positive side, you will get to learn production, editing, news, sports, promotions, marketing, and you'll likely even get a chance to get on the air. Once you start working at your college radio station, you'll understand why people want to get into this business. It can be rewarding, fun, entertaining, and you'll probably meet people that will remain your friends for the rest of your life.

On the negative side, you will also learn about the petty politics and ego battles you'll face in your radio career. Even this is a positive for a future producer. When you learn to navigate your way through the college radio station, you're actually training yourself to become a producer. Those same survival skills are essential.

There are eleven schools in the country that have commercial-licensed student-run radio stations. That is, they sell advertising time and the students are employees. The eleven schools are: The University of Illinois in Urbana-Champaign, Brown University, Dartmouth, Cornell, Princeton, Yale, University of Florida, University of Tennessee-Knoxville, Vincennes University, Harvard, and Howard University. This type of college radio station is the dream destination for someone seriously seeking a career in radio.

TAKING FULL ADVANTAGE OF YOUR COLLEGE RADIO EXPERIENCE

Getting a job at a college radio station may be as simple as asking. You probably won't be allowed to broadcast immediately, but there are so many departments of a radio station that might need your help. We recommend eventually finding your way into the production department if you want to be a producer some day. The skills you learn there (especially audio editing) will directly translate to your next radio job.

Our best advice is this: Sample every department. Learn as much as you possibly can. This is going to be some of the most fun you have in your life. You may even discover that you have what it takes to become a radio star.

The bottom line is that someone who works at a college radio station will graduate with four years of radio experience before they ever apply for a real radio job. Plus, they have a college degree. Do you think it would be possible to find a more attractive candidate for a first-time radio employee?

Rick Kaempfer worked at his college radio station (WPGU) at the University of Illinois from 1981–1985. He was on the air for three years, served a year as the program director, and worked in production and copywriting. That experience got him in the door at one of the biggest radio stations in Chicago shortly after he graduated school. His college radio experience also introduced him to people who remain his best friends to this day. Even now, twenty years later, they have a chat group on the Internet for WPGU alums. The group of people he met at WPGU has formed the basis of his networking contacts in the industry for the past two decades. Twenty years ago they worked at a college radio station, but today they run television newsrooms, anchor major-market morning newscasts, host highly rated major-market radio programs, and run entire radio stations.

WHAT ABOUT BROADCASTING SCHOOLS?

Nearly every city in America has one of these broadcasting schools now, and they do serve a purpose. We mentioned at the beginning of the chapter that you don't necessarily have to go to college to get a job as a radio producer. If you want to become a radio producer, and you can't afford college or you're at an age that makes going to college impossible, a broadcasting school is a legitimate option. They usually offer courses at night, and people who have contacts in the industry usually teach them. Broadcasting schools are a good place to go if you are thinking about changing careers. They can give you the training you need to learn the basics of radio broadcasting. Some excellent producers we know have taken this route.

The most important thing a broadcasting school can do is to help you receive an internship. This is a crucial step if you want to break into the business. In fact, it's so important that we're going to devote two complete chapters to acquiring an internship and taking advantage of it once you have it. With that in mind, we have some advice for broadcasting school students.

Over the years, we've both had interns from broadcasting schools and we've noticed a few trends. The younger students are usually more concerned about their grades at the broadcasting school than the internship they have acquired. There is nothing more meaningless than graduating first in your class from broadcasting school. On the other hand, if you treat the internship like a job, you may be able to go directly from broadcasting school to paid radio station employee. And isn't that what you wanted to do when you enrolled?

IS A COLLEGE EDUCATION AND COLLEGE RADIO EXPERIENCE ENOUGH?

In a few rare cases, it is. However, it's often necessary to take one more step. Unfortunately for the unconnected, radio is still a very incestuous industry. Once you are in the business, you can stay in it forever, but getting in is still a challenge.

If you have managed to lay down the educational base and gotten valuable experience at a college radio station, you have all of the skills necessary to become an excellent producer. In the next few chapters we'll show you what you need to do to convince the people hiring producers of that fact.

13

Getting Your Foot in the Door

OF COURSE, THIS BOOK IS A MEANINGLESS EXERCISE FOR A PRODUCER CANDIDATE if we don't tell you how to get that first job. If you've already been trying to get a paid producer or on-air position and you've been getting rejection after rejection, our sympathies are with you. Sometimes even having a college degree and radio experience isn't enough.

Rick Kaempfer was in the same boat. He had great college radio experience. He had a degree in the related field of advertising. He had an excellent audition tape. It wasn't enough. He couldn't get anyone to look at his resume or listen to his tape. That's when he heard about the radio catch-22. Stations like to promote from within, but it's impossible to get in.

Luckily for Rick, that was a myth. All he really needed was the radio password. The radio password is: "intern." When Rick discovered the password, he found his way in the door. That was eighteen years ago and he's been inside ever since.

We've touched on the internship issue in the previous chapter, but here is the real truth. If you want to break into radio, the internship is still the single most powerful tool at your disposal to help you to accomplish that goal. Yes, of course, we know this means working for free. That is undeniably true, but an internship is a highly prized position for one main reason. An intern isn't officially considered an employee, but he is "in."

When it's time to get a new paid employee, the really good interns nearly always get the first shot. That's the loophole in the famous radio catch-22. Next chapter we'll explain how you can become a really good intern, but first things first. Let's get you that internship.

GOING THROUGH THE PROPER CHANNELS

If you are a college student and your university offers an internship program in exchange for credit, by all means, do whatever it takes to get one through the proper channels. Universities have excellent connections with the broadcasting community, and most radio stations still prefer getting their interns this way. A simple visit to the person at your school who heads the internship program will send you on the correct path. If you don't know the correct person to ask, check with your dean.

When you begin to go through the proper channels, however, you may run into a few problems. Your school may have too many students trying for the same kind of internship, so they have to put you on a waiting list. Or, your school may not have the right kind of contacts to get you an internship at a radio station. Never fear. We call this a "paper wall." It's in your way, but all you have to do is punch through it. Opportunities abound on the other side of the paper wall if you know how to proceed.

MAKE YOUR OWN RULES

If your college internship contact tells you that you have to go on a waiting list or they don't have any contacts with radio stations, ask if you can secure an internship on your own. They will usually encourage the go-getter. There is no reason you can't get an internship on your own. Ask your school to give you the internship paperwork anyway.

If your school won't give you credit for a radio internship, tell them you are willing to do it for zero credit hours. With the paperwork from the school, it's still an official internship as far as the radio station is concerned. You just aren't getting credit for it. The school has nothing to lose by helping you.

If for some reason the school won't do anything to help you, you're still only hitting a paper wall. You should have no problem finding a radio station willing to take you on as unpaid intern. Some stations have specific rules governing who is eligible for an internship, but many of them don't. They would be very happy to get a college student as an intern because students make excellent interns (intelligence, flexible schedules, etc.).

What if you are out of school already, or you've never gone to school? Have you lost your best chance to use the radio password? No. In fact, some of the best interns we've ever had were older people looking to make a career change. Often these go-getters are the most desirable interns because they have been around long enough to develop a good work ethic, and they are extremely motivated to perform well. Because of radio station rules, they may not be considered interns, but they are doing the exact same work. For people like this, radio has managed to come up with another word that works just as well as intern: "volunteer."

GETTING IN: A QUICK HOW-TO GUIDE

Once you understand a few basic things about how radio stations work, getting an internship is not very difficult to do. You just have to be resourceful, persistent, and patient. We have a few hints that will make your search a successful one.

If you follow these six steps, you will get an internship. We guarantee it.

1. Make a list of the radio stations in your town
2. Make a list of the different radio shows on each station
3. Make a list of the department heads of each radio station
4. Write a letter to your top choices asking for an internship
5. Follow up with a phone call
6. If unsuccessful, move on the next radio station, show, or department and continue this process until all avenues are exhausted

Step 1: Make a List of the Radio Stations in Your Town

What stations are in your town? There are many different places to get this information. Local newspapers often list radio stations once a week or so, usually on Sundays. If you know when they do it, clip out the station list and work from that. If you don't know, move on to another possible source. I wouldn't bother looking in the yellow pages because many radio stations these days are too cheap to pay for an ad. You want to get a complete list.

We recommend checking out this Web site: *www.radio-locator.com.*

This site offers a free service that searches for radio stations based on formats and markets. Type in the name of the market (town) closest to you and you will get a list with every radio station in town. The list will have direct links to radio station Web sites. Check out each and every one of them. There may be stations in your town that you don't even know about.

Once you have the call letters, and you've checked out the Web sites, you can rank the stations based on your interests.

Helpful Hint: The cool stations are usually inundated with internship requests. Don't be a snob when you're trying to secure your first internship. If your favorite station says no, or doesn't return your call, keep moving down the list. You may learn more at a station that doesn't have interns as often as the cool stations, anyway. Don't worry too much about the format. The title of the chapter is "Get your Foot in the Door." Don't be too picky about whose door it is.

Step 2: Make a List of the Different Radio Shows on Each Station

In this case we're only referring to shows that may have producers. For instance, the morning show on virtually every station will need a producer (unless it's a nationally syndicated show based out of another market). You can also assume that every locally produced show on a talk station will need a producer (this includes news/talk, sports/talk, entertainment/talk, financial/talk, and whatever other kind of niche talk format is invented by the time this book comes out). Add to your list music shows with big-name personalities in any day-part, especially afternoon drive (usually 3–7 P.M. or 2–6 P.M.). After you've assembled this list, rank each show in order of interest. We'll help you out with this job a little later this chapter when we give you our list of the top four internships.

By now you must be assembling quite a list. Do you really think that you won't be able to get an internship with any of these stations or any of these programs? Fine, there are even more options available.

Step 3: Make a List of the Department Heads at Each of those Radio Stations

If you want to work as a producer, it's obviously most advantageous to work as an intern with the on-air side of the business. However, there is much more to the on-air side of radio than what you hear on the air. That's where Step 3 comes in.

In order to do Step 3, however, you're going to need to make a few calls and do a little legwork. You are trying to find the name of the marketing/promotion director, the production director, the program director, the news or sports director, the assistant program director/executive producer, and the producer of every show on your list from Step 2. Each of these people is involved in the on-air product, although you might not have heard of them.

Try going on the station Web site to see if it lists the names of the behind-the-scenes staff. Some stations do, and some stations don't. Fill in all the names you can. If your search hits a dead-end and you can't find the information via the Internet, it's time to call the radio station directly.

Start making your calls first thing in the morning, say 9:05 A.M. You don't need to speak to anyone other than the receptionist, and since you have done a little legwork before you called her, you'll be amazed at how receptive and friendly she will be as she gives you every name you need to finish up your list. After you finish with one station, move down the list of stations and call the next one, until you have all the names you need.

Again, when your list is complete, start ranking them in order of interest. Do you understand what each department does well enough to rank them? If so, feel free to skip ahead to Step 4. If not, we have some information that may help you rank them.

Helpful Hint: Don't call a receptionist of a radio station between the hours of 11 A.M. and 2 P.M. The receptionist may be at lunch, and the fill-in person may not know all the information you're seeking. The reason we suggest that three-hour window is because the lunchtime of the receptionist varies from station to station.

THE PROMOTION DEPARTMENT

The promotion or marketing department runs every radio station event. They are the people you see driving the station vehicles. They are the ones that send out the prizes. They coordinate the contests. They hang up the signs at remote broadcasts. They schmooze the clients at the radio station events. They pamper the personalities and the guests. And they need a lot of help. An internship in the promotion department can be very helpful. You will inevitably work closely with the hosts and the producers. Once you get to know them, you will have the inside track into the on-air side of the business.

Rick Kaempfer got his foot in the door at a major market radio station by writing an unsolicited letter to the promotion director of WLUP-FM; Sandy Stahl. In his letter, he mentioned that he had worked in college radio and loved the work, but had been unable to secure a job in his chosen profession. Sandy sent a letter back, asking him to come in for an informational interview. She pointed out that his letter had touched her, and that she was willing to do whatever she could to help.

Rick couldn't officially receive an internship because he was out of school, so she told him that he could come to promotions and work as a volunteer. While working for Sandy, he met the members of the on-air staff, and when an opening came up on one of the shows—*The Steve Dahl and Garry Meier Show*, Sandy personally recommended Rick for the position.

THE PRODUCTION DEPARTMENT

This is a busy, overworked, and undermanned department usually consisting of only one or two people. Every single commercial you hear has to either be recorded or transferred to a format that can be played on the radio by the production department. It's a time-consuming job, and production directors are rarely asked if they need intern help. The answer would nearly always be yes. Being an intern in the production department will provide an extra bonus. You will more than likely learn to work the equipment. This will make you more valuable when it's time to segue to the on-air side of the business.

THE PROGRAMMING DEPARTMENT

In this case, when we refer to the programming "department," we are actually referring to the programming management: the program director and the assistant program director (sometimes referred to as executive producer). A music station would also probably have a music director. Each of these people could use an intern, and each of them rarely gets asked. Being an intern for these people brings with it the added bonus of getting to know the most important people at the radio station. When it's time to get a producer, the program director will certainly remember the intern who did a great job for him.

Jim McInerney got his internship while he was a student at Columbia College. He impressed the music director of WLUP by knowing to file Lynyrd Skynyrd under *L* and Jethro Tull under *J*. That internship led to another internship with the producer of *The Kevin Matthews Show*. During his year-long internship with that show, he began to get paying shifts as a board operator. His first full-time paid position was as the board operator for the Howard Stern show in Chicago. From there he segued to a technical producer position for *The Jonathon Brandmeier Showgram*, and has since been the producer of the Buzz and Wendy show on WCKG. His producing career eventually came full circle when he was named the producer of the show he began his career with as an intern; *The Kevin Matthews Show*.

▶ ▶ ▶

Tom Sochowski went to broadcasting school after working as a carpenter. Through the broadcasting school, he landed an internship with the program director of WJMK-FM, Kevin Robinson. When there was an opening for an assistant producer on the morning show, Kevin immediately thought of his intern, Tom. Tom later converted that opportunity into a producer position at WCKG-FM, before moving on once again to ESPN radio. Kevin never forgot his former intern, however. When he was named program director of WZFS, and there was an opening for an executive producer, he called Tom once again and offered him the position.

THE NEWS/SPORTS DEPARTMENT

Some radio stations don't even have news or sports departments anymore. If they do, however, an internship in those departments would be extremely valuable. The news department is probably very small (unless it's a news/talk station). Because of the intimate size of the department, news or sports interns may get to do some real radio work. They may get to cover stories, get tape from newsmakers, or track down details on stories. As an added bonus, you'll be working alongside the on-air staff. Get to know them, and you may make an easy transition into a potential producer opening.

Jim Wiser was a student at Columbia College when he landed an internship at the Loop in Chicago. He was a sports intern, and the sports director Bruce Wolf put him to work getting tape in locker rooms after the games. He also helped out the news director Buzz Kilman. As it turns out, both of these department heads were sidekicks on the morning show. When a producer position became available, Jim got the job—producer of *The Jonathon Brandmeier Showgram*. He has since produced for Fox Television and currently produces the #1 rated morning show in Chicago—the Spike O'Dell show on WGN.

Step 4: Write a Letter to Your Top Choices Asking for an Internship

Now that you have the correct names, and you've ranked them in order of importance to you, be absolutely certain you have the correct spelling. Some people are very finicky about the spelling of their names. In fact, people with really difficult spellings are a little more understanding about misspellings than people with totally normal names. We knew a Garry who wrote "No Such Person, Return to Sender" on any envelope addressed to Gary. Another person with the last name of Greene got very upset when she received something addressed to Green. It sounds simple, but don't underestimate the importance of the correct spelling.

Now it's time to write a letter requesting an internship. Your letter shouldn't be lengthy. You only need a few sentences describing yourself and your desire to work in radio one day. Ask if the station offers an internship and say that you are available to work whenever the staff needs you. If you have any special qualifications or background, by all means mention that too (this is where your educational base comes in). The most important thing to remember is that your letter must look professional.

We know it's "old school" to write an old-fashioned letter via snail mail, but that's just the point. You will cut through the clutter by doing it this way. E-mails are too easy to delete. Faxes are too easy to toss in the garbage can by the fax machine. Letters are the best way to get the attention of the decision makers.

Step 5: Follow Up with a Phone Call

After you've sent the letter to the right person with the correctly spelled name, then what? You've done everything right so far, but you aren't there yet. You can't just sit around waiting for a return phone call. This is crucial. The busiest people have the least amount of time to call you. However, they also tend to need interns the most. If you call them to follow up on a professional letter, you will almost certainly get a return phone call.

If you don't get a return call, try calling a few days later. A few days after that give him one last strike. If no one returns your calls after three tries, cross him off, and move down the list.

Step 6: Continue this Process until All Avenues Are Exhausted

This is why you have the lists. If you still can't get an internship after trying the top ten or twenty names on your list, you'll have ten or twenty more names to choose from. When you are unsuccessful with one station, show, or department, all you need to do is move on to the next one. Feel free to send out a few letters at a time and check back with each of them simultaneously. What's the worst that can happen? Two job offers at once?

We've been suggesting this technique to producer candidates for years. No one has ever tried every single name on his list without being able to secure an internship. No one. Ever. That's our guarantee.

THE TOP FOUR INTERNSHIPS

We've already discussed some of the great internship possibilities and given you some real examples of people who took advantage of them. However, there are really four internships that we think are better than the rest.

The Producer

If you want to be a producer, doesn't it make sense to have an internship with a producer? The best way to learn how a radio show really works is to be there and watch it happen alongside the person producing the show. You probably think these are the most difficult internships to secure, right?

Wrong. A popular morning or afternoon show often operates completely autonomously from the rest of the station. A producer is never offered an intern, and if he were to receive a phone call or letter asking if he needed one, he would jump at the chance. Contact the producer directly. He will happily get you in the door to help and he will be motivated to teach you immediately—just to get some of the workload off his desk.

In the unlikely event the producer doesn't think he needs help, suggest a few ways you can help. Tell him you can do air checks for clients (an air check is a portion of a previous show put on tape or disc for clients of the radio station). Tell him you can help him keep a show log (a written record of everything that happens during a show). That should get his attention. If you sound like a producer, he'll want to have you help. We should know.

The New Gun in Town

If you keep an eye on the comings and goings of radio personalities in your town, you'll know if somebody new arrives. If your town has a radio/TV columnist, you should be reading her column religiously. That way, when the new radio personality's arrival is announced, your call will be among the first he receives. Nobody needs more help than the new gun. Offer to help indoctrinate him into your hometown. He will never forget the first person who helped him navigate his way through his new town. You never know. He may end up being a big star.

The Big Radio Star

This is not going to be the most exciting or the most rewarding internship, but it's going to look the best on your resume. It's also not that difficult to obtain.

Even if he already has legitimate interns through a school, he will want more help, especially with the pesky personal things a producer is too busy to do. You can call it a "gofer" position if you like, but you can also call it "producer in training." A host develops trust in people who cater to his personal needs (not *those* personal needs). If you knew the number of producers who started out this way, you wouldn't turn your nose up at it.

If he is a very big star, you can try to get an internship through his office. This is usually highly effective. The person running the office doesn't worry as much about following the rules and filling out the proper paperwork for college students. She just wants free labor— she doesn't care about the status of the student.

If the host is approachable and does a lot of public appearances and remote broadcasts, you may even be able to ask him face to face. Spontaneously "meeting" a host won't scare him off—especially if you tell him he needs someone to handle important things like getting sandwiches or answering fan mail. What else can you say that would get the attention of a radio host? You could offer to start up a fan club. Who wouldn't want to have a fan club? You could offer to start up a Web site to honor him. If you have those skills, let him know. This is a great way to get in the door.

John Swanson really wanted to work on *The Jonathon Brandmeier Showgram*. It was his favorite radio program. Everyone listened to Johnny B in Chicago. After hearing that the show was looking for an intern,

Swanson contacted Brandmeier's office directly and got on the interview list. Brandmeier gave him the internship because he liked the fire in his eyes. Because of his initiative, Swanson took a giant step to the front of the line. When the technical producer position became available not too long after he started his internship, Swanson was the natural choice. From there he has gone on to produce for Steve Cochran and Kevin Matthews, and is now the Executive Producer of *The Eric and Kathy Show* on WTMX—one of the top-rated shows in the city.

The Unknown Personality

What if a show doesn't have a producer because it isn't big enough? Perfect. If you intern for a show like that you'll become a de-facto producer. You won't believe how much you can learn in that situation. What if the station has a big-time morning show, but the afternoon host is a lesser-known personality who does less of a show? Call him! Many producers have gotten their first job by creating one that didn't exist. When you make yourself indispensable to someone, they will do whatever it takes to get you on the payroll. That's why the internship with the unknown personality is one of the top four internships you can have.

IT DOESN'T END THERE

Unfortunately, securing the internship isn't the end of the line. We've told you how to get that internship, but there are some very important things you must do once you get the internship. We've had hundreds of interns over the past twenty years and only a handful of them really had what it takes. And as you'll discover in the next chapter, it doesn't take much. If you have common sense, a halfway decent work ethic, and you handle yourself professionally, you got it. Remember, the internship is a job. Treat it like one.

14

TAKING ADVANTAGE OF YOUR OPPORTUNITY

THIS CHAPTER WILL GIVE YOU ALL THE INFORMATION YOU NEED TO TURN your internship into a paying job. But before we identify the ways to take advantage of your intern opportunity, we're going to help you keep your internship. You wouldn't think an intern could get fired. After all, he is working for free.

In fact, we've seen it happen so many times, we simply have to address the issue. Interns are given an amazing opportunity. They get their foot in the door, they meet people who can help them get full-time paying jobs in their chosen field, and they get free access to state-of-the-art facilities. They also get unfiltered access to some of the giants in the industry. Yet, they usually complain, say something inappropriate, do something inappropriate, or act like they own the place. It happens so often that an intern who doesn't do any of those things, even if he is not that talented, has the inside track at landing a paying job.

It's not only the intern's fault. Management at radio stations will rarely sit down with an intern and level with him about the proper etiquette in dealing with a radio star. Most of the errors and mistakes occur because of this. But, it's hard to blame the management. A program director or promotion director may not even realize what kind of behavior the star expects of the intern, because she has a much different relationship with the star. If she does know, she still won't tell the intern. She isn't being cruel or trying to set up the intern for failure, she is probably just embarrassed to spell it out. When we spell it out, you'll see what we mean.

Producers are very aware of the unwritten rules, because the host will inevitably tell us directly. When we get together in social gatherings with other producers, the conversation usually turns to the little quirks and rules each host decrees his producer must enforce. We can't really tell anyone else about them, so they come out in torrents of relief when we see each other. What we've discovered after hearing the same types of stories over and over again from producers in every part of the country is that radio stars all basically want the same thing. They want to be respected, and they want to be treated like a star.

THE UNWRITTEN INTERN COMMANDMENTS: DEALING WITH THE HOST

We both began our major-market radio careers as interns. We didn't know these rules when we walked through the door. However, we didn't break them. There are a couple of reasons for this. First of all, it's really not that hard to follow these rules. There is nothing unseemly about them. Second, we naturally treated the hosts with respect because we naturally respected them, and we treated the hosts as stars because we really thought of them stars. If you do the same thing, you won't have any problems.

The unwritten intern commandments are as follows:

▸ Thou shalt not "sass" a host, even jokingly, even if the host is jokingly "sassing" you.
▸ Thou shalt not speak to a celebrity guest unless spoken to.
▸ Thou shalt never repeat a story you hear the host or celebrity tell "off the air."
▸ Thou shalt not make any references at any times to the host's physical imperfections.
▸ Thou shalt not bug the host to pay for something just because he "makes a lot of money."
▸ Thou shalt never bug the host to put you on the air.
▸ Thou shalt not bring your friends in to see the show.
▸ Thou shalt not eat the free food before the host gets a crack at it.

We've seen some very smart interns fall victim to the unwritten intern commandments. We've seen interns accidentally break them even after having been warned repeatedly. It happens most often after an intern begins to feel a little comfortable. He starts joking with the host, who initially appears to be enjoying it. The intern forgets that he is not the host's peer, and begins joking with him like he would joke with his buddies. The host doesn't take kindly to being ribbed by someone who hasn't "paid his dues." That's usually when the hammer falls.

Here is a tip to make sure you never accidentally break the unwritten intern commandments. Imagine the host as Tony Soprano or any Joe Pesci character. You are allowed to get comfortable with him, but anything you say or do can still get you whacked without warning if you don't show the proper respect. It really isn't that hard to do.

THE UNWRITTEN INTERN COMMANDMENTS: DEALING WITH EVERYONE ELSE

Now that we've gotten the etiquette of treating a star out of the way, let's address the etiquette in dealing with everyone else at the radio station. If you have any common sense at all you'll naturally follow these rules. Nevertheless, it doesn't hurt to spell them out. These are rules any intern in any business should follow. Let's not forget that radio is a business too. And if you don't treat this internship the same way you would treat a job, no one will ever consider hiring you for a real job.

The other unwritten intern commandments are as follows . . .

- Thou shalt not complain about gofer tasks.
- Thou shalt not complain about (lack of) pay.
- Thou shalt not show up late or completely blow off work.
- Thou shalt not complain about the hours.
- Thou shalt not ignore basic human hygiene.
- Thou shalt not work on a personal project without permission.

Every paid employee at the radio station will expect you to live by those rules. You have to always keep in mind why you are doing this. Yes, you'd rather be doing something more rewarding than getting someone coffee at 4:30 A.M. for zero dollars, but think of the big picture. You can't complain about the pay, or the hours, or the gofer tasks because you knew what you were getting into when you took the internship.

If you didn't, let us spell it out. You are at the bottom of the totem poll. The bottom. There's no one underneath you. Just do what you're asked to do and do it with a smile. Even if you get frustrated occasionally, you're going to have a great time more often than not. Radio is fun. It's not like people will try to torture you or take advantage of you. Most people at most radio stations are very nice. And if you go in with a positive attitude, those people will notice. When the time comes, they will do whatever they can to help you get a paying job.

THE OPPORTUNITY TO LEARN

You'll thank us some day for teaching you what not to do, but what about the other side of the coin? If you are lying low, obeying the unwritten intern commandments, and doing your assigned duties with a good attitude, are you doing enough? No.

You have to learn as much as you possibly can while you're there. You speed up that process significantly by asking questions. Ask people to tell you about themselves. When you ask someone how they got into radio, you may get new insights into the industry. Ask people how they got a job at the station. You may get even more insight. Don't feel strange asking questions like that. People love talking about themselves.

If you have questions you want to ask a particularly busy person (like a production director or a promotion director), set up an appointment to meet with him. If you show the proper combination of respect and inquisitiveness, people will go the extra mile for you.

You can also learn a great deal by volunteering for absolutely everything. When you help out at live broadcasts, you will learn the inner workings of that particular show. When you help out at station events you will establish yourself as someone who can be counted on (and you'll do it in a very visible way). Volunteering for a remote or a station event will also give you insight into the people who listen to the radio station. That information will be extremely helpful when you become a producer.

What else can you volunteer to do? There is only one way to find out. Ask. Ask everyone. If you can find something to help organize, you will establish a reputation as an organizer. When it's time to hire a producer, they will remember that you did a great job organizing the music library or the old commercials. An organized person makes a great producer. If you can find a way to track down something they need for a show or event, do it. You will establish a reputation for being resourceful, another great producer trait.

This internship is your big chance. You want to do everything you possibly can to impress everyone you possibly can. Those are the kind of people that make it in this business, and anyone at a radio station can spot that type of intern from a mile away. Anyone you meet might be the person that recommends you for a paying job someday. Try to always keep that in mind.

GETTING THAT FIRST PRODUCER JOB

Making the leap from intern to producer is largely a matter of luck and timing. By impressing everyone at the radio station, you've improved your luck already. Now it's just a matter of timing, and recognizing that the time is at hand.

There are basically three different ways of becoming a producer. Any other way is really just a variation of these three. You can't really choose in advance which technique you will use. You have to let the circumstances dictate your methods.

Filling a Job Opening at the Radio Station

When a producer isn't working out or chooses to leave, you will be one of the first people to find out about it. That's the whole point of being "in." Even though legalities require that job openings be posted, if you are the first one in the door to pitch for the job, you have the advantage over everyone else.

Think about how attractive hiring you would be to any radio station. First of all, you're cheap. You've been working for free and haven't complained once. Instead of dealing with someone who will get into a lengthy negotiation, they know you will be excited to make money. Plus, they will feel good about rewarding you. Anytime you can reward a great intern it feels good. In addition to that, you are already one of them. You won't need to be taught "how we do things around here."

But the biggest advantage you have is that you know the host and he knows you. You should have already found out his quirks, what he likes or doesn't like about a producer, and what had gone right or wrong with your predecessor. This sort of knowledge can only be learned from within. That's why stations like to promote from within. That's why you've gone through this internship. It has all led up to this moment.

Mike Davis was an intern who got around. He was lucky enough to be interning at a station with many different shows, and he helped out on all of them, making himself a very visible intern. He also learned something from each of the producers with whom he worked. When the station decided to add one more host to the lineup to do an overnight show, Mike was the first one knocking on the program director's door. Because he had worked so hard, and helped out the station in so many ways, the station decided to give him a break. He was named the producer of the show.

Create the Position of Producer for a Show that Doesn't Have One

There are really two ways this can happen. We mentioned one of them in the last chapter when we listed the top four internships. This is the internship with the unknown or lesser-known host. Sometimes the radio station executives bring in someone they think has potential to grow into a big-time host. They don't want to invest in a full show staff at first, while they feel him out and give him room to grow. If you have been his intern and shown that you can take his show to the next level by producing it, the station executives may have noticed this too. They may have intended on naming a producer eventually, and your presence simply speeded up the process.

There is another way, too. It's possible to get a show with only one producer to expand to two producers. Sometimes a show is growing by leaps and bounds and becomes so big that the host and producer can't possibly manage to keep up. If you are the intern on that show, and you've taken a number of duties off the plate of the producer, you've probably made the show run more smoothly. If your timing is right and you've joined a show right on the cusp, creating that new position (technical producer or associate producer) may be a real possibility. Now you may have the host and the producer going to bat for you. And that never hurts.

Vince Argento got his internship by calling up the radio host's office and offering to be his "cabin boy." He was a college student at the time, near the beginning of his college career. He remained the intern/cabin boy for more than a year. When he finally told the host it was time for him to leave the show, he had become indispensable. The host found a way to get him on the payroll by naming him the technical producer. That was more than ten years ago, and Vince has been producing radio shows in Chicago ever since.

Take the Knowledge You've Acquired to Another Station

If you have been working at a radio station for an extended period of time for no pay, it's probably time to move on. Timing just hasn't been on your side. When you announce that you're planning on leaving, two different things can happen. The management or the host may offer you a paid job because they don't want to lose you. (See story about Vince Argento.)

However, that probably won't happen. In these corporate times, the money usually isn't there to create a new position. If you've been there for a long time, the program director knows she has taken advantage of your free labor and will feel guilty. If she doesn't offer you a job, thank her for the experience and immediately ask if she will be a reference. In this case, she almost certainly will agree. In fact, have a recommendation letter already printed up, ready to sign. She'll do it. While you're at it, ask her if she knows of any opportunities in the market, or if she knows anyone you can call. She just may give you the phone number that scores your first job.

As long as you walk out with a signed recommendation letter, you have the tools to pitch yourself for a paid producer position at another station. With that letter and the experience you've acquired during the duration of your internship, you will be a very desirable candidate for a paid producer job.

And that's the worst-case scenario after your internship. Not bad for a worst-case scenario.

15

FINAL PREPARATIONS

IF YOU'VE FOLLOWED OUR ADVICE, BY NOW YOU'VE SECURED YOUR FIRST job offer to become a producer. Now you're ready to hop in, roll up your sleeves, and get to work, right? Not exactly.

There are several details that need to be worked out before you accept that first producing job. We'll help walk you through that first negotiation. Then, once you accept the job, there is still some information you must know before you begin. In this chapter we'll tackle the non-technical information. We'll devote part 5 of this book to the rudimentary technical knowledge necessary to produce a radio show.

MONEY ISSUES AND BENEFITS

It's vitally important that all monetary issues are hammered out before you begin your job. If your job has emerged as a natural evolution within a radio station, the management might not sit down and go over all of the options available to you before you receive your first paycheck. Try not to let this happen. You aren't trying to rock the boat by asking for a clarification, you are merely making sure everything is spelled out. This is perfectly acceptable, even necessary.

Salary

Let's face it, this is your first producer position, and you won't have a great deal of negotiating power. If you don't want the job at their price, there are many others in line that do. It's simple supply and demand. You'll more than likely have to accept the salary that they offer. Typically, depending on the size of the market and the popularity of the show, a first-time producer will earn anywhere from $15,000 to $25,000 a year, with two weeks of paid vacation. There are exceptions where you can earn more or get more vacation time, but don't obsess about the salary for this first position. We'll tell you ways to get that figure up as you work your way through the business. It's not unheard of for experienced producers to make six figures. Now is not the time to let money get in the way. (See chapter 19 for tips on negotiating for your second job.)

Corporate Benefits

There are ways to get paid in addition to your salary. If you are working for a major corporation (and in this day and age, that is very likely), there may be a host of benefits available to you. It goes without saying that you should be receiving insurance (unless you have a part-time position). If you've priced private insurance lately, that is not a small expense. You may also be eligible to participate in the company's 401K plan. The only way to know for sure is to ask. In rare cases, profit sharing may be another benefit available to you. There are corporate rules and regulations regarding who is eligible for these benefits. Ask for an employee manual to see what other benefits may be available to you.

Producer Expenses

To offset the low salary, there are a number of things a producer can ask for that won't show up on the corporate ledger as salary. For instance, a producer will need a computer to perform his duties, and often those duties will need to be performed outside the office. You can ask the station to provide you with your own laptop. If you don't ask, you won't get it. A producer may also be asked to phone in live reports during the show occasionally. Ask for a cell phone. You may also have to subscribe to several newspapers and/or magazines that don't offer free press subscriptions. Ask the station to pay for these. It comes out of a different part of the budget. No one will be offended if you ask for any of these perks. If you don't get them, you may have pointed out things that can be used while negotiating a raise next year.

Other Ways to Increase Your Income

A producer may become a very visible part of a radio program. The host refers to him often, he comes on the air to explain various issues or incidents, or he may become a regular character on the show. When this happens, a producer can get more money by making personal appearances. Make sure to tell the sales department that you are available to make these appearances. Salespeople have trouble convincing hosts to show up at sales events. If a producer offers to go, it gives the sales department someone else to sell to clients. Most importantly, the client pays for this, not the radio station. Payment for a personal appearance can range from gift certificates to several hundred dollars.

A producer can also volunteer to help out on the weekends. Most stations need board operators (we'll explain what this in the next chapter) to run syndicated weekend programming. Depending on the market size, a board operator can earn anywhere from $8 an hour to $20 an hour to perform this skill, and you'll help out the radio station at the same time.

KNOWING THE HISTORY OF THE HOST

You must know as much as you can about the host before your first day on the job. That information is probably available on the station Web site. If not, it's available somewhere on the Internet. If he is a popular radio host, surely someone has written about him or interviewed him in the past.

What kind of material is he famous for? What specific bits or features has he done in the past? You must know the answers to these questions if you want to produce his show to the best of your ability. If you honestly exhaust all research avenues and you still can't find out what he has done, you can add these questions to the list of questions for the program director.

Never ask the host. He will probably be offended if you ask him directly. Regardless of where he is on the broadcasting ladder, he will assume that everyone knows where he has been. It's the performer's ego. Never ask him anything that implies you don't know who he is. It will start you off on the wrong foot with the one person that absolutely must trust you. There are exceptions to this rule, of course. We've worked with some unassuming performers who wouldn't care. On the other hand, we've also seen too many others that would care. Our best advice is to avoid asking the host directly. There is no downside to this strategy.

In this book we've told you many stories about the ego of the host. In all fairness, we should acknowledge that a host must have a big ego. It's impossible to perform without one. A host is asked to speak for four or five hours at a time. In order to convince yourself that you have that many interesting things to say, you must develop an ego. In order to risk embarrassment on a daily basis, you must develop an ego. In order to protect yourself from the inevitable criticism you'll receive, you must develop an ego. A host with an ego is not a bad thing. It's a necessary thing.

QUESTIONS YOU SHOULD ASK THE PROGRAM DIRECTOR

Each producer position is slightly different, and therefore we can't answer every question you may have. The program director of your radio station should be able to, however. Don't be afraid to ask her questions before your first day on the job. You will show her that you are thinking ahead, that you want to be as prepared as possible, and that you are responsible.

The question-and-answer session with the program director prior to your first day of work will set the tone for your relationship. Some of the questions we suggest are big picture questions while others involve the small day-to-day things. No question is too big and no question is too small. The only question we recommend avoiding regards the ratings.

Ratings are a very touchy subject around a radio station (unless the ratings are spectacular). The future of any program director hangs in the balance every month when the Arbitrends come out. (Arbitrends are the monthly reports from Arbitron.) Everyone at the radio station asks the program director about the ratings, and everyone thinks the program director should be getting better ratings. She is under constant scrutiny. You don't need to add to it, especially on your first day of the job.

If you really want to know the ratings, you can ask someone else at the station (the sales department, for instance, is intimately knowledgeable on the subject). If you don't feel comfortable doing that, you can find the information via the Internet, a radio trade publication, or a newspaper report. Ratings are reported to the public quarterly.

While it's true that your future may hinge upon ratings success, it's also true that a producer can do very little to alter the ratings. On your first day of the job, it should be the furthest thing from your mind. Your job is to make the radio show you're producing the best possible show it can be. Leave it to the program director to worry about the ratings. When you become a trusted part of the staff, the information will be readily shared with you.

For now, focus on the following questions.

Can I Have a Written Job Description?

Producer is a nebulous job title with ever-expanding duties. Get a written job description if at all possible. We don't know any producers who have actually received one, but we also don't know any producers who had the foresight to ask for one before they started on the job. The program director may actually sit down and write something out for you, but more likely than not she will just offer you vague descriptions. Write them down as she says them.

At the very least you will know what she expects of you. Also, when it's time to ask for a raise, you will have a list of expected duties to compare to your new list of actual duties. Often the program director or the host doesn't even realize how many things a producer does for a show. It never hurts to have a written record of what you were hired to do. Believe us, it will come in handy some day.

That advice comes to you from the benefit of hindsight. Hindsight is 20/20 only because you have your head in your hind the first time you do something. We learned the hard way so that you wouldn't have to.

Who Is Our Target Audience?

Program directors have a very definite idea about what kind of person represents their audience, for example, a forty-one-year-old mother, with two children and a dog, who drives carpool every morning. Sound ridiculously specific? This is the way the program director thinks. She crunches numbers all day long and has very specific data about the station's audience. Asking her a question like this shows her you think like she does. She may not say it, but having someone that thinks like a program director working on a particular show is her idea of a wonderful dream.

What Material Is Inappropriate for the Station?

In this case, we're referring to the internal station policies regarding show content. Where is the line? What are you not allowed to talk about? Most stations have their own rules in addition to the FCC guidelines. This could involve specific words you can't say, specific topics you can't cover, specific clients you can't criticize, or specific views you cannot espouse. (Religious or political stations have the most rules in this regard.)

Is There a Station Camera?

In this digital age, most radio stations have a digital camera on the premises to take pictures they can post on the station Web site. As a producer of a show that may be doing a remote or a charity event with listeners, or may have a celebrity guest in the studio, you should have access to that camera. It's a good way of promoting your show, and it shows management that you are thinking about everything.

In addition to the big-picture questions we mention in this chapter, there are also three minor questions that are important:

1. Where does the station keep the office supplies? You'll need to keep your own stash if you do a morning or nighttime show because everything is locked up.
2. Where does the station post the emergency numbers? Again, this is particularly important on a morning or nighttime show when no one else is actually on the premises.
3. How does the station handle contests? Each station handles this differently, and it will probably be the producer's responsibility.

GAINING THE PROGRAM DIRECTOR'S TRUST

While your relationship with the program director may not seem as important as your relationship with the host, don't lose sight of the fact that the program director is the host's boss. You must gain her trust while also gaining the trust of the host. That can be a delicate balancing act because the program director and the host often end up at odds. If you ask the questions we suggested you ask you can subtly gain the program director's trust from the very beginning. Gaining the trust of the host is a little more difficult. That only comes with time.

PART FIVE

TECHNICAL WORKSHOP

Part 5 is for the technical novice. If you have any doubts at all about the technical demands of the job, we've tried to explain each and every one of them here. We'll help you overcome your fear of control boards and editing software by stripping them down piece by piece and showing you their naked simplicity. We'll also help you establish a technical plan to implement your first day on the job, complete with a guide to maintaining an audio library.

You won't find all of these things anywhere except our neat and tidy little technical workshop. Come on in. But please, don't put any drinks on the consoles.

16

BECOMING CHAIRMAN OF THE BOARD

DON'T GET EXCITED BY THE TITLE OF THIS CHAPTER. WE'RE NOT PUTTING you on the fast track to the top of the radio business quite yet. But we are going to teach you how to run the board. Not the board of directors, the control board.

The board or console is the nerve center of the radio station. It's important you get to know its functions as soon as possible. It will become your friend. You will be spending more time with your new friend than you can ever imagine.

Yes, we realize that the board is a frightening console full of faders, switches, lights, and blinking thingies. Don't worry. It's only natural to be a little intimidated at first. We were. While it is true that boards are capable of doing many different things, they are essentially just the sum of their parts. Get to know the parts and you won't be frightened by the sum. When we break it down for you piece by piece you'll see it's not that bad. If you can hook up your receiver at home or you can figure out how to stop your VCR from flashing 12:00, you can figure out each piece of a board.

After we eliminate the fear of the board, we'll show you the rest of the radio studio. Item by item you'll realize that you can handle each one of them. By the time this chapter is over, you'll be ready to enter a radio studio without breaking into a cold sweat.

BREAKING DOWN THE BOARD: THE MODULE

The easiest way to think of a board is as one piece of equipment that controls every other piece of equipment in the studio (it's like the receiver for the entire studio). A board is a collection of modules. Each module of the board represents one of the pieces of equipment in the studio. Instead of looking at all of the modules on the board at once, look at the diagram of a single module (Diagram 16A). Not so bad, is it? When

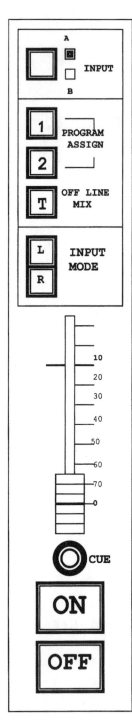

Diagram 16A

you know that each module represents something else in the studio, you have begun to decode the board. We'll give you a hand decoding the rest, but your biggest helper will be your logical mind. The modules are set up on the board in a very logical fashion.

The first module on the board is usually microphone one. The second is microphone two, etc. Remember one crucial thing: engineers put the board together. Engineers think logically. If you think logically too, you shouldn't have any problems at all.

But what are modules? We're going to break one down piece by piece. Every board is slightly different, but they will all have modules that are pretty similar to the module in Diagram 16A. A module basically consists of switches, faders, inputs, and outputs. Understand each of these elements and you understand the module.

Input

Look at the top section of Diagram 16A. There is a button labeled "Input." If it's not engaged (pressed in), it is considered Input A. If it is engaged, it's Input B. The input is really no different than the inputs in your stereo receiver. Something is plugged "in" to them. The input is the reason this module is being used at all. When you know what is connected to the input of a module, you know what the module controls.

To make it even easier to grasp this concept, most studios also label the inputs of each module. A quick glance at the input label will explain the entire module to you. ("Oh, module one is for microphone one!") If for some reason your station doesn't have any labels on the module inputs, you need to ask someone right away. Don't worry. That's not a stupid question. You can't be expected to know by osmosis what is connected to the module.

Keep in mind that the important stuff is usually connected to Input A. If the studio has been designed correctly, they won't have anything on Input B that needs to be used a lot. Or at the very least, it won't need to be used at the same time as whatever is connected to Input A.

Outputs

Look at the second section of Diagram 16A. There are two buttons labeled "program assign" and another button is labeled "off-line mix." These are the output buttons. Again, this is just like the output of your stereo receiver. While your stereo receiver sends the output to your speakers, there are three different places the output from a module is being sent: Program Assign One, Program Assign Two, and Off-Line Mix.

If the button is pressed in, the output is sent there. Program Assign One goes out of the board. Program Assign Two can go anywhere. For instance, it is often used for ISDN lines on remote broadcasts. (See chapter 11 for more about remote broadcasts.) Off-Line Mix goes to the telephone mix, hence the T on the button.

In the air studio, you want the output to go through the board. That's what will make it go on the air. Therefore, Program Assign One is the most important button. There are exceptions to this rule, and you'll learn them as your knowledge becomes more advanced, but the board beginner should always make sure the Program Assign One button is engaged (pressed in). You also want the output to go to the telephones, so people on the telephones can hear whatever is coming through the board. Therefore, the Off-Line Mix button should always be engaged too. (The Off-Line Mix also allows you to record telephone calls off the air.) Again, there are exceptions; but you'll also learn them as you go along in your career.

The output buttons may be labeled slightly differently on different boards. Some boards simply have a PGM button (which stands for program) and a UTL button (which stands for utility). The program button is the same thing as the Program Assign One button we write about in our example. The utility button is the same thing as the Off-Line Mix button from our example.

Input Mode

Look at the third section of Diagram 16A. There are two buttons, labeled L and R. As you might expect, these refer to left and right channels of a stereo broadcast. Neither button should be pressed in if you want the module to be in stereo. The great majority of the time, this is what you want. If neither button is engaged on every module, the whole board is in stereo.

For the purposes of this chapter, you shouldn't concern yourself about these buttons other than making sure they aren't engaged. There are times when you'll want to engage either the L or the R button, but these instances are rare. You'll learn those situations as they arise. (Just so you know what those buttons mean, if both buttons are engaged, this module is broadcasting in mono. If only the L button is engaged, the left side of the stereo broadcast is being broadcast in both the left and the right channels. If only the R button is engaged, the right side of the stereo broadcast is being broadcast in both channels.)

The Fader

The vertical list of numbers below the input mode portion of Diagram 16A refers to the volume levels. The knob at the bottom of those numbers is the fader (also known as a pot). It slides up and down. We could get wordy, but the fader can be explained in one sentence: It is the volume control of the module. If you set the fader to the reference line in our diagram (10 dB) you should have the perfect volume (or VU level) for this particular board.

Your board may have turning knobs (pots) instead of faders on the modules, but it's the same general concept. Look for the reference line, turn the knob to that level, and watch the VU meters to make sure it is properly calibrated to go to zero, which is the perfect setting on the VU meter. (VU, by the way, stands for volume unit, and the VU meter is usually located on the upright portion of the board.) Because the fader may not be perfectly calibrated to go to zero on the VU meter, just watch the VU meter when you adjust the levels. That's the important reading. It should be at or near zero. The fader is the device that lets you adjust that.

Fader knobs come in different colors for different types of modules. For instance, the virtual cart machine faders may be white, the microphone faders may be red, the CD players may be yellow, etc. The color-coding may be different on your board, but you'll see the different colors and that's the reason why.

Cue

The cue button on a module (see near the bottom of Diagram 16A) is used to listen to something on that module without putting it on the air. When the cue button is engaged, the speakers in the studio are disabled, and whatever is playing on that module will play on the cue speaker instead. Cue is really just a low-powered amplifier and speaker. The cue feature is used all the time, but here is a word of warning: When you want to adjust the levels (volume) of cue, the fader on that module will not do a thing. Instead, you should look for a "cue volume" knob. It will be near the volume knob for the entire board. Again, don't worry—explanation on the way.

On/Off Buttons

We don't really need to explain this one, do we? Needless to say, when you press "on" anything coming from that module will be "on" the air. When you press "off" it will be "off."

QUICK-CHECK MODULE TROUBLESHOOTING GUIDE

We can't really come up with everything that can go wrong on a module, but a few things come up often enough that we offer the following troubleshooting guide.

- If you press the "on" button and nothing happens, check to make sure that the input button is engaged correctly (it might need to be changed to A or B).
- If you press the "on" button and nothing happens, check to make sure "Program Assign One" or "PGM" is engaged.
- If you press the "on" button and nothing happens, and the above remedies still don't fix it, it's not the module; the main volume of the board may be turned down, or whatever you are playing may be damaged or blank. (Or something is really wrong.)
- If you press the "on" button and whatever you are playing sounds odd, you may be in mono. Check to make sure that the Input Mode buttons are not engaged.
- If your board seems to shut down for no reason, check to make sure that "cue" is not pushed in on any module.

BREAKING DOWN THE BOARD: INPUT SOURCES

Now that you know that each module represents a piece of equipment in the studio, what sort of equipment are we talking about? A typical radio studio will have a computer with virtual carts to play commercials, music, and audio clips or sound bites. It will also have another computer that is used to record and edit phone calls. In addition to those essential ingredients, a studio will probably have CD players, DAT and mini-disc recorders, a skimmer cassette recorder, a television, telephone lines, and a reel-to-reel system. Not to mention the biggest ingredient of all: the microphone.

Microphones

The number of microphones in the studio depends on the radio station and the studio. A typical production studio may only have one or two microphones. Many air studios, on the other hand, have as many as six or seven. Unless your station has an extremely unusual set up, each microphone will have its own module.

Microphone modules also have an extra knob called "Pan Control." This knob serves the same function as the input mode of the other modules. It's just a little fancier because it not only can choose stereo, left, or right, but it can choose degrees of left and right. Our advice: don't mess with the pan control.

All you need to know is which microphone is connected to which module. After you get the hang of that, don't think of anything except for "on" and "off."

Picture 16B

Computer: Audio Vault or RCS (Radio Computing Services)

Computers run nearly every radio station studio in America. If yours isn't, you've got a real dinosaur on your hands. Odds are it won't be long before you join everybody else.

The nerve center of the computer-operated radio studio is the audio vault or the RCS (or some other system that serves the same purpose). This computer system plays nearly everything you hear on the radio. All of the commercials, most of the music, and all of the audio clips (also known as sound bites and actualities) come from this system. It's very impressive and high tech, but it's really designed to mimic the radio station of the past.

Each element in the audio vault is nothing more than an audio computer file. However, the software makes each file look like the "carts" (an 8-track tape cartridge) that radio stations used to play. We call these virtual carts. They are labeled like carts used to be (title and length of song or commercial or whatever), and each virtual cart is assigned a different module on the board. Depending on the system, there are anywhere between four and eight different virtual cart machines.

Once a file has been dragged and loaded (like moving a computer file from one folder to another), it is ready to play through the board. Now all you have to do is press the "on" and "off" button on the module that corresponds to each virtual cart machine. We'll get into a much more thorough discussion of the audio vault (or related system) in chapter 18.

Computer: Phone Recorder and Editor

Another module is dedicated to the phone recorder/editor. There are so many different types of phone recorders and editors on the market that it would be impossible for us to mention every single kind. In chapter 17, we'll tell you more about how to record and edit a phone call but, for the purposes of this chapter, suffice it to say that every air studio has some sort of a computer that allows for digital editing of phone calls. Once a phone call is edited and highlighted on the screen, it also can be started on the board by simply pressing the "on" or "off" switch of the corresponding module.

Telephone Lines

Unlike the virtual cart machines of the computer, different telephone lines generally don't get their own modules. All of the request lines usually come over the same module. This is probably because some radio stations have as many as ten to twenty request lines coming into the studio. Can you imagine how big the control board would be if each line had its own module? The phone itself will probably have conferencing features so that more than one line can go on at the same time, but they will all come over the same module. There might be a separate module set aside for a special hotline, but that's about it.

OTHER EQUIPMENT THAT MAY HAVE DESIGNATED MODULES

If you work at a music station, CD players are definitely assigned their own modules. Even though many stations now play songs from the audio vault (or related system), computers are known to crash occasionally. If your station doesn't have backup CD players and the system crashes, you are up the river without a paddle. Hence, CD players.

As a producer of a personality/talk show, you won't be able to function without CD players. You'll use them for music beds (instrumental background music) and bumpers (instrumental music going in and out of commercials) all the time. By playing music beds and bumpers from CD instead of re-recording them into the vault, you will free up the limited number of virtual cart machines for other things. Most vault systems only have four to eight virtual cart machines.

Some stations also have a television hooked up through the board. This is fabulous if you are working at a radio station affiliated with a TV network and you are allowed to play television audio on the air. All you have to do is press "on" and the audio will come from that module. Other stations have mini-disc players hooked up to the board. Still others have old turntables or reel-to-reel tape players. These two items are slowly fading from the radio studio landscape. But if they are still there, you can be sure that they have their own module.

ISDN lines (digital phone lines) may have their own module (especially if one member of the show, like the traffic reporter, broadcasts remotely daily). Other modules may be set aside for remote broadcasts (chapter 11) or other studios at the radio station. Each board is different. If you have any questions about any of the modules on the board, ask someone who knows—the engineer.

Skimmer Cassette Recorder

We're sure there are some studios that have abandoned the skimmer cassette recorder, but we haven't seen it yet. It is probably just a matter of time before someone invents the skimmer CD, but for now this antiquated technology is still used.

What is a skimmer? This is a cassette deck that records only the spoken portions of the show. The microphone on/off switch activates it. A host doesn't want to be bothered listening to the songs and the commercials when he listens back to a tape of the show. He needs to hear the part he can control, the things he and the other members of the show said over the microphones. The program director also likes the skimmer cassette. She uses it to critique the host.

While the skimmer cassette is an important tool, it almost never has a module set aside for it on the board. Don't try to play it back from the skimmer cassette player. Listen to it elsewhere.

BREAKING DOWN THE BOARD: OTHER KNOBS, FADERS, AND SWITCHES

Of course we can't cover every single thing on a board because there are so many different possibilities. However, we must mention a few of them because they are so crucial. For instance, the entire board is controlled by one single volume control. You need to know where that is. It's usually all the way to the right or left of the board. In that same area you'll find the cue volume control and the headphone volume control. Most radio stations have separate headphone volume controls at each microphone position, but the person running the board has his headphone volume control right on the board.

MORE BOARD

Don't think that just reading this chapter will give you all the information you need to run a board. We're firm believers that you have to get into a real studio and get some hands-on practice. If you are in the midst of an internship, it's the perfect time to do it. Someone will be glad to show you how the board works. You just have to ask. Learning the board may lead to your first paying job. Former interns are often recruited to work as board operators.

If you are hired as a producer and you haven't yet been given the opportunity to run the board, you better pick it up quickly. Ask someone (we suggest the production director or the engineer) to give you a quick tutorial. This is important. Actually seeing your station's board being operated in front of you will answer any remaining questions you may have. Remember that each board is slightly different, so there is no shame in asking for a quick tutorial. With the background we provide in this chapter and your personal hands-on tutorial, you should have no problems at all.

DIGITAL BOARDS

The boards (or consoles) we describe in this chapter are all analog boards. Virtually every radio station in America still uses an analog board. However, that will be changing over the next few years. Companies like SAS, Klotz, and Harris (to name a few) are on the vanguard of digital consoles. These consoles still have modules, but no audio goes through the board. It's all done by fiber optics. It's very high tech, but the bottom line is this: the digital board will still be the sum of its parts. It will still serve the same function as the analog boards we describe in this chapter.

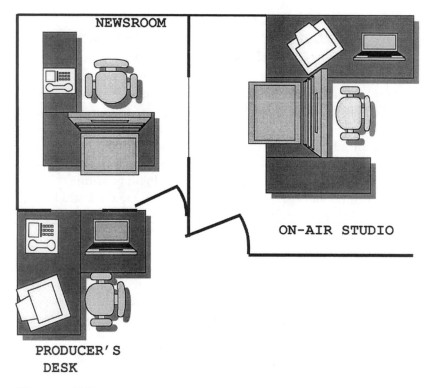

NEWSROOM

ON-AIR STUDIO

PRODUCER'S DESK

Diagram 16C

AIR STUDIO SET UP

Take a look back at Picture 16B (page 170). That's the studio of WTMX Radio in Chicago. See where the producer sits? No? Hmmm.

At most radio stations, the producer sits in a separate booth so that he can screen phone calls. In Diagram 16C we've shown you the bird's eye view of what this studio looks like, including the producer booth/area.

Hopefully our sample diagram will put a picture in your mind when we start discussing the show in progress. Can you see why it's essential to be as prepared as possible for each show? Depending on the studio setup at a radio station, the producer may or may not even be able to make eye contact with the host. (For instance, in Diagram 16C, he cannot.) Thankfully, there are two technical features of the studio that allow the producer and host to communicate: the intercom and the phone screener.

The Intercom

Most radio stations have intercom technology. The producer must merely press the intercom button in his producer booth and he will be able to talk into the host's headphones without going on the air. In most cases, the host will have the option of putting the producer on the air by potting the intercom up on the board. If you aren't sure whether or not the intercom module is potted up, be very careful about what you say.

To be honest, the intercom shouldn't be used too extensively while the host is talking on the air. It may distract him. We only use it in cases of emergency or clarification.

The Phone Screener

Another method of producer-host communication during the show is the phone screener. The phone screener is a monitor that has spaces corresponding to each of the phone lines. The producer has the keyboard and a computer monitor in the producer's booth, while the host has a corresponding computer monitor in the air studio on which he can see whatever the producer types. Most phone screeners have spaces for the name of the caller, the town he is calling from, and what he is calling about. They also have spaces for the producer to write notes to the host during the show. This provides an effective means of communication. (We discussed this extensively in chapter 5 and chapter 10.) However, most in-show communication between producer and host still takes place during commercial breaks the old-fashioned way, face-to-face.

KNOWING THE STUDIO

While you will need to know the air studio like the back of your hand, most of your time will be spent in another studio: the production studio.

What will you be doing in the production studio? Editing. Lots of editing. This is the technical skill that most often frightens fledgling producers. It won't frighten you after you read the next chapter.

17

DIGITAL EDITING

EDITING IS ONE OF THE BASIC SKILLS A PRODUCER IS EXPECTED TO MASTER. The amount of editing a producer must do depends on the format (for instance, at some talk stations this is done by an engineer or production director), the size of the show and station staff (some shows have technical producers who handle all technical duties), the availability of studios, and several other factors, but every producer will at least need to know how to do this. Luckily for you, this job is much easier today than it was only a few years ago.

Editing used to be a nightmare. Before the dawn of digital editing, we had to splice reel-to-reel tape together. The following paragraph describes a simple edit.

We listened for moments of silence on the tape, toggling the tape back and forth over the tape head with the speakers at full blast until we got it in the perfect place of absolute silence, used a white grease pencil to mark the exact spot, and then found the other place to edit and repeated the process. After we had our two spots marked exactly, we sliced each piece with a razor and spliced the tape back together with a tiny sliver of splicing tape. Then we listened back to it. If it wasn't perfect, we were on the floor, looking for that piece of tape we just cut off, swearing at the stars above.

To get a looped musical cart, we had to. . . .We're sorry, we can't even go there. It's much too painful of a memory.

The dawn of digital editing saved us and will save you from this horrible experience. Now it's all done on a computer screen. If you have any computer experience at all, you've been cutting and pasting since you clicked on your first computer. That is essentially what editing is all about. In this chapter we'll tell you the very basics of editing, tell you a little bit about the industry standard for editing, and give you the resources you'll need to improve. Any person that masters digital editing is very marketable. You want to be that person.

BASIC DIGITAL EDITING PRINCIPLES

There are hundreds of editing software packages in radio, but all of them work on the same basic premise. You download or record audio into the computer editing system, it comes up on the screen as a sound wave, you edit it by cutting and pasting it to your specifications, you mix it, you save it, and then you transfer it to another system that will play the edited product on the air. Sound complicated? It's not at all.

As we did with the board, it's probably easiest if we break it down step-by-step.

Downloading/Recording Audio into the Computer

Before you begin recording, you need to set up a session on the editing software. If it's your first time, you'll want to have someone do this for you (the production director is always a good choice). This will create your own folder of files on the editing system. Now you're ready to record your first file.

The original audio source (VCR tape, mini-disc, CD, etc.) needs to be potted up on the control board. Play it once to set the levels of the VU meters on the editing software. You'll see the levels moving. Just make sure that they aren't too low or too high. (Don't worry, it's easy to figure out if they are too low or too high—the VU meters will peak in the red if they are too high and they'll barely move if they are too low). Once they are set at the right level, simply press record and play the original source of the audio through the board. This is really no different than starting the record feature of a VCR tape, a cassette tape, or any other kind of audio recording you have ever done. It's quite simple, really. (In chapter 18 we'll tell you about getting that original source of audio.)

You can tell if it's recording because it will look different than it looked when you set the levels. The way it shows that is, although recording differs from editing software to editing software, it's always very obvious (it's highlighted in red, or it's flashing, or something equally obvious). After you finish recording, listen back to make sure it sounds right and watch the levels on the VU meters. If you are satisfied with the way it sounds and looks, you are ready for the next step.

Editing on the Computer Screen

Once the audio file is on the computer editing system, it will appear in sound wave form. (See Diagram 17A.) Editing on the computer has two huge advantages over the archaic tape editing we mentioned at the beginning of this chapter. For one thing, you can now see and hear the quiet spaces (as opposed to only hearing it). This is a huge

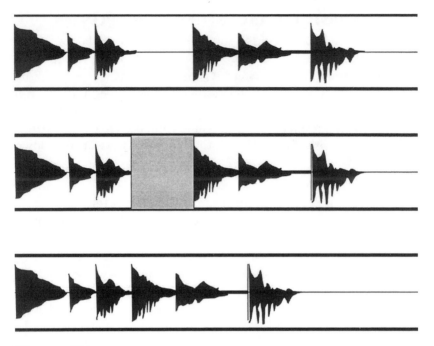

Diagram 17A

advantage when it comes time to cut. For another thing, you can undo anything you accidentally cut out because it's still in the computer. That's worth its weight in gold.

Look closely at Diagram 17A. This is a typical sound wave as it appears on the Pro Tools editing software. In the first sound wave, see the space where the levels go to zero? That is the silent space. You have to edit from that space if you want your final product to sound seamless. For the purposes of this demonstration, let's assume we are trying to get rid of that silence because the person speaking has an unnatural pause in his delivery. The sentence on the sound wave sounds like this: "I went . . . to the store."

You want to make the sentence sound a little smoother. Simply go just past the last sound right before the silence, and make a marker by clicking there on your mouse. (This is where your cutting and pasting computer experience will pay off.) After you mark it, drag to the spot just before the sound resumes and release. That will highlight the section you want to edit out (as you would in a document file on a computer). The second part of Diagram 17A shows what this would look like. When your desired edit is highlighted, press delete. Gone. That's it. The space will be gone, and the two separated sections will automatically move together as it looks in the bottom sound wave of Diagram 17A. The sentence will no longer have a pause. It will sound like this: "I went to the store."

It's as simple as that. Listen to the results. It probably sounds seamless. If it doesn't, you may have cut too closely to one of the words, or taken out a breath of the person speaking. Don't like it? No problem. Press undo just as you would on your home computer. It's back to its original form, ready for you to try again.

> Two helpful hints when editing audio: 1. Try to edit just after a breath, so it sounds like the person speaking is taking a breath to say the new line you are pasting. 2. When you are editing music, you need to look for a drum beat. These will stick out like sore thumbs on the sound wave. If you edit from drumbeat to drumbeat, it will sound seamless.

Mixing

If you only recorded the file on two tracks (for stereo), you won't really need to mix it at all. Mixing only comes into play if you have also recorded a separate track for music, or you've added other elements. You'll need to have someone show you how to do this. It will depend on the editing software.

Transferring the File

Once a file has been saved, you highlight it on the screen, and pot up (turn up the fader) the editing computer on the board for playback. Because you will be recording it into another computer system, you're simply going back to step number one. The only difference is you won't be recording into editing software, you will be recording into a vault (or related system).

Check the levels on the VU meter, press record on the vault, press play, name and save the file, and voila! You've done it. In chapter 18 we'll get into more details of handling the vault system. There are a few tips we can give you to make sure that everything is organized properly.

PRO TOOLS

Although there are hundreds of editing software packages, there is one that has become the production studio standard: Pro Tools. The company DigiDesign, a subsidiary of AVID, makes Pro Tools, a well-known video editing program. There are other programs in widespread use like

Adobe Audition (formerly known as Cool Edit Pro), but Pro Tools is the top of the heap. While Pro Tools is the industry standard for production studios, it isn't really used in air studios. It's more of an editing software package for production professionals. The editing software in air studios is mainly used for editing recorded phone calls. This is where you will run into the many different brands of editing systems. (VOX PRO, Sound Forge, etc.)

The good news is that all of them use the same general principles we outlined in this chapter. You open files, record, find the dead spots, mark them, highlight them, and cut and paste. Then you name the file, save the file, and play it back on the air.

It's simple, especially if you are computer savvy. You'll be able to pick up editing in no time at all.

ONE MORE COMPUTER SYSTEM

There is still one more computer system you need to master: the vault. This is where you will be storing all of the audio you acquire during your producing stint at this particular radio station. While this is the easiest computer system to master, it's also essential that you go into your first day on the job with a plan for maintaining your audio library. We'll give you some valuable tips in chapter 18.

18

CREATING AN AUDIO LIBRARY

ONE OF A PRODUCER'S PRIMARY RESPONSIBILITIES IS CREATING AND maintaining an audio library. For the purposes of a producer, the audio library includes everything that is used to create the sound of the show (like sound effects, news clips, movie clips, etc.) plus the archives of best of shows, but doesn't include music or commercials. But where does this audio library come from?

There are several different ways to accumulate audio. Different radio stations in different-sized markets have different technical capabilities, and you'll have to adjust to the equipment of your radio station. To get television audio, you can use a high-tech TiVo system installed at the radio station, or you can use a TiVo system installed at home. You can use a VCR installed at the radio station, or you can use a VCR installed at home. Plus, there is always the Internet. We'll explore each of these possibilities in this chapter.

Once you have begun to accumulate audio, you'll need to put it into the vault (or some other related computer-based system like RCS). That's a subject we will explore in depth. Because the vault will hold every single piece of audio you ever bring to the radio station, you'll need to have a very organized system in place from your first day on the job. Two years from now you may need to use that same clip, and you'll need to find it in a few seconds. If you aren't organized, this becomes an impossible task.

And audio comes in many forms. You will be recording every single show. Where do you keep all of that audio? Only the best segments will need to be saved in the vault. What's the best way to organize the stuff you save? Where do you keep the raw show tapes you don't save in the vault? This chapter will answer these questions, as well as help you organize your ever-growing CD collection. You'll have to be able to find whatever you need in a matter of seconds. If you aren't organized, it won't happen.

In the introduction of this book we told you that the word producer was actually an acronym (*p.r.o.d.u.c.e.r*). If you remember, the *o* in the acronym stands for Organizer. That's one letter you don't want to ignore. In this chapter we'll concentrate on organizing your audio. That's one of the biggest battles you'll face, and you'll need to be on top of this your very first day on the job.

AUDIO ACCUMULATION HARDWARE

In the upcoming chapters we'll give you all sorts of examples of things you'll need to record, but there are really only two sources of this audio: television and the Internet.

Some radio stations haven't equipped their studios to deal with the demands of a producer. They are more concerned with producing commercials (for clients who don't have advertising agencies), having working microphones, and being able to deliver their music and/or news product. That is understandable. As a producer, you have two choices. You can ask the station to adjust the studio to your needs, or you can adjust yourself to the studio's needs. Your answer to that question depends on your radio station. We'll tell you how to do it either way, just in case.

Adjusting the Studio

The best way of getting audio from television is by doing it directly at the radio station. All you need is cable television and TiVo. If the DVD (TiVo now can record directly onto DVD) is hooked up through the production studio board (given its own module), you have the best possible setup: digital audio that you can transfer directly into the digital editor.

Unfortunately, most stations will not have this setup if you don't ask for it. If you explain that TiVo will give you digital audio and point out that it will sound much better on the air, they may go for it. If not, having a VCR will have to suffice. Most stations will at least have a VCR in the production studio. If not, they can probably be convinced to add one.

Simply set the VCR or TiVo before you leave for the day (again, later in the book we'll give you examples of what you should record). If you want to save yourself time, you should also watch the program at home. Make notes about which clips you're going to need. Mark the time they occur. That way, when you come in the next morning to get the audio from the DVD or VCR tape, you'll be able to find it quickly.

Once you have found the clip, pot up the fader on the VCR or DVD module, play the tape through the board, and record it into the editing software (we describe this process thoroughly in chapter 17). You'll probably want to shorten or edit the clip slightly and make sure that the beginning and ending sound perfect. Once you do that, you're ready to load (record) it into the vault. We'll get into more detail about the vault a little later in this chapter.

Adjusting to the Studio

If your station is unwilling to add a VCR, DVD, or TiVo to your station's production studio, you are going to have to create a recording system at home. This has a few advantages and many disadvantages, but you do what you have to do to accomplish your daily duties.

If you can afford it, we highly recommend that you get TiVo. TiVo will record every TV program you need. It will also record it digitally, ensuring the best possible sound quality. If your station doesn't have a DVD player, you'll still want to record TiVo onto some other digital source. Otherwise, it kind of defeats the purpose of having TiVo. A mini-disc player is affordable, and most radio studios are equipped to handle mini-discs.

Now you need to treat your stereo receiver like the board at the radio station. If you hook up your television and the mini-disc player to your home stereo receiver, you can record directly from the TiVo to the mini-disc. Press the "TV" button on your receiver (or "DVD" if your TiVo is hooked up there), and make sure the sound is coming through the receiver. Cue it up to the exact spot, press "record and play" on the mini-disc, and then "play" on the TiVo. It's as simple as that. If you are able to pull this off, it is the best-possible home-studio setup.

However, if your station doesn't have mini-discs, or you can't afford TiVo, you may have to settle for sound quality that isn't quite top of the line. This is the way we did it for years. All you need is a VCR, a cassette recorder, and a stereo receiver. Believe it or not, there are some advantages to doing it this way. As you watch a program that is recording, you can hit the record button again on most VCRs. Instead of re-recording the same show, this will record an index/marker on that spot. When you want to retrieve a particular audio clip, simply hit the minus (−) index button and it will rewind exactly to the place you want, saving lots of time. Now all you have to do is cue up the video-tape to the exact spot, press "record and play" on the cassette tape, and "play" the videotape.

If you are bringing in a mini-disc or a cassette to the radio station the next day, you will still need to load this clip into the editing software to make sure you edit it for airplay. The sound quality of a mini-disc will be excellent because you are going from digital to digital. However, if you are bringing in a cassette, you are bringing in sound that is at least three generations removed from the original sound (video to cassette to editing software). The listeners will hear a slight hiss. Your host will hear it too. Using this technique should be a last resort.

If at all possible, try working toward one of the better sound quality techniques we mentioned earlier in this chapter. It may take some time for you to convince the station to hook up TiVo at the station, and it may take time for you to save up the money to put together the right setup at home, but VCRs and cassettes aren't going to be around very much longer anyway. In the long run, you really have no choice.

After all, it is radio. Sound quality should matter.

DOWNLOADING AUDIO FROM THE INTERNET

Downloading audio from the Internet is something you can do in virtually every radio studio. Your production studio will undoubtedly be hooked up to the Internet. When you find a Web site that has audio clips (for instance movie clips are available at *www.moviewaves.com* or *www.moviesounds.com*), you simply need to download these files directly into the production studio computer (or the air studio if you are on the air at the time). Once the clip is in your computer, you can transfer it to the editing software and edit it right there. After you edit it to the length you're seeking, you can load (record) it into the vault.

The same process occurs when you get clips from news feeds. The wire service at your station probably receives a daily supply of actualities (audio clips of newsmakers) automatically downloaded directly into the news computer. If your station has a computer network, you can very easily transfer these actualities directly into the editing software.

Remember that downloaded audio files are really just computer files. If you know how to get a computer file from one computer to another in a computer network, you know how to transfer an audio computer file.

RECORDING THE SHOW EVERYDAY

Before we get into the nitty-gritty of the vault, we should mention another kind of audio: your show. As we mentioned a little earlier in this chapter, you simply need to make sure you record every single show. The big question is: what do you record it on, and how do you save it?

We like to record each show on several sources. Again, you are looking for the best possible sound quality. Mini-discs now have a five-hour capability (plus they are tiny and easily stored). If you keep track of when the important moments occurred on a particular show, transferring them from mini-disc is a great choice.

Some stations choose different digital ways to record their shows. They may burn a CD for every hour of the show. This is a little more of a pain because you have to replace the CD every hour and if it's not re-recordable, you will quickly accumulate an unwieldy pile of CDs. Some stations use DAT. If possible, find a way to tape the show digitally using one of the techniques we described above.

However, some stations still use analog. They may record their programs on BETA tape because they like the sound quality and length, or they tape them on a VCR because a videotape can go for hours. Some stations simply rely on cassette (see the section on Skimmer cassettes in chapter 16). These analog methods are better than nothing. The bottom line is you have to record the show.

Regardless of the form your recording of the show takes, you want to save the best portions in the vault. Choose the portions of your show that you think you might want to play back at a later date. For instance, high-lights from celebrity or newsmaker interviews should be saved in case that celebrity or newsmaker is in the news again. You'll be able to access it in seconds. Also, classic moments of the host screwing up or a listener saying something hilarious or profound should be kept in the vault in a form that is ready for airplay. Just as you prepare the audio from televi-sion, movies, the Internet, and the news feeds, you'll want to record first the "best of" highlights into the editing software. You'll edit it to the length you seek, and then you'll be ready to load it into the vault.

As for the actual raw-show tape (or CD, or videotape, or mini-disc, etc.), you need to have a system in mind to keep these organized as well. Keep a log of what happens on the show, and keep that log with the tape of the show. That way if you ever need to retrieve something that didn't seem valuable at the time, you can find it quickly. We suggest keeping all of your shows just in case. Keep them organized chronologically. It's the only way.

RECORDING INTO THE AUDIO VAULT

Now that you know what you are loading into the vault (or RCS or related system), it's time to tell you how to load (record) something into the vault. It's amazingly simple. Pot up the editing computer on the board. Press "record" on the vault computer. Play the edited clip from the editing computer (through the board), and press "stop" on both computers when it's done. That's it.

You should be able to figure this out technically in seconds. It's the way you label it that can come back to haunt you. That's why we're going to get into a rather thorough explanation.

AUDIO VAULT LABELING

In order to do a good job labeling all of your clips in the vault, you need to know how the vault is used. Take a good look at the vault system in the air studio. Look at what is showing on the monitor. On one side of the screen you'll see the virtual cart machines. These are the devices that actually play the audio from the computer through the board. On the other side of the screen you'll see various tabs, like computer folder tabs. That's exactly what they are. These are the categories of the different audio clips in the system; for instance, commercial log, music log, show log, etc. You simply click on the folder you need and drag the virtual cart across the screen into a virtual cart machine. That's how you play it on the air.

If you wanted to, you could create your own tabs for the different kinds of audio you put into the vault. Many shows do it this way. For instance, they have a tab for movie audio, another for television, another for newsmakers, or sports, or something else. A tab is very easy to create. However, if you do it this way, you must enter the tab description every time you load something into the vault. And there are some things that just don't seem to fit into a category—leaving you scratching your head when it comes time to find it.

There is another way, and it's even easier. Look for the tab that says "All" or something just as obviously inclusive of everything. When you click on the "all" tab, every single clip in the vault is listed in alphabetical order. Now all you have to do is click on the search engine. Type in the first letter of your clip and the list goes to the beginning of that letter. Type in the second letter and it narrows it down further. If you type in the first three letters of anything, you'll be able to find it in seconds. Plus, if you search in the "All" tab, it doesn't matter how it's been categorized. It only matters that you know the first few letters.

In the 1980s, *The Jonathon Brandmeier Showgram* in Chicago used all sorts of audio clips, sound bites, and actualities. In the pre-search engine days, everything was put on "cart" (which is short for tape cartridge—about the size of an eight-track tape). Brandmeier's show had over 5,000 carts—so many that they didn't all fit in the air studio. John Swanson was the technical producer of that show and spent most of each show running back and forth between offices looking for carts. For people who went through the old system, the new system of "searching" is a gift from heaven.

CONSISTENT LABELING

Because this is such an easy way to find things, producers think that they don't have to spend too much time coming up with the correct label. After all, type in Osbourne and you'll find all the Ozzy Osbourne clips in a second. On the other hand, what if you labeled it under Ozzy? Or *The Osbourne's*? Now you have to look somewhere else and you've added a few unnecessary seconds to your search.

It doesn't really matter how you decide to label your clips, but it does matter that you are consistent from the very start. If you decide to name the clip after the person talking, do that. (Many news/talk stations do it that way). If you decide to name the clip after the title of the show or movie you got it from, do that. If you decide to name it after the subject matter, do that. If you want to categorize them chronologically (we wouldn't suggest it—but it's possible), do that. The key is to always do it exactly the same way so you can find it quickly.

Also, try to be very descriptive in your labeling. For instance, during the hey-day of the *The Osbourne's*, personality/talk morning shows had hundreds of clips from that show. If you simply typed in "Osbourne," it wouldn't have been enough. You also need to say something about the content of the clip. Something like "Osbourne—Throws Rocks" would help you find that clip much more quickly. You don't have a lot of room on the label, so you can't get too wordy, but that doesn't mean you can't get descriptive. In fact, you have to. If you last in a job for a few years (Rick Kaempfer produced the same show for ten years), you'll have such a huge audio library that you will be completely lost if you aren't descriptive enough.

A good example of this involves the "best of" clips you save from your show. Some of these you'll decide to save in other places (like archiving them on CD or DAT), but there will be plenty "best of" clips in the vault. If you name all of them after the host, forget about finding what you need quickly. If you name all of them after the guest, how will you know it's a clip from the show and not from something else? You need to figure out how to label those clips, make sure they are descriptive, and then stick to that plan. It's absolutely essential.

Helpful Labeling Hints: If you decide to organize your audio clips by title, be sure you never start it with the word "The." Remember that the computer organizes the clips in a strictly alphabetical way. You'll be looking for Osbourne under O, and won't think to look under T for *The* Osbournes. Also, be careful of using quotations when you type in a label. You have been trained to put TV show and movie titles in quotes. However, if you do that on a vault label, your clip will be alphabetized by the quotation mark and not the first letter. You'll never find it there. Spelling is also crucial. We knew a producer who spelled so badly and inconsistently that he often had trouble finding clips (for instance, Seinfeld was spelled S*i*enfeld, etc.). Misspell the end of the label all you want—just make sure those first few letters are correct.

ORGANIZING YOUR CD LIBRARY

While your CD library will never be as big as your audio clip library, it will become big enough to be unmanageable in no time. You will need CDs for all sorts of things. CDs with music beds (instrumental music played under the host's voice) set the mood for the topic, CDs with bumpers (instrumental music played into and out of commercials) keep the show upbeat and moving, and some CDs contain songs that your host likes to play.

How do you manage to keep this strange assortment of CDs organized? Well, since you don't have a CD search engine, we suggest you choose categories. Here are a few possible categories from some of our CD collections.

- Music with lyrics (by artist)
- Music with lyrics (various artists/compilation CDs)
- TV themes
- Movie soundtracks
- Instrumental (various)
- Seasonal
- Sports themes
- Comedy
- Eras or decades (60s, 70s, 80s, etc.)

Of course, you can categorize them further if you like, but those categories will probably suffice.

Categorizing them isn't enough, of course. You need to find them quickly. If you look at a mismatched drawer full of "Music with lyrics—by artist" CDs, you'll never find what you want. You should still alphabetize within each category.

If you are storing the CDs on a shelf, additionally color-coding the CDs could help. For instance, all of the seasonal CDs could have a green sticker, and the movie soundtracks could have a red sticker, etc. This way, if you aren't the person putting away the CDs, they get put back in the right place. Once a CD is misfiled (depending on how large your collection is), it may take you quite a long time to find it. If you color-code it—an intern or an assistant can help you find CDs more quickly and, more importantly, put them away correctly.

PART SIX

CLIMBING THE LADDER

Let Led Zeppelin sing about a *Stairway to Heaven*. That's a little beyond our means. All we have is this simple ladder. Like Led Zeppelin, we can't tell you exactly what awaits you at the top, but we do know about a few possibilities.

In part 6, we're talking to the battle-tested producer who has learned all the lessons we have, but still hasn't managed to climb the ladder to a satisfying height. It's not too late. Here, we'll hold the ladder. Go ahead and take a look at what you can find all the way at the top.

19

THE PRODUCER LADDER

IF YOU DO ALL OF THE THINGS WE'VE SUGGESTED IN THIS BOOK, YOU WILL more than likely become a very good producer. What happens when the quality of your work doesn't match the quality of your pay? It might be time to move on.

That is often a very difficult thing for a producer to do. We've talked to many producers who reach this point and still can't pull the trigger. And it's usually for understandable reasons.

- I've helped to build this show.
- The host needs me.
- I can't start all over again.
- There aren't any other shows I want to produce.
- I'm not good enough.

All of these reasons seem real. None of them are. We'll play the part of therapist this chapter as we explain why.

To increase your salary, you really need to have another job offer. Whether you decide to stay and produce the same show, leave to produce another day-part, or leave to produce a competitor, it's the only way. If you use the tried and true techniques we lay out for you in this chapter (which by the way, will also work in just about every other business), it can happen to you.

HOW NOT TO IMPROVE YOUR SALARY

It's human nature to work hard and expect to be rewarded. But in business, and a radio station is definitely a business, that's not the way it works. Put yourself in the corporate owner's shoes. The less you make the more profit they make. And if you're working hard, that's even better. That means things are getting accomplished, and they still don't have to pay the price. Don't feel bad, it's nothing personal. They look at every employee the same way. That's pure capitalism.

You might be running into a brick wall because you've forgotten that. While you think you have tried every conceivable approach to increase your pay, you haven't. You've only tried every conceivable incorrect approach. You pointed out how many hours you are working. You pointed out the amount of money the station makes on the show you produce. You pointed out that the host can't do the show without you. You pointed out how much money the host is being paid. You pointed out that you are barely scraping by on the little money you make. All of these mean nothing to them if you don't give them an incentive.

Are they cold-hearted? No. They are businessmen. You aren't a person to them when you discuss salary. You are the producer position, and they only have so much money slotted for that position. If you only talk to them, you'll start believing that too. You'll accept their low pay and you'll start to think that producing a show is a dead-end job. It's not. It's not the job's fault, and it's not the employer's fault. It's yours.

You aren't thinking like a capitalist. If you want to increase your salary, you have to change your mindset. It's a simple case of supply and demand. If someone else demands your services, suddenly you are worth more money, despite what they tell you the producer position should be paid. And that's the only way it can happen.

If your problem with your current position is your salary, it's time to look for something else. We don't mean quit—look for something else. You may discover there is a better job waiting for you. You may discover that other stations think you are worth considerably more money. You aren't the same person that accepted this first producer job. You are now a veteran, and the rules have changed. When another station shows your management that they consider you an asset, your management may begin to look at you differently.

BUT I CAN'T LEAVE THIS SHOW

We have all felt this way. When you work on a show and develop a great rapport with the host, it's hard to leave. But if you are making a substandard wage, you have to consider it. What is the alternative? Stay forever and make no money? If you are waiting for the radio station to suddenly reward you, you will wait forever. What is their incentive? Remember to think like a capitalist. That's the way they think.

There are highly paid producers in their second or third or fourth job who are making very good money. For them, the issue isn't money;

it might be boredom. Have you been with a show for so long that you've lost your edge? Has the challenge completely faded? Are you going through the motions? Do you dread doing the same features over and over and over again? If that rings a bell, you are a bored producer. You may think that you can't leave your current show, but you also owe it to yourself to see what else is out there.

Realizing that the issue is probably money or boredom, let's take another look at the excuses we hear from disgruntled producers who won't take a look at what else is out there.

I've Helped to Build this Show

If you are so bored doing the job that you can do it in your sleep, or you haven't been challenged in years, what difference does it make that you helped build the show? If you are not being paid enough despite having built the show, what difference does it make that you helped build the show? If you don't feel the passion for the show, or the show doesn't feel the passion for you, this reason rings hollow. Try to look at it objectively. Don't let the fact that it's easier not to look dissuade you. There is no downside to looking.

The Host Needs Me

Do you really think that the host couldn't survive without you? If so, why isn't he kicking in some salary to this underpaid producer he so desperately needs? He's probably not underpaid. If he really needs you, he should cough up some dough. If you are bored, why isn't he giving you more challenging assignments? You are serving his needs before you serve your own needs. Wouldn't you say your priorities are slightly misplaced? There is nothing wrong with having a great relationship with the host, but if you aren't making enough money to keep you happy, or you are so bored that you dread going to work, the relationship is meaningless. He isn't on your side if he insists you stay under those circumstances. He's only in it for himself.

I Can't Start All Over Again

We hear this one often from producers who have grown too comfortable in their positions. The reason you aren't looking for another job is pure laziness. Even though you are bored or you're not making enough money, you won't try to better your situation because you think it will be too much work to start producing another show. If you believe this, you've forgotten one very important point. You will never have to start all over again. You are now a veteran producer. You are starting with enough knowledge to eliminate almost all of the growing pains.

Yes, you will be taking a new job. But you won't have to relearn everything you already know. You'll skip right to the good part. You won't be bored anymore, and you'll be making more money.

There Aren't Any Other Shows I Want to Produce

If this is really true, you might want to skip to the next chapter. That chapter discusses other careers you might want to consider.

On the other hand, if you are bored and don't think there is another challenge out there, consider these possibilities. Are you confining yourself to the same format? If you've only done personality shows, have you considered trying a talk show? It could be the new challenge you seek. If you've only done morning shows, have you considered an afternoon show? The different hours may be the ticket to your happiness. If you've only done shows in your own market, have you considered shows in bigger markets? What about nationally syndicated shows? The next step is always out there if you want to look for it. As for your salary, are you making six figures? If not, you haven't reached the top of the ladder yet. Keep reaching and you will find another challenge that may interest you and may pay you more.

I'm Not Good Enough

If you really believe this, you may be working for an abusive host. We've seen this phenomenon before—up close and personal.

There are hosts (and program directors for that matter) who keep you in line by keeping you down. This is classic abusive behavior, and we're happy to say that it doesn't exist as much as it used to. If your self-esteem has taken a big hit since you took this job, you may be working for one. You may not even realize it. It's the hostage syndrome. Hostages tend to feel for their kidnappers because it's the only way they can mentally survive. We've seen producers in the same position. Ask yourself these questions.

- Do you have to tiptoe around the host because you're afraid he'll bite your head off?
- Do you have to alter your behavior every day to match his changing moods?
- Do you get the same amount of grief on days you prepare extensively as you do on days you don't?
- Does he badmouth you on the air?
- Does he get personal in his attacks?

- Does he constantly remind you that you are lucky to have this job?
- Does he react badly when good things happen to you?
- Does he seem to get a perverse joy in humiliating you?

By now you know if we're talking about you. You need to move on more than anyone else. People that are abusive don't change. He'll be abusive tomorrow, he'll be abusive next year, and he'll be abusive five years from now. You have to get away. You may be surprised by what you find. Sometimes the grass really is greener, and sometimes it is way greener. If the host or program director is publicly abusive, the rest of the radio community knows it. If you have survived in that situation for a while, you have achieved the respect of everyone in town. Just wait until you interview for another position. You won't believe the reaction.

HOW DO YOU LOOK FOR ANOTHER PRODUCER JOB?

If you have done your job correctly, you will have drawn the attention of another radio station or show. They may not know your name, but they know your work. Program directors might not understand exactly what makes a great producer, but they know a well-produced show when they hear one. Realizing that will give you the confidence you need to sell yourself.

Spread the Word Directly

The most obvious way to get the word out is to apply for any opening in town. When it becomes known that you are available, the calls may start coming to you. At the very least, you are getting in the door and letting the rest of the radio community know what you do.

No opportunity is too small. Go all out for each and every one. The job that appears to be in the wrong format may actually be in a format you should be considering. The job that appears to pay too little may actually pay more than you are making now. Keep one thing in mind during this process. There is no downside to letting people at other radio stations know what you do. The program director you impress today for the wrong job may someday hire you for the right job. Look at every job opportunity as a chance to put out a press release about yourself.

We have always found interviewing to be a positive experience even if the job is wrong or you don't get an offer. You will learn from your mistakes. You will discover what people are looking for. You will expand your horizons. You will learn to think outside the box.

Of course, it's better to go for jobs that interest you or may pay more money. How do you know? The higher the profile of the show, the more money you can make. The better the day-part, the more money you can make. The bigger the market, the more money you can make. Your experience will also play a factor in the money offer. The more experience you have, the more money you can make. There are exceptions to all of these rules, of course, but for the most part that's the way it works in this business.

Spread the Word Indirectly

After you've been in the business a few years, you will have made contacts at radio stations all over the dial. The radio community in every town is amazingly small. Everyone knows everyone. The person working at your station today will be working at another radio station tomorrow. Soon you'll have friends at every station in town.

If you are unhappy in your current position, let your friends in the business know about it. If they recommend you for a position, you can negotiate from a completely different perspective. Now you have leverage. You have a job, you have a recommendation, and they are calling you. You'll be amazed at the difference in the money offer when people come after you.

If someone actually calls you, always agree to talk to him. Nothing bad can come from it. If you get an offer for more money, you can take it or use that offer to negotiate a raise at your current station. If you get an offer for less money, you'll find out that you are making more than other producers. That may change your perspective completely. If you don't get an offer at all, you will still get the word out about yourself and have an opportunity to learn from your interviewing mistakes.

WHAT DO YOU DO WHEN YOU GET ANOTHER OFFER?

You'll probably have to negotiate with the other radio station before that offer comes. There are important tips to remember when you negotiate.

Never give out a salary figure first. Do whatever you can to avoid this. They will also be trying to get you to say a number first. We call this the negotiating mambo. They'll try to pin you down on your current salary. The second you give them a figure, you are taking money off the table. Come up with a non-committal phrase and stick to it. Tell them you make as much as they would expect a top producer to make.

They won't be offended. They know what you are doing because they are doing the exact same thing.

Once they actually give you an offer, you need to counteroffer. Say that you were really hoping to make ten thousand more. If they don't increase the offer immediately, say that you will have to think about it. After all, you already have a job, and while this is an attractive offer, there are many things to consider. They may blink and increase the offer. If they don't, this is the highest they will go. (You may find that if you eventually reject that offer, they will go even higher. Again, this is a win-win situation.)

Now that you have the highest possible offer, it's time to go back to your radio station. Tell your program director about the offer and see her reaction. That will tell you all you need to know. If she wants to talk to you about it, she may consider matching it. Now you are doing another negotiating dance. You will want your current station to top this offer because the other station obviously appreciates your abilities more. You have the leverage now. Don't blow it by accepting less or equal money than the other offer.

Of course it's important that you are willing to accept the other offer. If you aren't willing to take the other job, don't make the mistake of using it as a bluff. The program director may just tell you to take it. If she does, take it. Don't hesitate. Your suspicions about your current job were right all along. You will be much happier elsewhere.

AFTER THE TOP STEP

There may come a time in your producing career when you decide you've had enough. If you honestly look within yourself and decide that you aren't interested in the job anymore, or you think that you've reached the top of the ladder and there is nowhere else to go in producing, it's time to try something else.

Despite the fact that your producing career may be ending, you will leave the field with some great memories. More importantly, your producing career has given you skills that can help you excel in many other fields. In the next chapter, we'll show you just how diversified you really are. Hopefully this will help you see some possibilities you hadn't even considered.

20

FUTURE CAREERS FOR EX-PRODUCERS

ONCE YOU'VE PRODUCED RADIO SHOWS FOR A WHILE, YOU MAY DECIDE to try your hand at something else. That sort of restlessness happens to everyone in every field. It's human nature.

We've spoken to so many radio producers over the years who reach this point without realizing the many different directions this producing experience can take them. Instead of exploring their industry and beyond, they remain producers. They get comfortable and bored, and, eventually, they get unhappy.

It doesn't have to be that way. Within the radio business and outside the radio business, former radio producers are flourishing. They have become managers, executives, entrepreneurs, and artists. And those are just the ex-producers we personally know. In case you haven't considered where this career can eventually lead you, it's time that their stories are told.

THE NEXT STEP INSIDE THE RADIO BUSINESS

The producer has a unique opportunity within the radio business. Very few radio positions acquire the depth of experience that a radio producer gets. He has to learn about every single department just to do his job. He dabbles in promotions, production, sales, engineering, and programming.

You may find that you have skills or interests that make you an ideal candidate to transition into another department. By all means, explore that. Ex-producers are working at every level of radio today, including station managers, sales managers, and program directors. Let's take a look at some of the departments that make for the easiest transition.

Host

If you get a break to host your own show, you may decide that you have been behind the scenes long enough. Some of the best air personalities in the country are former producers. If you think about it, this is an easy transition to make. A producer must think like a host during every show he produces. He comes up with material and considers how that material can be used on the air. If he also has the personality and ability to communicate these ideas himself, he will make an excellent host.

Dan McNeil was the executive producer of the Chet Coppock show in the late eighties and early nineties. The show was a sports-talk show on an entertainment-talk station (in the days before the sports-talk format was created by WFAN in New York). When Chet Coppock would go on vacation, McNeil was asked to fill in. McNeil took full advantage. When the sports-talk station WSCR began assembling their on-air staff, McNeil was offered the full-time position of afternoon drive co-anchor. He has since moved on to ESPN Radio, but twelve years after leaving his producer position, he is still one of Chicago's most popular sportscasters.

There are scores of other sports/talk hosts in the country who have followed a similar path. Other examples in Chicago include WSCR's Jesse Rogers and Jonathon Hood. Both of them were producers who took advantage of temporary fill-in slots and parlayed them into their own shows. In news/talk radio, one of the most popular hosts in Chicago is ex-producer Roe Conn. His talk show is one of the highest rated programs in the city. Jimmy Baron was a personality/talk producer in San Diego and Chicago before becoming a co-host of a very popular show in Atlanta.

Those are just a few examples from our hometown, but we're guessing you know of several more examples from your town. If you have the talent, and being a producer has given you the opportunity to get on the air, becoming a host is viable and realistic goal.

Marketing/Promotion Director

As the producer of a big-time radio show, you have been working closely with the marketing/promotion director on every major promotion at your radio station. Depending on the situation at your station, you may have even co-opted some of the promotion director's duties just to help out. For instance, you may be handling all of the publicity for the show you are producing. If this is an area that interests you, you've probably asked enough questions over the years to learn the other parts of her job. If the position ever opens up, you may decide to go for it.

Cindy Gatziolis began her career as the producer of *The Larry Lujack Show*. She later made the move into promotions, eventually being named the marketing/promotions director of WLUP and later WMAQ radio. We'll mention what she is doing now when we get to some of the possibilities outside of radio.

The Production Director

A producer does production work on a daily basis. He learns how to edit, how to mix, and how to work all of the equipment. Sometimes the producer does more complicated production projects than the production director. Many times, the producer will work so closely with the director that he will become the vacation replacement for the production director. That happened to one of the writers of this book.

It's not hard to imagine it going to the next level. For instance, Jim McInerney was one of the producers for several different shows in Chicago (including Jonathon Brandmeier's and Kevin Matthews'), but production was always his specialty. When the production director position became available at his radio station (WCKG), he was given the job.

Program Director

In many ways the producer is the program director of the radio show he produces. He works closely with the program director to make sure the show shares the program director's vision. He directs the flow of the show, calms and soothes the egos, and becomes the point person for every other department at the station. When you think about it, going into management is probably the most natural transition for a producer.

Jack Silver was the producer of the Rick Dees show in Los Angeles, and he is a perfect example of this transition. Since ending the producing portion of his career, he has been a program director in Chicago, Los Angeles, and San Diego. Lorna Gladstone began her career as a radio producer and has since been the program director of radio stations in Chicago and Minneapolis. Mitch Rosen began his career as the producer of an overnight show in Chicago. He also has gone on to become a program director. Further examples of this natural transition are too numerous to mention. We guarantee at least a few of the program directors in your town began their careers as producers too.

THE NEXT STEP OUTSIDE THE RADIO BUSINESS

Sometimes when you work in one industry for too many years you stop seeing the possibilities in other related fields. Again, because producers have such diversified backgrounds within the radio business, they also acquire a full palette of applicable skills for other businesses.

In the introduction of this book we said that the word producer was actually an acronym. The letters P, R, O, D, U, C, E, and R all represented the first letter of different duties the producer is expected to perform (Psychologist, Researcher, Organizer, Director, Understudy, Creative writer, Engineer, Right-hand man). Throughout the book we've also told you about many of the other producer duties. Just about any one of the skills a producer acquires while carrying out those duties can lead to a different career. Here are a just few examples.

TV Producer

What's the difference between producing a radio show and a local television show? Very little. In fact, a segment producer for television is only responsible for one segment per show. We know several radio producers who have made the switch. They tell us that radio is actually much more demanding and difficult. On some TV talk shows, a segment producer is only responsible for one show a month. The duties are basically the same. The producer books the guests, coordinates the segments, and helps the host perform the material to the best of his ability.

Jim Wiser was the producer of *The Jonathon Brandmeier Showgram* in Chicago. While he was producing that show, Bob Sirott appeared as a guest host. Sirott was impressed with Wiser's preparation and abilities, and when Sirott got his own morning television show a few years later, he asked Wiser to come aboard as a segment producer. There are stories like that throughout the television industry. Ex-radio producers make the transition to television very well.

Advertising

We've already covered the production skills a producer acquires. Some producers also become skilled writers. Combining the two talents is a natural progression for a career in advertising.

Rick Kaempfer and his technical producer Vince Argento (along with salesman David Stern) started their own advertising agency in 1999 when they were still producing *The John Landecker Show*. At first they focused on writing and producing ads exclusively for radio and ran this company as a side project. They have since expanded into other media, and their company is flourishing (*www.amishchicago.com*). The combination of their production skills, writing ability, and knowledge of the media business has helped make this business a success.

Public Relations

As we've said, a radio producer is basically the publicist of the show he produces. The producer also deals with other publicists every single day on the job. Throughout the years it's only natural that he will make contacts and develop friendships with people in this industry. Since a producer can write and can offer a special insight into the way the other side thinks, he can be an extremely valuable asset in public relations. That's why many producers make the leap into working at a public relations agency.

Earlier in this chapter we mentioned former Larry Lujack producer Cindy Gatziolis. Since leaving radio promotions, she has gone into public relations. Her current position is Director of Public Relations for the Mayor's Office of Special Events in Chicago.

Consultant

When you reach the top of the producer ladder it's only natural to become a radio consultant. Many ex-producers have done that. But we know one ex-producer who has become a different kind of consultant altogether. His name is Brendan Sullivan and he was once a producer and writer for *The Jonathon Brandmeier Showgram* in Chicago.

We asked him to explain exactly what his company "Creativity Coach" (*www.creativitycoach.net*) does. It's a great example of thinking outside the box.

"I took my ten years of experience and blended it into another career," Brendan tells us. "My job as a producer was to create material. Sometimes it was as simple as presenting the host with an interesting real story from the news. Often it entailed much more, including writing and voicing taped re-enactments, voicing a character live on the show, writing material for the host to deliver, or suggesting tie-ins to ongoing segments of the show. I was able to use this experience to help create my own career as a creativity coach. I help organizational teams to create more dynamic ideas, more productive meetings, stronger client relationships, and a healthier, more positive work environment. I take a lot of the same skills I used to create radio ideas, and coach others on how to develop and apply these skills to the corporate world."

We're betting you hadn't considered that as a possibility.

Writing

We've given you a few examples of how to use your writing skills in other fields (like public relations and advertising), but anyone who has to come up with something like 10,000 ideas is probably capable of doing even more with his writing skills. You can write for television, magazines, newspapers, and just about anything else. In chapter 1 we told you about Steve Dale, one of the early modern-day producers. He is now a writer for the *Chicago Tribune*.

We even know two producers who have become authors.

THE RADIO PRODUCER'S HANDBOOK

At the very least we have given you some food for thought in *The Radio Producer's Handbook*. The job of the radio producer is a challenging, difficult, frustrating, and rewarding job. You will learn so much, and you will polish and refine practical skills that will help you become a success at whatever you choose to do in the future.

You may decide to climb the producer ladder and become the best producer you can be. Or, you may decide to follow your radio dream wherever it takes you. You may even decide to branch out into something new and exciting. The possibilities are endless.

The book is not.

APPENDIX A:
GLOSSARY OF RADIO TERMS

ACTUALITY. A short piece of spoken audio from a newsmaker. News departments use this term most often.

ADOBE AUDITION. An editing software used by disc jockeys, newscasters, and producers to do quick edits during the course of a radio program. Formally called **Cool Edit Pro.**

AIR MIX. Headphone setting as it sounds on the air. This is post-compression (see **compressor**) and post-delay (see **delay**). See **program mix** for the alternate headphone setting.

AIR PERSONALITY. Another term for radio host. This usually refers to someone on the air at a music station or personality/talk station. It is not the personality equivalent of "air guitar."

AIR STUDIO. The studio that is currently on the air. Many studios at the radio station can be put on the air, and most stations designate one studio for this, but any studio that is currently on the air qualifies.

AIR TALENT. See **air personality**. Some stations just prefer this term.

ARBITRON. The king of the radio ratings services. It uses a diary system to judge who is listening to the radio, when they are listening, and for how long.

AUDIO CLIP. A short piece of spoken audio. This can be a clip of a newsmaker, from a television show, or from a movie. See **drop-in**, **sound bite**, and **actuality**.

AUDIO VAULT. See **vault**.

AUDITION TAPE. Telescoped recording showcasing talents of air personality.

AVERAGE QUARTER HOUR. A typical fifteen-minute period on the radio. Often **ratings** are discussed in terms of listeners per average quarter hour.

BARTER. Trading commercial airtime for goods or services.

BENCHMARK. A radio segment that airs at the same time every day or week.

BIT. From the comedy term "bit," referring to a humorous radio **segment**. A very common term in personality/talk.

BOARD. Short for control board. Also see **console**. Essentially the mixing board in the studio that controls all sound, including microphones.

BOARD OPERATOR. Person that works the controls of the **board**.

BUMPERS. Instrumental music played into and out of commercial breaks as a transitional device.

CALL LETTERS. The three or four letters that identify the radio station. East of the Mississippi all call letters begin with *W*. West of the Mississippi all call letters begin with *K*.

CANS. Slang term for headphones. The grizzled radio veterans use this term.

CART. Short for tape cartridge. These are nearly obsolete now, although some radio stations in smaller markets still use them. As recently as fifteen years ago, they were industry norm. Nearly everything heard on the radio was played on a cart. They look like mini 8-track tapes (also obsolete). See **virtual cart**.

COMMERCIAL LOG. Official list of daily commercials broken down by hour and by **segment**. The commercial log remains in the **air studio**.

COMMERCIALS. See **spot**.

COMPRESSOR. A processing device that doesn't allow as much fluctuation in the levels of the signal. It's like an automatic or electronic hand on the volume knob of the signal making sure that's it's never too high or never too low.

CONSOLE. See **board**.

CONTEST BOOK. Usually a three-ring binder kept in the **air studio** to keep track of contest prizes and winners.

COOL EDIT PRO. See **Adobe Acrobat**.

COST PER POINT. An advertising term, literally meaning the dollars spent per **gross rating point**. Calculated by dividing cost by the **gross rating points** (GRPs).

CUE. A device (small amplifier and speaker) that allows listening to audio off the air. There is usually a cue button below every single **pot** or **module** on the **board**.

CUME. A ratings term, meaning the cumulative unduplicated total audience over two or more time periods.

DAT. Digital audiotape.

DAY-PART. The time of day of a particular show. For instance, mornings, middays, afternoons, evenings, overnights. See **time slot**.

DELAY. A device which allows a radio program to broadcast a signal a few seconds after it occurs in case something needs to be edited out (i.e., swearing callers, etc.)

DEMOGRAPHICS. Listeners categorized by age, income, location, and a number of other factors.

DROP-IN. See audio clip and **actuality** and **sound bite**.

EDITING SOFTWARE. See **Pro-Tools, Vox Pro, Adobe Audition, Cool Edit Pro**. Computer software that allows digital editing of audio.

FADER. See **pot**.

FCC. The Federal Communications Commission; the governing body of the broadcasting industry.

FORMAT. A radio-station's genre, i.e., news/talk, alternative rock, rap, etc.

FREQUENCY. The total number of times an individual hears an ad; an advertising term.

GENERAL MANAGER. The person in charge of the radio station.

GROSS IMPRESSIONS. The total number of times an advertising message is heard, including duplicate times by the same person.

GROSS RATINGS POINTS. An advertising figure calculated by dividing **gross impressions** by the target population and multiplying the sum by 100. Also known as GRPs.

HARMONIZER. A device that changes voice pitch and adds effects to a voice.

HOST. The person who performs the radio program on the air.

HOTLINE. The in-studio phone line dedicated to important calls; not given out to the public.

IFB. Interrupted foldback; also known as **talkback**. A device that allows a remote broadcast to communicate to the studio through the microphone (via phone line).

IMAGING. The sound packages a radio station uses to identify itself and create an image.

INPUT BUTTON. Used to identify which piece of equipment is fed into a certain **module**. Some modules have two input buttons, labeled A and B.

INPUT MODE. Used to identify whether a **module** is in stereo or mono, and whether or not the stereo is balanced or not.

INTERVIEW PREP SHEET. A fact sheet with background information, questions, and angles on an interview subject.

ISDN. Integrated Services Digital Network; a digital phone line.

JOCK. Short for disc jockey. No one says disc jockey anymore.

LEVEL. Amount of volume units; audio measurement.

LINERS. Promotional announcements written by the radio station; read by the host.

LIVE COPY. Commercial material read over the air; not pre-recorded.

MARTI. A device that transmits a remote broadcast directly to the transmitter tower.

MINI-DISC. A recordable CD player that uses miniature discs; also made in portable form.

MODULE. Each individual **pot** or **fader** position on the board (includes **input, output,** on/off switch, and **input mode.**)

MUSIC BED. Instrumental music played underneath an announcer's or **host's** voice.

MUSIC LOG. A computer-generated daily list of a radio station's music; prepared by music director or program director.

OPERATING LOG. An in-studio sign-on/sign-off sheet that also keeps track of transmitter readings; an FCC requirement. Also known as **program log** or **transmitter log.**

PGM. Short for **program.** In this case it refers to the program button on the control **board.**

PHONE SCREENER. Computer screen for phone calls; allows producer to type in names and short messages about each caller. The person screening the calls can also be called the phone screener if that is his only job at the radio station.

PHONER. Topic used to solicit phone calls; also used to identify a phone interview with a guest (as opposed to in-studio, etc.)

PITCHING. Suggesting segments to the host.

POT. Short for potentiometer; a **fader** switch on the control **board.** Also used as a verb. **Pot** it up and the volume goes up. Move it down and it would be **potted** down.

PREP SHEET. A detailed written segment-by-segment preview of a radio show; usually prepared by the producer.

PRODUCTION. Audio creation using studio equipment. Also the department of the radio station that creates (or transfers into an airable version) the **commercials, promos,** and **imaging.**

PROGRAM MIX. Headphone setting directly from the **board;** pre-**delay** and **compression.**

PROGRAM DIRECTOR. The person responsible for final decisions on programming matters (i.e., personnel, music, etc.)

PROGRAM LOG. See **operating log.** Also known as **transmitter log.** Different radio stations use different terms, but it's always one of these three.

PROGRAMMING. The material or content that airs between the commercials. Also the department at the radio station in charge of content.

PROMOS. Recorded **commercials** for a radio station event or feature. Some stations also use this term to describe **liners.** At such a station, the term **recorded promo** is used.

PRO TOOLS. The industry standard editing software from the Digidesign company.

RADIO SEGMENT. See **segment.**

RATINGS. The percentage of the targeted population tuned to a station or program. See **Arbitron.**

RCS. Another computer system comparable to the **vault**.

REACH. The unduplicated number of people exposed to a medium.

REMOTE. A broadcast from a location outside of the radio studio.

REVERB. A device that allows a voice to have an echo-effect.

RUNDOWN SHEET. The daily list of segments for a particular show.

SEGMENT. The block of time between commercial breaks; used to identify different portions of a particular radio show.

SEGUE. Transition between topics or songs.

SFX. Abbreviation for sound effects.

SHARE. The percent of people with radios turned on who are listening to a particular radio show or station. (Is not a percentage of total audience because it only counts those with their radios on.)

SOUND BITE. See **actuality**, **drop in**, and **audio clip**.

SOUND FORGE. A brand of digital editing software.

SPOT. Standard industry term for paid **commercial**.

TALKBACK. See **IFB**.

TIME-SLOT. See **day-part**.

TIVO. Device that programs and records television shows digitally on computer hard drive or DVD.

TRAFFIC. Radio station department in charge of scheduling commercials.

TRANSMITTER. Antenna used to broadcast radio station's signal. Usually located on top of tallest building in city. In rural area referred to as **transmitter tower** because it is freestanding.

TRANSMITTER LOG. See **program log**, **operation log**. Different radio stations use different terms, but it's always one of these three.

UTILITY. The device on the control **board** that sends sound from each particular **pot** to the phone.

UTL. **Utility** button on the control **board**.

VAULT. The audio library of everything contained in the computer; **commercials**, songs, etc.

VECTOR. Analog phone line used to transmit a remote broadcast.

VIRTUAL CART. Computerized file of one piece of audio. Named after obsolete **cart**. When radio switched from **carts** to computers, engineers designed the computer files to look like the old carts so that it was less intimidating to old radio veterans.

VOX PRO. An editing software used to edit recorded phone calls.

VU METER. Volume units. Gauge for measuring volume in decibels.

WARM LINE. Direct phone line to the producer; not given out to the public.

APPENDIX B:
SCHOOLS WITH STUDENT-RUN RADIO STATIONS
(By Region)

NORTHWEST

(*Alaska, Washington, Oregon, Idaho, Montana*)
Central Washington University (Ellensburg, WA)
Centralia College (Centralia, WA)
Eastern Oregon University (La Grande, OR)
Green River Community College (Auburn, WA)
Linfield College (McMinnville, OR)
Montana State University (Bozeman, MT)
Montana Tech (Butte, MT)
Oregon Institute of Technology (Klamath Falls, OR)
Oregon State University (Corvallis, OR)
Pacific Lutheran University (Tacoma, WA)
Portland State University (Portland, OR)
Reed College (Portland, OR)
University of Alaska—Fairbanks (Fairbanks, AK)
University of Idaho (Moscow, ID)
University of Montana (Missoula, MT)
University of Oregon (Eugene, OR)
University of Puget Sound (Tacoma, WA)
University of Washington (Seattle, WA)
Washington State University (Pullman, WA)
Western Montana College (Dillon, MT)
Western Washington University (Bellingham, WA)
Whitman College (Walla Walla, WA)
Whitworth College (Spokane, WA)

WEST

(*California, Colorado, Hawaii, Nevada, Utah, Wyoming*)
Adams State College (Alamosa, CO)
Cal Poly State University (San Luis Obispo, CA)
California State University (Turlock, CA)

California State University—Fresno (Fresno, CA)
Central Wyoming College (Riverton, WY)
Chabot College (Hayward, CA)
Colorado State University (Fort Collins, CO)
Fort Lewis College (Durango, CO)
Loyola Marymount University (Los Angeles, CA)
Mount San Antonio Community College (Walnut, CA)
Palomar Community College (Oceanside, CA)
Pikes Peak Community College (Colorado Springs, CO)
Saint Mary's College (Moraga, CA)
San Diego State University (San Diego, CA)
Santa Clara University (Santa Clara, CA)
Stanford University (Palo Alto, CA)
University of California—Berkley (Berkley, CA)
University of California—Davis (Davis, CA)
University of California—Irvine (Irvine, CA)
University of California—Los Angeles (Los Angeles, CA)
University of California—San Diego (San Diego, CA)
University of California—Santa Cruz (Santa Cruz, CA)
University of Colorado (Boulder, CO)
University of Hawaii (Honolulu, HI)
University of Northern Colorado (Greeley, CO)
University of San Francisco (San Francisco, CA)

SOUTHWEST

(*Arizona, New Mexico, Texas*)
Amarillo College (Amarillo, TX)
Arizona State University (Tempe, AZ)
New Mexico State University (Las Cruces, NM)
Northern Arizona University (Flagstaff, AZ)
Rice University (Houston, TX)
Sam Houston State University (Huntsville, TX)
San Antonio College (San Antonio, TX)
Stephen F. Austin State University (Nacogdoches, TX)
Texas A&M University (College Station, TX)
University of Texas (Austin, TX)
West Texas A&M University (Canyon, TX)

MIDWEST

(*Illinois, Indiana, Iowa, Kansas, Michigan, Minnesota, Missouri, Nebraska, North Dakota, Ohio, Oklahoma, South Dakota, Wisconsin*)
Alma College (Alma, MI)

Augustana College (Sioux Falls, SD)
Baker University (Baldwin City, KS)
Ball State University (Muncie, IN)
Black Hills State University (Spearfish, SD)
Carroll College (Waukesha, WI)
Central University of Iowa (Pella, IA)
Cleveland State University (Cleveland, OH)
College of Wooster (Wooster, OH)
Columbia College (Chicago, IL)
Cornell College (Mount Vernon, IA)
Culver-Stockton College (Canton, MO)
DePauw University (Greencastle, IN)
Doane College (Crete, NE)
Elmhurst College (Elmhurst, IL)
Findlay College (Findlay, OH)
Grinnell College (Grinnell, IA)
Heidelberg College (Tiffin, OH)
Henry Ford Community College (Dearborn, MI)
Illinois Institute of Technology (Chicago, IL)
Illinois Wesleyan University (Bloomington, IL)
Iowa Central Community College (Fort Dodge, IA)
Iowa State University (Ames, IA)
John Carroll University (University Park, OH)
Kenyon College (Gambier, OH)
Knox College (Galesburg, IL)
Lake Forest College (Lake Forest, IL)
Lake Superior State University (Sault Saint Marie, MI)
Lewis University (Lockport, IL)
Luther College (Decorah, IA)
Manchester College (North Manchester, IN)
Marietta College (Marietta, OH)
Marquette University (Milwaukee, WI)
Miami University (Oxford, OH)
Michigan State University (East Lansing, MI)
Michigan Technological University (Houghton, MI)
Milwaukee School of Engineering (Milwaukee, WI)
Missouri Valley College (Marshall, MO)
Morningside College (Sioux City, IA)
Northland Community & Technical College (Thief River Falls, MN)
Northeastern Illinois University (Chicago, IL)
Northwest Missouri State University (Maryville, MO)
Northwestern University (Evanston, IL)
Oakland University (Auburn Hills, MI)
Oberlin College (Oberlin, OH)

Ohio Wesleyan College (Delaware, OH)
Olivet College (Olivet, MI)
Otterbein College (Westerville, OH)
Panhandle State University (Goodwell, OK)
Park University (Parkville, MO)
Parkland College (Champaign, IL)
Principia College (Elsah, IL)
Purdue University (West Lafayette, IN)
Rose-Hulman Institute of Technology (Terre Haute, IN)
Saint Cloud State University (Saint Cloud, MN)
Saint John's University (Collegeville, MN)
Saint Mary's University of Minnesota (Winona, MN)
Saint Olaf College (Northfield, MN)
Saint Xavier University (Chicago, IL)
Simpson College (Indianola, IA)
South Dakota State University (Brookings, SD)
Southern Illinois University (Carbondale, IL)
Southwestern College (Winfield, KS)
Tri-State University (Angola, IN)
Truman State University (Kirksville, MO)
University of Chicago (Chicago, IL)
University of Dayton (Dayton, OH)
University of Detroit Mercy (Detroit, MI)
University of Evansville (Evansville, IN)
University of Illinois (Urbana-Champaign, IL)
University of Indianapolis (Indianapolis, IN)
University of Iowa (Iowa City, IA)
University of Kansas (Lawrence, KS)
University of Michigan (Ann Arbor, MI)
University of Minnesota (Minneapolis, MN)
University of Minnesota (Saint Louis Park, MN)
University of Missouri (Columbia, MO)
University of Missouri (Rolla, MO)
University of Nebraska (Lincoln, NE)
University of Oklahoma (Norman, OK)
University of South Dakota (Vermillion, SD)
University of Toledo (Toledo, OH)
University of Wisconsin (Madison, WI)
University of Wisconsin—Platteville (Platteville, WI)
University of Wisconsin—River Falls (River Falls, WI)
University of Wisconsin—Stevens Point (Stevens Point, WI)
University of Wisconsin—Whitewater (Whitewater, WI)
Valparaiso University (Valparaiso, IN)
Vincennes University (Vincennes, IN)

Wabash College (Crawfordsville, IN)
Wabash Valley College (Mount Vernon, IL)
Washington University (Clayton, MO)
Western Illinois University (Macomb, IL)
Western Michigan University (Kalamazoo, MI)
Wheaton College (Wheaton, IL)
William Jewel College (Liberty, MO)
William Penn College (Oskaloosa, IA)
Winona State University (Winona, MN)
Wright State University (Fairborn, OH)

SOUTHEAST

(Alabama, Arkansas, Florida, Georgia, Kentucky, Louisiana, Mississippi, North Carolina, South Carolina, Tennessee, Virginia)
Abraham Baldwin Agricultural College (Tifton, GA)
Arkansas Tech University (Russellville, AR)
Auburn University (Auburn, AL)
Austin Peay State University (Clarksville, TN)
Centenary College (Shreveport, LA)
Central Carolina Community College (Erwin, NC)
Chattanooga State Technical Community College (Red Bank, TN)
Clemson University (Clemson, SC)
Copiah-Lincoln Junior College (Wesson, MS)
Cumberland University (Lebanon, TN)
Duke University (Durham, NC)
East Carolina University (Greenville, NC)
Embry-Riddle Aero University (Daytona Beach, FL)
Emory & Henry College (Emory, VA)
Flagler College (Saint Augustine, FL)
Florida State University (Tallahassee, FL)
Freed-Hardeman University (Henderson, TN)
Furman University (Greenville, SC)
Gaston College (Dallas, NC)
Georgia College (Milledgeville, GA)
Georgia Southern University (Statesboro, GA)
Georgia State University (Atlanta, GA)
Georgia Tech University (Atlanta, GA)
Guilford College (Greensboro, NC)
Hampden-Sydney College (Hampden-Sydney, VA)
Hendrix College (Conway, AR)
High Point College (High Point, NC)
James Madison University (Harrisonburg, VA)
Lincoln Memorial University (Harrogate, TN)

Longwood University (Farmville, VA)
Louisiana State University (Baton Rouge, LA)
Mary Washington College (Fredericksburg, VA)
Middle Tennessee State University (Murfreesboro, TN)
Milligan College (Elizabethton, TN)
Mississippi State University (Starkville, MS)
Mississippi Valley State University (Itta Bena, MS)
North Carolina State University (Raleigh, NC)
Northwestern State University (Natchitoches, LA)
Rollins College (Winter Park, FL)
Sweet Briar College (Sweet Briar, VA)
Tennessee Technological University (Cookeville, TN)
Tulane University (New Orleans, LA)
University of Florida (Gainesville, FL)
University of Georgia (Athens, GA)
University of Kentucky (Lexington, KY)
University of Louisiana at Monroe (Monroe, LA)
University of Miami (Coral Gables, FL)
University of Mississippi (University, MS)
University of North Carolina (Chapel Hill, NC)
University of North Carolina—Greensboro (Greensboro, NC)
University of Richmond (Richmond, VA)
University of the South (Sewanee, TN)
University of South Carolina (Columbia, SC)
University of Tennessee (Knoxville, TN)
University of Tennessee—Martin (Martin, TN)
Valdosta State University (Valdosta, GA)
Vanderbilt University (Nashville, TN)
Virginia Tech (Blacksburg, TN)
Virginia Wesleyan College (Norfolk, VA)
Volunteer State Community College (Gallatin, TN)
Wake Forest University (Winston-Salem, NC)
Western Carolina University (Cullowhee, NC)
Western Kentucky University (Bowling Green, KY)
Wilkes Community College (Wilkesboro, NC)

MID-ATLANTIC

(*Delaware, Maryland, New Jersey, New York, Pennsylvania, Washington D.C., West Virginia*)
Adirondack Community College (Glen Falls, NY)
Albright College (Reading, PA)
Alfred University (Alfred, NY)
Allegheny College (Meadville, PA)

Bethany College (Bethany, WV)
Bloomsburg University (Bloomsburg, PA)
Burlington County College (Pemberton, NJ)
California University of Pennsylvania (California, PA)
Camden County College (Blackwood, NJ)
Carnegie Mellon (Pittsburgh, PA)
Cayuga County Community College (Auburn, NY)
Cazenovia College (Cazenovia, NY)
Centenary College (Hackettstown, NJ)
City College of New York (New York, NY)
Clarion University of Pennsylvania (Clarion, PA)
Clarkson University (Potsdam, NY)
Colgate University (Hamilton, NY)
College of New Jersey (Trenton, NJ)
College of Staten Island (Staten Island, NY)
Cornell University (Ithaca, NY)
Corning Community College (Corning, NY)
Dickinson College (Carlisle, PA)
Drew University (Madison, NJ)
Drexel University (Philadelphia, PA)
East Stroudsburg University (East Stroudsburg, PA)
Edinboro University of Pennsylvania (Edinboro, PA)
Elizabethtown College (Elizabethtown, PA)
Elmira College (Elmira, NY)
Franklin and Marshall College (Lancaster, PA)
Fredonia State University (Fredonia, NY)
Gannon University (Erie, PA)
Genesee Community College (Batavia, NY)
Geneva College (Beaver Falls, PA)
Gettysburg College (Gettysburg, PA)
Hamilton College (Clinton, NY)
Hartwick College (Oneonta, NY)
Herkimer County Community College (Herkimer, NY)
Hofstra University (Hempstead, NY)
Howard University (Washington, D.C)
Indiana University of Pennsylvania (Indiana, PA)
Ithaca College (Ithaca, NY)
John Hopkins University (Baltimore, MD)
Juniata College (Huntington, PA)
Kean College (Union Township, NJ)
Kings College (Wilkes-Barre, PA)
Kingsborough Community College (Brooklyn, NY)
Lafayette College (Easton, PA)

Lehigh Carbon Community College (Schnecksville, PA)
Lehigh University (Bethlehem, PA)
Long Island University (Brookville, NY)
Luzerne County Community College (Nanticoke, PA)
Lycoming College (Williamsport, PA)
Lyndon State College (Lyndonville, VT)
Manhattan College (Manhattan, NY)
Mansfield University of Pennsylvania (Mansfield, PA)
Marist College (Poughkeepsie, NY)
Marshall University (Huntington, WV)
Marwood College (Scranton, PA)
Millersville University (Millersville, PA)
Monmouth University (West Long Branch, NJ)
Montclair State University (Upper Montclair, NJ)
Mount Saint Mary's College (Emmetsburg, MD)
Muhlenberg College (Allentown, PA)
New York University (New York, NY)
Nyack College (Nyack, NY)
Penn State University (State College, PA)
Pennsylvania College of Technology (Williamsport, PA)
Plattsburgh State University (Plattsburgh, NY)
Point Park College (Pittsburgh, PA)
Princeton University (Princeton, NJ)
Ramapo College of New Jersey (Mahwah, NJ)
Rensselaer Polytechnic Institute (Troy, NY)
Richard Stockton College (Pomona, NJ)
Rider College (Lawrenceville, NJ)
Rochester Institute of Technology (Henrietta, NY)
Rowan University of New Jersey (Glassboro, NJ)
Saint Bonaventure College (Saint Bonaventure, NY)
Saint Lawrence University (Canton, NY)
Seton Hall University (South Orange, NJ)
Shepherd College (Shepherdstown, WV)
Shippensburg University (Shippensburg, PA)
Skidmore College (Saratoga Springs, NY)
Slippery Rock University (Slippery Rock, PA)
State University of New York at Albany (Albany, NY)
State University of New York at Cortland (Cortland, NY)
State University of New York at Oswego (Oswego, NY)
State University of New York at Stony Brook (Stony Brook, NY)
Susquehanna University (Selinsgrove, PA)
Swarthmore College (Swarthmore, PA)
Syracuse University (Syracuse, NY)

Union College (Schenectady, NY)
University of Maryland (College Park, MD)
University of Pennsylvania (Philadelphia, PA)
University of Pittsburgh (Pittsburgh, PA)
University of Scranton (Scranton, PA)
Utica College of Syracuse University (Utica, NY)
Vassar College (Poughkeepsie, NY)
Villanova University (Villanova, PA)
Washington and Jefferson College (Washington, PA)
Westchester Community College (Valhalla, NY)
Westchester University of Pennsylvania (Westchester, PA)
Westminster College (New Wilmington, PA)
West Virginia Technical College (Buckhannon, WV)
West Virginia University (Morgantown, WV)
Widener University (Chester, PA)
Wilkes University (Wilkes-Barre, PA)
William Paterson University of New Jersey (Wayne, NJ)

NORTHEAST

(*Connecticut, Maine, Massachusetts, New Hampshire, Rhode Island, Vermont*)
Amherst College (Amherst, MA)
Bates College (Lewiston, MA)
Bentley College (Waltham, MA)
Boston College (Newton, MA)
Boston University (Boston, MA)
Bowdon College (Brunswick, ME)
Brandeis University (Waltham, MA)
Bridgewater State College (Bridgewater, MA)
Brown University (Providence, RI)
Bryant College (Smithfield, RI)
Castleton State College (Castleton, VT)
Central Connecticut State University (New Britain, CT)
Colby College (Waterville, ME)
Colby-Sawyer College (New London, NH)
College of the Holy Cross (Worcester, MA)
Connecticut College (New London, CT)
Curry College (Milton, MA)
Dartmouth College (Hanover, NH)
Dean College (Franklin, MA)
Eastern Connecticut State University (Willimantic, CT)
Emerson College (Boston, MA)
Fairfield University (Fairfield, CT)

Framingham State College (Framingham, MA)
Goddard College (Plainfield, VT)
Grove City College (Grove City, PA)
Harvard University (Cambridge, MA)
Holyoke Community College (Holyoke, MA)
Husson College (Bangor, ME)
Massachusetts College of Liberal Arts (North Adams, MA)
Massachusetts Institute of Technology (Cambridge, MA)
Middlebury College (Middlebury, VT)
Mount Holyoke College (South Hadley, MA)
New England College (Henniker, NH)
Nichols College (Dudley, MA)
Northeastern University (Boston, MA)
Plymouth State College (Plymouth, NH)
Providence College (Providence, RI)
Quinnipiac College (Hamden, CT)
Roger Williams University (Bristol, CT)
Saint Michaels College (Colchester, VT)
Salem State College (Salem, MA)
Springfield College (Springfield, MA)
Springfield Technical Community College (Springfield, MA)
Stonehill College (Easton, MA)
Thiele College (Greenville, PA)
Trinity College (Hartford, CT)
Tufts University (Medford, MA)
University of Connecticut (Storrs, CT)
University of Maine (Fort Kent, ME)
University of Maine (Oromo, ME)
University of Maine—Farmington (Farmington, ME)
University of Massachusetts (Amherst, MA)
University of Massachusetts—Dartmouth (North Dartmouth, MA)
University of New Hampshire (Durham, NH)
University of New Haven (West Haven, CT)
University of Rhode Island (Kingston, RI)
University of Southern Maine (Gorham, ME)
University of Vermont (Burlington, VT)
Vermont Technical College (Randolph Center, VT)
Wellesley College (Wellesley, MA)
Western Connecticut State University (Danbury, CT)
Western New England College (Springfield, MA)
Williams College (Williamstown, MA)
Worcester Polytechnic Institute (Worcester, MA)
Yale University (New Haven, CT)

Appendix C:
Sample Celebrity Interview Prep Sheet

JAMIE LEE CURTIS

She will be here from 8:30—9 A.M. Our intern Tom will meet her downstairs. She is here today publicizing her children's book *Where Do Balloons Go?* (Both of you have copies of the book by your chairs.) Check page 28 for the highlighted portion. She is appearing today at Borders from 12:00 to 12:30. If she isn't here by 8:30, the cellular phone of the book publicist is (555)-555–5555.

Intro: ("God Save the Queen" instrumental in and under, snooty British delivery) "Ladies and Gentlemen, it isn't often that we are joined by such an esteemed guest. As if it weren't enough to be born into Hollywood royalty, our next guest is now also a bona fide baroness. Would you please welcome Lady Haden-Guest."

Questions:
- How did you get to be a baroness? (Her husband Christopher Guest inherited the Barony in 1996).
- Are you like the baroness in *Sound of Music*, trying to take Captain Von Trapp away from the kids and the governess/nun? (AUDIO: *Sound of Music*/ Baroness: "Why, you're blushing Fraulein Maria.")
- How did you meet your husband? (The legend is that she saw his picture on the front of a magazine and sent her telephone number to his agent.)
- The Baron has done some truly great movies like *Spinal Tap*, *Waiting for Guffman*, *Best in Show*, and most recently *A Mighty Wind*. (AUDIO: *Spinal Tap*: "These go to eleven.)" Out of all of his movies, you've only made one cameo, and that was in his *Spinal Tap* sequel. How come he never casts you in his movies?
- Do you consider yourself to be an actress/author or an author/actress?

- Your latest book is called *Where Do Balloons Go?* Can I read this section to the audience, because I think it's really beautiful? (page 28) You won a Grammy award for the spoken word version of this book didn't you?
- Where did you get the idea for this book?
- You've come a long way, Jamie Lee Curtis. It doesn't seem like that long ago that a young Jamie Lee was known as the scream queen. (AUDIO: *Halloween*/Jamie Lee screams.)
- What was the best thing and worst thing about being in those movies?
- Of all the movies you've made, I have a favorite. I think it's one of the best movies of the eighties. You were fantastic in *A Fish Called Wanda* (AUDIO: *A Fish Called Wanda*/Jamie Lee calls Otto stupid.) Do you have a favorite?
- I also liked the movie you did with the Governor of California. How strange is it having a friend living in the Governor's mansion?
- You did a couple of nude scenes in the eighties, but recently you did a pictorial that was even more courageous. This one shows what you would look like without a hairdresser, or special lighting, or makeup. You are Mary's hero. What made you decide to do that?
- *Freaky Friday* was a big hit for you last year. Mary and her daughter went to see that together. With that movie, you've tapped into the teenage audience. With your books you've tapped into the younger kid audience, and people my age still love you from your earlier movies. How do old people feel about you? Tell me they hate you. Otherwise that's too much love for one person.
- [Only if we have time.] Let's play a word-association game with some of the stars you've worked with in the past. I'll say a name and you tell me what you most remember about what it was like working with that person: John Travolta (*Perfect*), Richard Lewis (*Anything But Love*), John Cusack (*Grandview USA*), Eddie Murphy (*Trading Places*), Dan Ackroyd (*Trading Places*), Tom Arnold (*True Lies*), Ron Silver (*Blue Steel*), Donald Sutherland (*Virus*), Kevin Kline (*A Fish Called Wanda*), John Cleese (*A Fish Called Wanda*), Michael Palin (*A Fish Called Wanda*), Danny DeVito (*Drowning Mona*), Bette Midler (*Drowning Mona*), Leslie Nielson (*Prom Night*).

Close: "OK, before you go, I want to give you a little quiz. This is just a little test we like to do to see how dedicated actors were to their acting roles. Let's see how well you remember the names of the characters you played. I'll say the character name, you tell me the movie. Helen Tasker (*True Lies*), Wanda Gershwitz (*A Fish Called Wanda*). Now some harder ones . . . Kim Hammond (*Prom Night*), Queen Camilla (*Rudolph the Red Nosed Reindeer and Island of Misfit Toys*). OK, this one will stump you: Linda Frey (guest starring role on *Charlie's Angels* in 1976). At least I didn't ask about the "Hardy Boys/Nancy Drew Mysteries." You were Mary, by the way. Thanks for coming Jamie Lee."

APPENDIX D:
SAMPLE PREP SHEET—THE LARRY & MARY SHOW

Date: May 21

6:10—MARY'S DAILY INSPIRATION
The intro jingle is filed under "Mary." The music bed is filed under "Inspiration." The last four days have been about: Smiles (Tues.); Appreciation (Wed.); Children (Thurs.); Peace (Fri.).

6:20—GOVERNOR'S STORY
Story synopsis: "According to yesterday's *Chicago Sun-Times*, the governor only paid $28,000 in taxes during the last fiscal year, the same amount as the typical sanitation worker." Possible punch line: I guess that's only fair, they both do about the same thing—they deliver garbage.

6:40/6:50—PET EATS MAN'S PAYCHECK
Story synopsis: "Willie Nordstrum of South Bend brought home his paycheck last Friday and left it on the coffee table so he could change his clothes before going to the bank. When he returned, the paycheck was gone. The doors were all locked, and no one else was in the house, except his dog Buster. At first Willie thought Buster moved it somewhere in the living room. He looked at all of Buster's favorite hiding places—nothing. Finally he found the corner of the paycheck under the couch. It had been bitten off. Now that Willie knew where his paycheck was, he just had to wait for it to come back out. The next day when he took Buster for a walk, lo and behold, it popped out . . . nearly intact. Willie picked it out of the pile with his plastic baggie, brought it home and washed it off, endorsed it, and took it to the bank. They cashed it."

(AUDIO: Paul Lynde/*Bye Bye Birdie*: "There's nothing as wholesome as a pet"/:02.)

(AUDIO: *Welcome Back Kotter*: Kotter reads note from Epstein's mother about the dog eating his homework/:12.)

Phoner: "Buster isn't the first pet to eat something he shouldn't have. (Kotter audio). Give us a call at 591-WJJJ and tell us your story."

7:10—PRESIDENT MISSPEAKS

Story Synopsis: "Dateline: Bombay, India. The President was making his first visit to India. While speaking to the Indian prime minister he leaned over and asked him a question. Reporters were wondering what the question was and finally cornered the embarrassed Prime Minister. "He wanted to know why they call us Hoosiers in India," the Prime Minister admitted.

(PARODY SONG)

7:20—PHONE INTERVIEW: HOG-CALLING CHAMPION

His name is Chester Beauregard. We're calling him at his home number (555-555-5555) at 7:15. He won the grand prize at this year's Arkansas State Fair. He's seventy-seven years old. Among his quotes in the article. . . . "I've been calling hogs in these parts since before most of them other fellas were born." And "My wife Gladys is always tellin' me that I'm full of hot air, and I guess I just proved her right."

Questions:
- Do you have a favorite pig with which you practice?
- Did you win a trophy? (If yes, where are you going to put it?)
- Did Gladys do anything special for you after you won?
- Are you going to defend your title?
- Any advice for all the young hog callers out there?

7:40/7:50—CHILDHOOD NICKNAMES

Mary will tell the story of her daughter Dottie getting upset because some of the kids in her neighborhood have been calling her "Snottie."

(AUDIO: *Animal House*—Giving nicknames to Flounder and Pinto/:22.)

(AUDIO: *Airplane*—"Don't call me Shirley"/:03.)

(AUDIO: *Simpson's*/Homer—"Wait, let's make sure nothing rhymes with Bart before we name him. Cart, Dart, E-art. All clear."/:13.)

PHONER: "Dottie is being called Snottie. When I was a kid, my arch enemy called me Scary Larry. What nicknames were you called? Tell us your story at 591-WJJJ."

8:10—LARRY AT THE BLOOD BANK

Message: "There is a blood shortage. Come out and give blood and say hello. I'll be tapping a vein too." Time: 3 P.M.—6 P.M. Address: 303 N. Main Street.

8:20—DUMB CROOK FILE

Intro jingle filed under "Dumb." Music bed: Dragnet instrumental. (TV Themes CD 1 Cut 5.)

Story 1: "Bank robber Jim Davis waited until just before he entered the bank before putting on his mask. That's when he realized his one fatal flaw. He forgot to cut eyeholes into the mask. After bumping into people he finally made it up to the teller and handed her the note asking for cash in small bills. He didn't see her wave for the security guard, didn't see her push the panic button, and didn't see her put stacks of empty deposit slips into his bag instead of money. He didn't see the police waiting for him outside the door either. But he felt them when they put on the cuffs.

Punch line: And they say justice is blind.

Story 2: "Convenience store customer Bobby Franks was being carded for a liquor purchase when he decided to rob the store and asked for all the money in the register. The clerk handed him the money as he memorized Bobby's name and address from the driver's license sitting on the counter. When the police picked him up they recovered all $44 and both uneaten Slim-Jims."

Punch line: Imagine how fast they would have found him if he had taken a good picture and didn't under-report his weight by twenty pounds.

Story 3: "Burglar Jeffrey Appleton thought he was making a routine house burglary in Riverville. Unfortunately for Jeff, he was breaking into the home of mobster Vinnie 'The Bull' Argento. Mr. Argento was having a poker party with his bodyguards 'Rocco' Alfreddi, 'Face-Crusher' McGintty, 'Anvil Fist' Nicholson, and the Chief of Police."

Punch line: Needless to say, he was busted. And after that, he was arrested.

8:40/8:50—IN-STUDIO INTERVIEW: RICHARD SIMMONS

He is coming here after being interviewed on Fox TV. They promised he would be out by 8:30 and it's only a ten-minute walk. Be prepared to go to spots first if he isn't here yet.

Richard is promoting his line of dolls that he sells via The Home Shopping Network. The dolls are called "Collection of the Masters," and they are reproductions of the dolls that Richard has in his 300-plus doll collection. We promised we would talk about the dolls, and that we would not talk about his feud with Howard Stern.

Intro: "Would you please welcome to the program, the first guest we've ever had named . . . Milton. Is that really your given name?"

Questions:
- Remember the "Free to Be You and Me" special from the seventies, hosted by Marlo Thomas? It made a hit out of this song (AUDIO: "William wants a doll.)" Were you collecting dolls already when that show came out?
- Out of all the dolls in your collection, which one is your most treasured and why?
- You've done "Sweatin to the Oldies," "Disco Sweat," and "Platinum Sweat," but you haven't done an exercise video to the music of your favorite singer—Barbra Streisand. How come? Doesn't she rock enough?
- Did you ever hear from her after you went on *Saturday Night Live* and parodied her songs? (AUDIO: *Saturday Night Live* (from '94)/ Singing Streisand parody "People who need pizza"/:15.)
- Tell us how your video "Groovin' in the House" ended up in the movie "What Women Want."

Closing Question:
- I know you aren't an actor, but you have acted in a few television shows. In the eighties you appeared in the TV show *Fame* (AUDIO: *Fame*/Richard Simmons/:12). In the nineties you appeared in the TV show *The Larry Sanders Show* (AUDIO: *Larry Sanders*/Richard Simmons/:09), and just last year you appeared on *Arrested Development* (AUDIO: *Arrested Development*/Richard Simmons/:13). Tell me we won't have to wait another decade to see you act again. (Or to appear on our show again.)

9:10—NUDE MAN CLIMBS SKYSCRAPER

Story Synopsis: "Downtown Detroit came to a standstill yesterday as a French Canadian named Jean Claude Chateaubriand, wearing nothing more than a pair of gloves and a pair of climbing shoes, climbed a skyscraper. Police were waiting for him when he got to the top of the building and arrested him for creating a disturbance."

Punch line: Onlookers were not as impressed with his climbing skills as they were with his ability to open a window without using his hands or feet.

9:20—MONDAY MOVIE MANIA
Theme Song is filed under "Monday." It has a trailing bed after initial jingle. Don't fade it out, it fades automatically.

Question: "The movie *Rocky 7* opened to record box office numbers over the weekend. You probably know that *Titanic* is the #1 box office hit of all time. But what is the number one box office hit of all time after the figures are adjusted for inflation? 591-WJJJ. First caller wins a 52-week Blockbuster video card."

Answer: *Gone with the Wind*. When adjusted for inflation, that movie has grossed over $1 billion dollars at the box office.

(AUDIO: *Gone with the Wind*/Rhett Butler... "Frankly, my dear, I don't give a damn.")

9:40—CALL TO MAYOR MEISTERBURGER
We are calling his office at 9:35. His press secretary Melvin Glickenhoffer will patch us through to the Mayor. (555-333-5555.)

(AUDIO: Instrumental "Happy Birthday.")

The Mayor is sixty years old today. Mary is ready to sing her sultry "Mr. Mayor" rendition of the song. Remember that the Mayor isn't very good on the air, keep it short.

- Mr. Mayor, are you and Mr. T celebrating your birthdays together again this year?
- Mr. Mayor, any progress on that Larry & Mary statue?

9:50—SIGN OFF/TEASE TOMORROW'S SHOW
"Don't miss tomorrow's show, because we'll have Sean Hayes calling from the set of the hit show *Will & Grace*, plus we'll be doing our regular Tuesday feature 'Give me a break.' Will your office get the break tomorrow? Tune in and find out."

APPENDIX E:
USEFUL WEB SITES

www.amishchicago.com. Web site of author Rick Kaempfer's advertising agency. Includes news about the authors.

www.ananova.com. Offbeat news stories from the U.K.

www.assignmenteditor.com. Useful links to newspapers, newspaper columnists, wire services, magazines, search engines, and other Web sites.

www.bonehead.oddballs.com. Offbeat news stories from around the globe.

www.digidesign.com. Home page for Pro Tools digital editing software. Contains information about editing classes and certification, plus downloads of editing software available.

www.drudgereport.com. Useful links to newspapers, newspaper columnists, wire services, magazines, search engines, and other Web sites.

www.eonline.com. E! Television's site; celebrity gossip and news.

www.imdb.com. Biographies and complete filmographies of film stars.

www.karaokegalore.com. Karaoke of nearly every hit song.

www.karaokewh.com. Karaoke of nearly every hit song.

www.moviesounds.com. Downloadable audio clips from famous movies.

www.moviewaves.com. Downloadable audio clips from famous movies.

www.oldradio.com. Information about the history of radio.

www.princetonreview.com. Matches students to universities with specific majors.

www.radio-locator.com. Provides call letters and formats of every radio station in America.

www.thesmokinggun.com. Uncovers details of newsmakers and celebrity arrests and other skeletons in closets.

www.tvtome.com. Biographies and complete listings of television appearances by television stars.

www.whitehouse.gov. Official web site of the White House.

BIBLIOGRAPHY

American Heritage Dictionary of the English Language. 4th ed. Boston: Houghton Mifflin, 2000.

Bartlett, John. *Bartlett's Familiar Quotations: A Collection of Passages, Phrases, and Proverbs Traced to Their Sources in Ancient and Modern Literature.* 17th ed. Edited by Justin Kaplan. Boston: Little, Brown, 2002.

Beers, Mark H. *The Merck Manual of Medical Information.* 2nd ed. New York: Simon & Shuster, 2003.

Brook, Tim and Marsh, Earle F. *The Complete Directory to Prime Time Network and Cable TV Shows: 1946—Present.* 8th ed. New York: Ballantine Books, 2003.

Chase's Calendar of Events: The Day to Day Directory to Special Days, Weeks, and Months. Edited by the Editors of Chase's. New York: McGraw-Hill/Contemporary Books. Published annually.

Dolgins, Adam. *Rock Names: From ABBA to ZZ Top: How Rock Bands Got Their Names.* Revised ed. New York: Citadel Trade, 1995.

Green, Jeff. *The Green Book of Songs by Subject: The Thematic Guide to Popular Music.* 5th ed. Nashville, TN Professional Desk, 2002.

The New York Public Library Desk Reference. 4th ed. New York: Hyperion Press, 2002.

Panati, Charles. *Panati's Extraordinary Origins of Everyday Things.* Reissue ed. New York: Harper & Row, 1989.

Roget's 21st Century Thesaurus. Nashville: Thomas Nelson, 1992.

Spignesi, Stephen J. *The Odd Index: The Ultimate Compendium of Bizarre and Unusual Facts.* New York: Penguin USA, 1994.

Videohound's Golden Movie Retriever 2004. Edited by Jim Craddock. Farmington Hills, MI: The Gale Group, 2003.

Wetterau, Bruce. *Congressional Quarterly's Desk Reference on American Government: Over 600 Answers to Frequently Asked Questions.* 2nd ed. Washington, DC: Congressional Quarterly Books, 2000.

Whitburn, Joel. *The Billboard Book of Top 40 Hits.* 7th ed. New York: Watson-Guptill Publications, 2000.

Who's Who: An Annual Biographical Dictionary. New York: St. Martin's Press. Published annually.

Wood, Clement. *The Complete Rhyming Dictionary.* Revised edition. New York: Dell Publishing, 1992.

World Almanac and Book of Facts. New York: St. Martin's Griffin. Published annually.

ABOUT THE AUTHORS

RICK KAEMPFER

Rick Kaempfer was the executive producer of *The John Records Landecker Show* on WJMK-Chicago from 1993 to 2003. During his tenure, *The John Records Landecker Show* won the Achievement in Radio Award as Best Morning Show in Chicago (1997) and the Radio & Records Award as the Best Oldies Morning Show in America (2001, 2002). From 1987 to 1991, Kaempfer was also the producer of the top-rated *Steve Dahl & Garry Meier Show* on WLUP Chicago.

Kaempfer has a diverse writing background. He has written hundreds of radio bits, scripts, and parody songs in his career, and won numerous writing awards for his freelance writing projects for magazines and advertising agencies. He is particularly proud of his national writing award in 1999 (for his essay "Living Life to Its Fullest"), and his award winning work for A.M.I.S.H. Chicago Advertising, an agency (specializing in radio advertising) that he co-founded in 2000. While Rick continues to consult morning shows and morning show producers, he is now working full-time as the Senior Creative Vice President of that agency (*www.amishchicago.com*).

Rick lives in suburban Chicago with his wife Bridget, and his three sons, Tommy, Johnny, and Sean.

JOHN SWANSON

John Swanson is the executive producer of *The Eric and Kathy Show* on WTMX-Chicago. Under his tutelage, the Eric and Kathy show has been a ratings juggernaut, attaining top-five status in the highly competitive morning drive time slot for the past four years. He has been the only producer for the entire run of this very successful show. In 2001, Swanson was nominated as producer of the year.

Before coming to WTMX, Swanson served as the executive producer of the highly acclaimed *The Kevin Matthews Show* on WLUP-Chicago and *The Steve Cochran Show* on WPNT-Chicago. He got his producing start as the technical producer of the top-rated *The Jonathon Brandmeier Showgram* on WLUP.

Swanson lives in suburban Chicago with his wife, Cheryl, and their two children Jonathon and Ava.

INDEX

ABC/Disney corporation, 40
abusive hosts, 196–197. *see also*
    hosts
Aykroyd, Dan, 22
actors, 16–17. *see also* celebrity
    guests
    movie publicity, 18–21
    television, 21–22
Adobe Audition, 180
advertising, 131, 203
Affleck, Ben, 19, 29
air studio set up, 174–175
Allen, Tim, 16
Almost Salinas (movie), 30
AM radio, 4
Andrews, Julie, 19
AP wire service, 38
Arbitrends, 159
archives, 35, 89–90. *see also* audio
    libraries/clips
Argento, Vince, 64, 154, 203
Arthur, Bea, 17
athletes, 23–24
audience participation, 46–60.
    see also phone segments
audio libraries/clips, 180,
    181–189
    CD libraries, 188–189
    equipment for, 182–184
    from the Internet, 184
    interviews, 35
    organization of, 186–189
    phone segments, 58–59
    of radio shows, 89–90, 101,
        184–186
    television events, 40
audio vaults, 171, 185–187

Baron, Jimmy, 201
Basic Instinct (movie), 29
Belushi, Jim, 22
benchmark bits, 51, 69–70
benefits, corporate, 157
BETA tapes, 185

Biondi, Dick, 4
Bit Exchange, 43
Bitboard, 42–43
Blanco & Peace Enterprises,
    Ltd., 24
board operators, 5. *see also*
    control boards
    checklist for remote
        broadcasts, 121–122
    hourly wage of, 158
Bon Jovi, Jon, 124–125
book tours, 17–18, 23
boredom, 195
Brady, Wayne, 16
Brandmeier, Jonathon, 4
    audio clips, using, 186
    Brendan Sullivan working
        with, 70–71, 204
    "Crack Me Up Line" bit, 69
    Jim McInerney working for,
        144, 202
    Jim Wiser working with, 145
    John Swanson working with,
        147–148
Brenner, David, 16
Britain, Ross, 43
broadcast journalism, 130
broadcasting schools, 136
broadcasts, remote, 117–125. *see
    also* remote broadcasts
Brokaw, Tom, 18
Brooks, Mel, 18, 34
Bullock, Sandra, 19
business major in college,
    133–134
Buzz and Wendy show, 144

cable television shows, 22
call-in participation, 46–60. *see
    also* phone segments
cameras, 160
Cantu, Richard, 81
career changes, 200–205
    advertising, 203

consultants, 204
hosts, 200–201
production directors, 202
program directors, 202
promotion directors, 201–202
public relations, 203–204
TV producers, 203
writing, 204
Carey, Drew, 22
Carlin, George, 16
Carol Fox & Associates, 24
Carter, Jimmy, 23
Casey Kasem, 4
Castellaneta, Dan, 22
Cattrall, Kim, 18
CD discs/players, 172, 185,
    188–189
celebrity guests, 11–25
    actors, 16–17
    athletes, 23–24
    book tours, 17–18
    comedians, 15–16
    contact information
        management, 83
    contacting local venues for,
        12–13
    merging interests with, 12
    movie publicity, 18–21
    musicians, 13–14
    phone calls, 88
    politicians, 22–23
    sample interview prep sheet,
        222–224
    television stars, 21–22
cellular phones, 31–32
Chicago Sun-Times (newspaper), 37
Chicago Tribune (newspaper), 37
Clark, Dick, 22, 31
Clark, Wesley, 23
classical music, 4
Clear Channel corporation, 4
Clinton, Hillary, 23
Cochran, Steve, 148
coffee machines, 99

college, 129
  majors useful for radio, 130–134
  radio stations at, 134–136, 212–221
Collins, Joan, 32
comedians, 15–16
commercial logs, 97–98
communications major in college, 130–131
computers, 171, 176–180
confidence, 73
Conn, Roe, 201
consoles, 165–175. see also board operators
contact information management, 82–84
contests
  logs for, 98–99
  music trivia, 70
  prize winners as audience, 123
  station policy about, 161
  writing up, 67
control boards, 165–175
  CD players, 172
  checklist for remote broadcasts, 121–122
  computers, 171
  cue buttons, 169
  digital, 174
  faders, 168
  input modules, 166–167
  intercoms, 175
  microphones, 170 (see also microphones)
  modules, 165–166
  output modules, 167
  phone screeners, 175
  skimmer cassette recorders, 172–173
  stereo broadcasts, 168
  studio set up, 174–175
  troubleshooting guide, 169
Coppock, Chet, 201
corporate benefits, 157
corporations, 4
country music, 14
Cousin Brucie, 4
Crawford, Cindy, 18
"Creativity Coach," 204
"critic list" for movie screenings, 19
Cromwell, James, 19
Cronkite, Walter, 18
Crowe, Russell, 21
Cruise, Tom, 19
Cruz, Penelope, 19
cue buttons, 169
current events, 132

Curtis, Jamie Lee, 18, 222
Curtis, Tony, 18
Cusack, John, 19

Dahl, Steve, 4
  comedy-talk show on WLUP-AM, 15
  Rick Kaempfer working with, 143
Daily Herald (Chicago newspaper), 37
Daily Southtown (Chicago newspaper), 37
Dale, Steve, 6
Damon, Matt, 19, 29
Danson, Ted, 22
Davis, Mike, 153
Dearborn, Bob, 5
Dees, Rick, 4, 202
delay system, 101–102
delays in transmitting, 32, 120
Derek, Bo, 18
DigiDesign company, 179
digital boards, 174
digital editing, 176–180
Disclosure (movie), 29
Douglas, Michael, 19, 29
Drudge Report, 38, 41
Dukakis, Michael, 55
DVD recorder, 182

e-mail, 97
Ebert, Roger, 18
Eden, Barbara, 17
editing, 176–180
education, 129–137
  college majors, 130–134
  internships, 152 (see also internships)
  student-run college radio stations, 134–136, 212–221
Edwards, Tommy, 70
electronic devices for organization, 86
"The Empire Carpet Man Strikes Back," 64
engineers, 5
English major in college, 133
equipment, 119. see also control boards
The Eric and Kathy Show (radio program), 15, 69
  John Swanson working on, 148
  remote broadcast of, 121
ESPN radio, 144
etiquette for interns, 150–152. see also internships
expenses, 157

faders, 168
Family Ties (television program), 28
Fatal Attraction (movie), 29
fax machines, 99
FCC (Federal Communications Commission), 101–102
feature stories, 62–63
Ferguson, Eric, 20
Ferrell, Will, 19
Flying Saucer (recording), 64
FM radio, 4
Ford, Harrison, 20
friendly kiss-offs, 56–57

Gatziolis, Cindy, 201, 204
Gibson, Mel, 19
Gingrich, Newt, 23
Giuliani, Rudolph, 23
Gladstone, Lorna, 202
Goodman, Dickie, 64
Gore, Al, 23
Grammar, Kelsey, 22
Grant, Hugh, 19
The Greaseman, 4
guests, 11–25, 63. see also celebrity guests

Hanks, Tom, 19
Harkin, Nick, 24
harmonizer, 101
Harper, Valerie, 27
Harrison, Sean, 105
headphones, 100
Heaton, Patricia, 18
Heffner, Hugh, 18
Henner, Marilu, 17, 27
Heston, Charlton, 18
Hewitt, Jennifer Love, 19–20
history major in college, 132
hoaxes from callers, 54–55
home run call, 59
Hood, Jonathon, 201
hosts
  abusive, 196–197
  callers, dealing with, 58–59
  egos of, 158
  interviews, 26 (see also interviews)
  meeting with producers, 87
  pitching ideas to, 74
  producers becoming, 200–201
  as producer's boss, 7
  producers' knowledge of, 158
  quirks, dealing with, 149–151
  relationship to, 195
  setting up phone segments, 49–51
hotline, radio, 55

Hunt, Bonnie, 22
Hurley, Elizabeth, 20

I Love Lucy (television program), 3
ideas for shows, 36–45, 90
    Internet, 41–42
    magazines, 38–39
    newspapers, 36–38, 96–97
    personal life, 44–45
    for phone segments, 47–49
    prep services, 42–44
    remote broadcasts, 122–123
    television, 39–41
    wire services, 38, 96
Idle, Eric, 18
IFB (interrupted foldback), 120–121
Imus, Don, 64
in-studio interviews, 30–31
input modules, 166–167
Integrated Services Digital Network (ISDN), 120
intercoms, 175
Internet, 28, 68
    audio clips from, 184
    newspapers, 37
    at remote broadcasts, 118
    television, 41
    web sites for ideas, 41–42
    wire services, 38
Internet Movie Database (IMDb), 28
internships, 138–155
    broadcast schools, 136
    contacting radio stations, 140–142, 145–146
    departments that have, 142–144
    hosts, relationships with, 149–151
    obtaining through schools, 138–139
    as opportunities to learn, 152
    with producers, 146
    producers, transition to, 153–155
    with radio personalities, 147
    staff, relationships with, 151–152
interrupted foldback (IFB), 120–121
interviews, 26–35. *see also* celebrity guests
    archiving, 35
    closing, 29
    in-studio, 30–31
    loosening up interviewee, 26–27
    phone, 31–32
    recorded, 33–34

research for, 27–29
sample prep sheet, 222–224
satellite, 32
ISDN (Integrated Services Digital Network), 120, 172

Jackson, Michael, 66
job descriptions, 159–160
jobs, changing, 197–198
Jones, Chuck, 9
journalism, 130

Kaempfer, Rick, 15
    advertising agency begun by, 203
    booking John Travolta, 20
    college education of, 138
    "The Empire Carpet Man Strikes Back" bit, 64
    handling news of World Trade Center attack, 81
    internship of, 142–143
    John Mahoney and Virginia Madsen interview, 31
    long-form radio specials, 69
    Marilu Henner interview, 27
    personal life, 44–45
    producing recordings, 90
    remote broadcast from Dominican Republic, 124
    Use Your Glove (parody song), 66–67
    working at college radio station, 135–136
karaoke, 65–66
Keiling, Leslie, 81
Kid Rock, 14
KILF-AM station, Dallas TX, 3
Kilman, Buzz, 144
King, Larry, 18
KOWH station, Omaha NE, 3
Kraddick, Kidd, 4

labeling audio clips, 186–188
Landecker, John, 4, 20
    "The Empire Carpet Man Strikes Back" bit, 64
    handling news of World Trade Center attack, 81
    interviewing Marilu Henner, 27
    Michael Douglas interview, 29
    remote broadcast from Dominican Republic, 124
    serenading Martha Stewart, 18
    Use Your Glove (parody song), 66–67
The Larry & Mary Show, 77–80, 105–116, 225–229

Led Zeppelin, 191
Leno, Jay, 16, 40
Letterman, David, 40
Lewis, Richard, 16
liberal arts major in college, 131–133
Lichtenstein, Jim, 41
Linkletter, Art, 45
listener participation, 46–60.
    see also phone segments
"live copy," 98
local venues, celebrity guests at, 12–13
location broadcasts, 117–125.
    see also remote broadcasts
Long, Shelly, 17
long-form radio specials, 68–69
Lopez, Jennifer, 20
Lucas, George, 64
Lujack, Larry, 4, 70, 201

Madsen, Virginia, 30
magazines, 38–39
Maher, Bill, 16
Mahoney, John, 22, 30
mail, 99
Malden, Karl, 18
marketing, 133
Marti unit, 120
Martin, Dave, 5
Martin, Steve, 16
materials for shows. *see* ideas for shows
Matthews, Kevin
    Jim McInerney working for, 143, 144, 202
    John Swanson working for, 148
McCartney, Paul, 14
McCormick, Maureen, 17
McInerney, Jim, 143–144, 202
McLendon, Gordon, 3, 4
McNeil, Dan, 201
McNeil, Don, 4
Meet the Press (radio program), 11
Meier, Garry, 4, 15, 143
microphones, 100–101
    as part of control board, 166, 170
    at remote broadcasts, 118
Miller, Dennis, 16
mixing, 179
money issues, 156–158
Moore, Mary Tyler, 17, 27
movie publicity, 18–21
Mr. Jaws (recording), 64
Murray, Bill, 20
Murray the K, 4
music, editing, 179
music logs, 98

music radio, 3, 4
musicians as celebrity guests, 13–14. *see also* celebrity guests
My Favorite Husband (radio program), 3

National Public Radio, 68–69
negotiations for producer jobs, 156–161
  knowledge of host, 158
  money issues, 156–158
  program director, questions for, 159–161
  salaries, 198–199
New York, NY, 17
New York Times (newspaper), 37
Newhart, Bob, 16, 34
news, 34, 35
  feature stories, 63
  internships in department, 144
  last-minute check for, 96–97
  using for phone segments, 47–49
  wire services, 38, 96
newspapers, 36–38, 96–97
Newsweek (magazine), 39
Notting Hill (movie), 19
Nugent, Ted, 14

O'Day, Dan, 43
O'Dell, Spike, 145
off-line mix, 167
oldies popular music, 14–15
on-location broadcasts, 117–125. *see also* remote broadcasts
operating logs, 103
output modules, 167

pan control, 170
parody songs, 65–67
Patrick, Butch, 81
Peace, Lissy, 24
personal appearances, 157
PGM button, 167
Philbin, Regis, 22
Phillips, Wally, 4
phone book management, 82–84
phone calls to radio stations, 142
phone interviews, 31–32, 34
phone lines
  into control board, 171–172
  ISDN lines, 172
  for remote broadcasts, 121
phone recorders/editors, 171
phone screeners, 103, 175
phone segments, 46–60
  coaching callers, 57–58

home run call, 59
hosts setting up, 49–51
material for, 47–49
preparing host for caller, 58–59
recording, 58–59
Red Alert System for bad callers, 51–57
Pinchot, Bronson, 17
pitching material, 72–74
planning shows, 74–81
  flexibility, 80–81
  prep sheets, 77
  rundown sheets, 75–76
  sample show, 77–80
political science, 132
politicians, 22–23
Powell, Colin, 23
pre-show preparation, 95–104
  maintenance checklist, 97–99
  production, 95–96
  studio checklist, 99–103
prep services, 42–44
prep sheets, 77, 104, 225–229
Presley, Elvis, 66
Presley, Lisa Marie, 66
press releases, 45
press secretaries, 22
Pro Tools editing software, 179–180
production work, 88–89
  internships, 143 (*see also* internships)
  pre-show, 95–96
  production director, 202
program assign, 167
program directors, 7
  internships with, 143
  producers becoming, 202
  questions for, 159–161
Project Greenlight, 29
promos, 89
promotion directors, 201–202
public relations, 203–204
  book publishers, 17–18
  celebrity guests, 12 (*see also* celebrity guests)
  comedy clubs, 16
  contact information, 83
  local venues, 13
  majoring in college, 131
  movies, 18–19
  press releases, 45
  television, 21
  theaters, 17
publicists. *see* public relations
publicity stunts, 68
publishers, 17–18

Pulp Fiction (movie), 20
Purtan, Dick, 64
radio computing services (RCS), 171
radio format, 3
  filling rundown sheets, 76
  matching to celebrity guest, 13, 14–15
radio personalities. *see* hosts
radio segments, 61
radio stations. *see also under individual stations*
  hierarchy, 6
  student-run college, 212–221 (*see also* college)
  website listing, 140
Rather, Dan, 18
ratings of radio shows, 159
RCS (radio computing services), 171
reality television shows, 21–22
recorded interviews, 33–34
recordings, editing, 177–179
recordings of shows, 90. *see also* audio libraries/clips
Red Alert System for bad callers, 51–57
reference library for research, 68
Reindeer Games (movie), 29
Reiner, Carl, 18, 34
Reiser, Paul, 18
remote broadcasts, 117–125
  checklist for board operator, 121–122
  content of show, 122–123
  live audiences, 123–124
  staffing, 124
  technical issues, 117–119
  technical language, 119–121
research. *see also* ideas for shows
  for interviews, 27–29
  reference library for, 68
Reuters wire service, 38
reverb, 101
Rivers, Joan, 16
Roberts, Julia, *19*, 20
Robinson, Kevin, 144
Rogers, Jesse, 201
Romano, Ray, 18
Rosen, Mitch, 202
Ross, Marion, 17
rundown sheets, 75–76, 105

salaries, 156–157, 193–199
  negotiating, 198–199
  obstacles to increasing, 194–197
  searching for new jobs, 197–198
sales, 7

Sambora, Richie, 124–125
Sandler, Adam, 16
satellite broadcasts, 32, 120
Schwimmer, David, 22
Seinfeld, Jerry, 16
September 11, 2001, 80–81
Shannon, Scott, 4
Shearer, Harry, 16
Sheppard, Cybil, 18
Short, Martin, 16
Siegel, Matt, 4
Silver, Jack, 202
Simmons, Richard, 18
skimmer cassette recorders,
    172–173
Smothers, Tommy, 16
Sochowski, Tom, 144
Spacey, Kevin, 20
speech communications, 133
Spirit (movie), 29
sports, 144, 201
staffing, remote broadcasts,
    119, 124
Stahl, Sandy, 142
Stairway to Heaven (Led
    Zeppelin), 191
Starr, Ringo, 15
stereo broadcasts, 168
Stern, Charlie, 105
Stern, David, 203
Stern, Howard, 4, 144
Stewart, Martha, 18
Stiller, Ben, 20
stories for phone segments,
    50–51. *see also* phone
    segments
Storz, Todd, 3
student-run college radio
    stations, 134–136, 212–221
studios, 85, 99–103. *see also*
    control boards
Sullivan, Brendan, 70–71, 204
Swanson, John, 15
    audio clips used for *The Jonathon
        Brandmeier Showgram*, 187
    booking Russell Crowe, 21
    Harrison Ford interview, 20
    remote broadcast of *The Eric
        and Kathy Show*, 121
    as "Swany the Love
        Chicken," 68
    working with Jonathan
        Brandmeier, 147

tape editing, 176
target audiences, 160
technical aspects of producing
    control boards, 165–175 (*see
    also* control boards)
    digital editing, 176–180

remote broadcasts, 117–119
    terms for remote broadcasts,
        119–121
telephone. *see under* phone
television
    impact on radio, 3
    networks, 21–22, 41
    producers, 203
    as source for ideas for shows,
        39–41
    taping, 91
theater major in college, 132–133
theaters, 17
30 Odd Foot of Grunts (musical
    group), 21
"This American Life" program,
    68–69
Thomas, Marlo, 17
Time (magazine), 39
time management, 81–92
    archiving shows, 89–90
    ideas, 84–85
    meetings with host, 87
    phone book organization,
        82–84
    phone calls, 88
    production bits, 89
    production work, 88–89
    promos, 89
    researching ideas, 90
    scheduling day, 86–91
    studio organization, 84–85
    television taping, 91
    to-do lists, 85–86
    writing, 90–91
TiVo systems, 181, 182, 183
Top 40 radio, 3
Travolta, John, 20
turntable operators (TTO), 5
Tvtome.com, 28

universities. *see* college
University of Illinois, 135–136
UPI wire service, 38
U.S. News & World Report
    (magazine), 39
USA Today (newspaper), 37
Use Your Glove (parody song),
    66–67
UTL button, 167

Valentine, Scott, 28
Van Dyke, Dick, 17
VCRs (videocassette recorders),
    181, 182, 183
Vector, 120
Viacom corporation, 4, 40
videocassette recorders (VCRs),
    181, 182, 183
virtual carts, 171

voice mails, 83–84, 99
volume control, 168
volunteering, 139, 152

Wall Street Journal (newspaper), 37
Walsh, Joe, 15
WCFL station, Chicago IL, 5
WCKG-FM station, Chicago IL,
    144, 202
Web sites, 231
    for colleges, 130
    posting pictures on, 160
    for radio stations, 124, 140
Web sites for news ideas, 41–42
Wendt, George, 17
WIND station, Chicago IL, 5
Winfrey, Oprah, 22
Winston, Fred, 5–6
wire services, 38, 96
Wireless Flash, 43
Wiser, Jim, 144
WJMK-FM station, Chicago
    IL, 144
WLUP-AM station, Chicago
    IL, 15
WLUP-FM station, Chicago
    IL, 142, 143, 201
WMAQ-AM station, Chicago
    IL, 202
Wolf, Bruce, 144
Wolfman Jack, 4
WPGU station, University of
    Illinois, 135–136
writing for shows, 61–71, 90–91
    benchmark bits, 69–70
    career change, 204
    contests, 67
    feature stories, 62–63
    Jonathon Brandmeier's
        suggestions, 70–71
    journalism, 130
    long-form radio specials,
        68–69
    parody songs, 65–67
    produced bits, 64
    stunts, 68
WSCR-AM station, Chicago
    IL, 201
WTMX station, Chicago IL,
    15, 21
    John Swanson working
        at, 148
    remote broadcast of *The Eric
        and Kathy Show*, 121
    remote broadcast on
        Halloween, 124–125
WZFS-FM station, Chicago
    IL, 144

X-Radio, 43

Books from Allworth Press

Allworth Press is an imprint of Allworth Communications, Inc. Selected titles are listed below.

VO: Tales and Techniques of a Voice-Over Actor
by Harlan Hogan (paperback, 6 × 9, 256 pages, $19.95)

Technical Film and TV for Nontechnical People
by Drew Campbell (paperback, 6 × 9, 256 pages, $19.95)

The Health & Safety Guide for Film, TV & Theater
by Monona Rossol (paperback, 6 × 9, 256 pages, $19.95)

Career Solutions for Creative People
by Dr. Rhonda Ormont (paperback, 6 × 9, 320 pages, $19.95)

Writing Television Comedy
by Jerry Rannow (paperback, 6 × 9, 224 pages, $14.95)

Directing for Film and Television, Revised Edition
by Christopher Lukas (paperback, 6 × 9, 256 pages, $19.95)

The Best Things Ever Said in the Dark: The Wisest, Wittiest, Most Provocative Quotations from the Movies
by Bruce Adamson (hardcover, $7^1/_2$ × $7^1/_2$, 144 pages, $14.95)

Makin' Toons: Inside the Most Popular Animated TV Shows and Movies
by Allan Neuwirth (paperback, 6 × 9, 288 pages, 82 b&w illus., $21.95).

The Directors: Take Four
by Robert J. Emery (paperback, 6 × 9, 256 pages, 10 b&w illus., $19.95)

Creative Careers in Hollywood
by Laurie Scheer (paperback, 6 × 9, 240 pages, $19.95)

Please write to request our free catalog. To order by credit card, call 1-800-491-2808 or send a check or money order to Allworth Press, 10 East 23rd Street, Suite 510, New York, NY 10010. Include $5 for shipping and handling for the first book ordered and $1 for each additional book. Ten dollars plus $1 for each additional book if ordering from Canada. New York State residents must add sales tax.

To see our complete catalog on the World Wide Web, or to order online, you can find us at
www.allworth.com.